Easy-to-Make
CLOTH DOLLS
& All the Trimmings

Jodie Davis

Williamson Publishing • Charlotte, Vermont 05445

DEDICATION

In memory of my sister,
Peggy-Lynne,
Whose laughter lives on.
1963-1989

Library of Congress Cataloging-in-Publication Data

Davis, Jodie, 1959–
  Easy-to-make cloth dolls & all the trimmings Jodie Davis.
      p. cm.
  Includes bibliographical references.
  ISBN 0-913589-53-5 : $13.95
  1. Dollmaking. 2. Cloth dolls. 3. Doll clothes. I. Title.
TT175.D38 1990   90-48286
745.592'21 — dc20   CIP

Cover illustration: Loretta Trezzo Braren
Cover and interior design:
Trezzo-Braren Studio
Photography: Stephen Ostrowski
Project diagrams: Jodie Davis
Printing: Capital City Press

Manufactured in the United States of America
2 3 4 5 6 7 8 9

CONTENTS

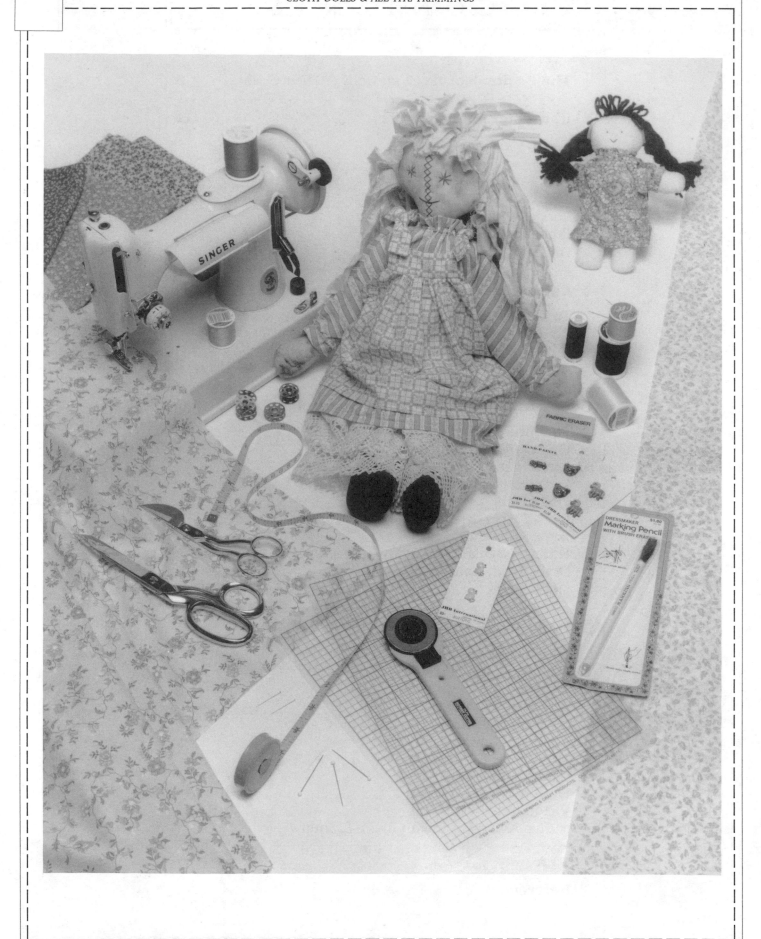

CHAPTER ♥ 1
THE
BASICS

*H*ere are all the essentials for constructing the dolls and clothes in this book. Anyone with the desire to make any of these wonderful dolls can feel comfortable with these projects. However, you might find the excellent general sewing reference books listed in the bibliography useful. They are available from your local library or bookstore. These books give a thorough review of sewing basics, should you feel the need. The projects in this book are listed from the simplest to the more challenging (dolls around the world in chapter 6). Before you begin, assemble all of the tools and materials needed for your project, and then follow the instructions one step at a time.

GENERAL SUPPLIES

Essential

Sewing machine: Although the dolls can certainly be stitched by hand, a sewing machine will speed the process considerably and result in dolls with stronger seams.

Bent-handle dressmaker's shears: A good quality shear, 7" or 8" in length, is recommended for general sewing purposes. Reserve these shears for cutting fabric only, as paper will dull them quickly.

Scissors: Used for cutting paper, cardboard, and other materials, these inexpensive scissors will save your shears from a lot of wear and tear.

Dressmaker's tracing paper: Used for transferring markings from patterns to fabric.

Dressmaker's tracing wheel: A device used with the tracing paper.

Straight pins or paper weights: To hold paper pattern pieces in place as you cut out the fabric.

Hand-sewing needles: For general hand sewing. Choose fine, size 10-8, sharp for lightweight fabrics such as calico, and medium, size 8-6, sharp for heavier fabrics such as corduroy, flannel, and denim.

Embroidery needle: For embroidering the dolls' faces.

Glue: A general purpose white glue made for fabric, felt, wood, and paper is available at any fabric, dime, or crafts store under a variety of brand names.

General purpose thread: The all-purpose size 50 will fill most of your general hand and machine sewing needs. Some people insist on cotton thread, but I find that polyester or cotton-wrapped polyester are stronger and slide through the fabric more easily.

Paper: For clothing and other patterns. 5" or longer dollmaker's needle: Needed for thread-jointing the doll.

Nice to Have

Seam ripper: A sharp, pointed tool used to tear out temporary basting stitches and seams. I list this as non-essential because you can substitute the thread clipper listed below, but you'll want to at least have one or the other.

Pinking shears: Cuts a ravel-resistant zigzag, used for finishing seams. A good choice is the 7½" size.

Thread clippers: A variation on a small pair of scissors, thread clippers are made by a number of companies and are handy for trimming threads at the sewing machine, for clipping into seam allowances, and for making buttonholes. If you do much sewing, I recommend a pair highly.

Thimble: This is listed as non-essential though many, including myself, will argue that this little piece of equipment is necessary to guide the needle and to guard against painful pin pricks.

HOW TO TRANSFER PATTERNS

All of the patterns in this book are shown in their actual size. I suggest that you make your doll patterns out of a heavy cardboard, such as oaktag or cereal boxes, since accuracy is extremely important. By tracing around cardboard pieces, you will transfer the patterns very accurately. Heavy paper will suffice for the clothing patterns, as these will be pinned to the fabric and then cut out.

On all illustrations in this book, the wrong side of the fabric is shown as shaded. The right and left of the pattern is the same as doll's right and left.

MATERIALS

Tracing paper

Dressmaker's tracing paper

Cardboard or paper for patterns

INSTRUCTIONS

1. Lay a piece of tracing paper over the pattern in the book. Carefully trace the pattern onto the tracing paper, including all pattern markings.

2. Lay the cardboard (for clothing patterns, heavy paper) on your work surface (not the dining room table!). Place a sheet of carbon paper on top and your tracing over that. To avoid the possibility of slippage you may wish to tape the two top sheets to the bottom cardboard or paper, or to the work surface. With a pencil or dressmaker's wheel, trace the pattern, pressing firmly. Pick up a corner of the two top layers to be sure that the pattern is being transferred clearly to the bottom surface. Transfer all markings to the pattern.

3. Cut out your pattern. Mark the name of the pattern piece and the name of the doll or garment on it.

4. For patterns that are in more than one piece, butt the cut edges together and tape them before cutting your fabric.

> *TIP: Manilla envelopes and zip lock sandwich bags are great places to store your patterns. Label them and store them away for lots of future use.*

SEWING TECHNIQUES

Darts
Fold the fabric along the center line of the dart, right sides together. Beginning at the raw edges or widest point of the dart, sew the dart along the broken lines to the point; backstitch to secure the stitching. For clothing, press the dart to one side.

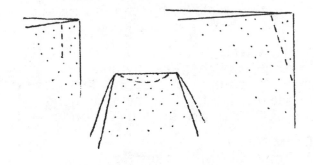

Gathering
Using a long stitch, make a row of stitches between the marks indicated on the pattern, leaving the thread tails long enough to grasp so you can pull them. Repeat close to the first stitching. Pin the two pieces together, matching the dots on the two pattern pieces as indicated. Pull up the threads to gather the fabric and loop the thread tails around the pins at either end. Adjust the gathers evenly and smoothly. Baste the seam. Stitch the seam.

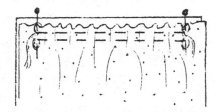

Trimming and Clipping Seams
After stitching a seam, seam allowances are trimmed and clipped for a number of reasons. For clothing, trimming with pinking shears reduces the bulk of the seam and, in some fabrics, prevents raveling of the raw edges. For clothing and dolls, clipping into the seam allowances of convex (outward) curves permits the edges to spread when the item is turned right side out. Notching the seam allowances on concave (inward) curves allows the edges to draw in when the item is turned right side out. Trimming across corners insures a smooth, finished seam and square, crisp corners.

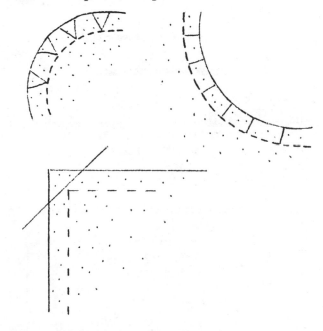

Elastic Casings

The casing is a tunnel of turned under fabric enclosing flat elastic which is stretched to fit snugly around the body.

To make an elastic casing, the edge of the garment is pressed under ¼". Then the edge is turned and pressed under an additional ¾" or to the desired amount.

The lower edge of the casing is then machine stitched in place, leaving a ½"-wide opening for threading the elastic. Machine stitch a second row of stitching close to the top fold.

Cut a length of elastic as indicated in the instructions for the garment. Attach a safety pin to one end of the elastic, push it into the casing and work it through, being careful not to twist the elastic.

Safety pin the two ends of the elastic together, overlapping them ½ inch. Try the garment on the doll. Adjust the elastic if necessary. Your doll's measurements may vary according to how you stuff it, so it is best to check the fit. Machine-stitch the ends of the elastic together, back and forth, to secure them. Pull the elastic into the casing. Machine-stitch the opening closed, being careful not to catch the elastic in the stitching.

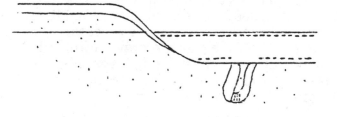

STITCH DICTIONARY

Basting Stitch

This long (¼" by hand or longest possible by machine), temporary stitch is used for both marking and for stitching fabric pieces together to make sure it fits properly, before the final stitching.

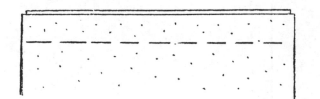

Running Stitch

This stitch is similar to the basting stitch, although it is a shorter, even stitch used for fine, permanent seaming.

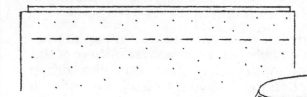

Topstitch

Longer than a regular sewing stitch, the topstitch is applied from the right side of the finished item. It can be for decorative or functional reasons (sometimes both) and is often used to secure casings, zippers, facings, and more.

Overhand or Whipstitch

Used to join two finished edges, as when closing the turned under edges of the doll's ear, legs, and arms.

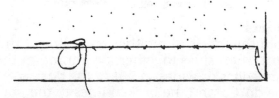

Slipstitch

This almost invisible stitch is made by slipping the needle through a fold of one fabric and then taking a stitch in the second fabric.

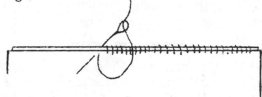

Staystitching

Staystitching is simply a row of small machine stitches along the seam line used to keep the fabric from stretching.

Satin Stitch

Decorative stitches, usually of colored thread or embroidery floss, made right next to one another to cover the underlying fabric. This is used for doll eyes and mouth.

Cross Stitch

A simple X of embroidery floss.

PREWASH

Before cutting fabric, wash, dry, and iron it according to the manufacturer's instructions. This will avoid shrinkage and running of colors when the finished item is washed.

TEA-DYING FABRICS

To give fabric an aged look, steep tea bags in a large bowl or sink with enough hot water to cover the fabric, making a strong, dark infusion. Saturate the fabric with hot water and then immerse in the tea. Soak the fabric, stirring it frequently. Remove the fabric from the tea and rinse it until the water runs clear. Hang to dry or run through the dryer. If the fabric isn't dark enough, dye it again. Press.

SEWING THE DOLLS

A short machine stitch is recommended for sewing the dolls. Since a lot of strain will be placed on the seams, especially around the tight curves of the hands and feet, these smaller stitches add the strength needed to withstand stuffing and hugging.

STUFFING

The art of stuffing is a learned skill. First, start with a quality stuffing — one of even, fluffy consistency. Always begin at the extremities (hands or toes), packing the stuffing in tightly, using smaller bits for smaller parts. Graduate to larger chunks of stuffing as you progress to the larger parts of the doll. To produce less lumping, use handfuls of stuffing. Pack the stuffing as you add it, continually checking for lumps and evenness. Hold whichever part you're working on at arms length to check for symmetry. You may have to unstuff your first attempts to get it right. Whipstitch the openings closed, once you are satisfied with your work.

Just take your time. With a bit of experience you will develop a feel for stuffing and it will progress more quickly.

HAIR

The possibilities for doll hair are endless. First, there is yarn. Regular knitting yarn offers many colors and sizes. The finer yarns work well for many of the dolls, especially the small ones. But don't limit yourself to the offerings of a general merchandise store. A visit to a specialty yarn shop will provide inspiration from the fascinating yarns in intriguing color, textures, and materials.

Various hair products are available from craft stores and through mail order craft suppliers. Pretty Hair® is a baby fine material which comes in long strands. This is the best approximation to baby hair. Torn muslin (as for Prudence), chenille, folk wool (a cross between wool yarn and Feel-O-Fleece), even Spanish moss, are all used for doll hair.

SIGNING BOTTOMS

As the finishing touch, sign and date your doll's bottom as an artist signs a painting. Use a permanent marker such as a Sharpie. After all your loving work, you should let your doll display your name proudly.

IMPORTANT: When making any doll or clothing for a young child (four years or younger), do not use buttons, snaps, pompons, beads, or other decorations which could be pulled or twisted off and swallowed. Instead, embroider features and use velcro closures.

CHAPTER ♥ 2

CHARACTER 18-INCH DOLLS

*S*tarting with a simple, one piece head and body pattern, you can interchange hand and feet patterns, stencil the appropriate face, and stitch up a custom-made outfit, to transform one doll pattern into a charming collection of assorted personalities: a cheerful clown, a humble elf, jolly old Santa Claus, well-loved boy and girl raggedy dolls, Prudence — a true rag doll, a crow-catching scarecrow, and a precious little girl playing dress-up.

All dolls stand 18" tall when finished, excluding hats.

CLOWN

Bring cheer to a loved one with this fun-filled fellow. Sit him on a shelf, hang him over a child's bed, place a bunch of balloons in his gloved hand or a dove on his shoulder; however he is displayed, this clown is sure to brighten all lives he touches.

Bright fabrics suitable for children's clothing are perfect for the clown's costume. For a hobo-type clown doll, select muted tones. Mix and match stripes, prints, bold dots, patchwork fabrics — whatever suits your fancy. To facilitate removal of clothing for little fingers, use velcro rather than snaps on the front opening of the clown's jacket.

Construction of the doll is simplified by sewing the gloves and shoes as one with the arms and legs.

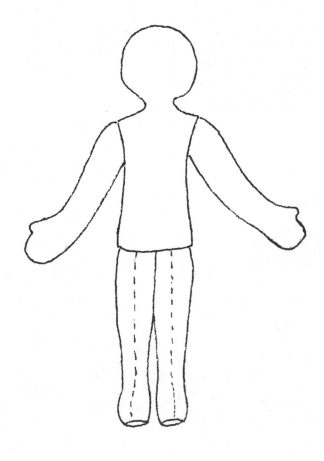

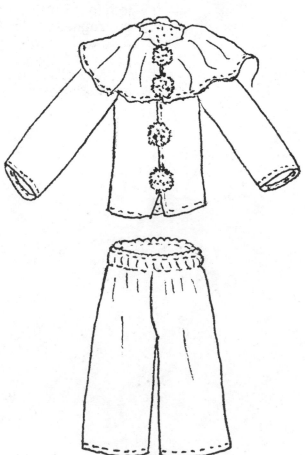

MATERIALS

For the doll:

⅓ yard muslin	Matching thread
Matching thread	One ¾" coverable button for the nose
Acrylic paints: red and white	One skein red yarn
Stencil brush	Matching thread
Heavy paper or stencil plastic	Thin cardboard
X-acto® knife	**For the clothing:**
Black fine tip permanent marker, such as a Sharpie	⅓ yard jacket fabric
One 6" piece of ¼" dowel	Scrap of fabric for jacket ruff
Fray Chek®	⅜ yard pants fabric
Polyester fiberfill stuffing	Matching thread
Scrap of red and white striped fabric for legs (or to match clothing)	¼"-wide elastic
Scrap of red wool for gloves and shoes	Thin cardboard
Two ½" black buttons for eyes	Four 1" pompons
	Four snaps

INSTRUCTIONS

Note: All seam allowances are ¼" unless otherwise instructed.

Make the patterns and cut out the doll and clothing pieces according to the instructions in chapter 1. Cut the ruff (collar) for the jacket from contrasting fabric 4" x 30".

To make the doll:

1. Face: Transfer face stencil pattern onto heavy paper or stencil plastic. For reference, draw in the outline of the head, neck, and shoulders on the stencil. Using the X-acto® knife, cut out the face features. Lay the stencil over one muslin head. Using a dry brush and a small amount of paint, stencil the features as follows: Stencil eyes white, nose and mouth red. When dry, draw in the lines of the mouth as indicated on the pattern using the permanent marker.

2. Head and body: Pin front of body (stenciled) to back of body (plain), right sides

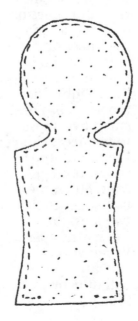

facing. Stitch, leaving an opening between the dots at the bottom of the body, as indicated on the pattern. Clip seam allowances along curves.

Turn. Stuff the head firmly. Poke a hole into the stuffing with a pointed object. Insert a 6"-long dowel approximately 3" into the stuffed head. Stuff the neck firmly around the dowel, packing the stuffing with a wooden spoon as you go. Continue stuffing the body until it is full and firm. Handstitch the bottom opening closed.

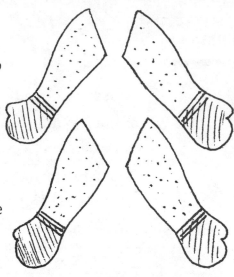

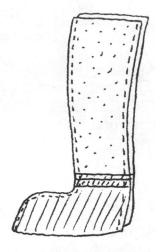

3. Arms: Sew four gloves to four arms, right sides together, making sure the thumbs are on the inside curve of arm and that there are two sets of opposing arms. Press seams open.

Right sides facing, match two stitched sets of legs and shoes. Sew the front and back seams, leaving the bottom of the shoes and the tops of the legs open. Repeat for remaining set.

Matching the large dot to the front leg seam and the small dot to the back seam, pin and stitch soles to bottom of shoes. Clip curved seams. Turn. Stuff firmly to within 1½" of the top of the leg.

Turn ¼" to the inside at the top of the legs. Whipstitch opening closed. Whipstitch legs to bottom of body.

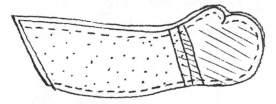

Pin and stitch arms and handstogether, right sides facing.

Clip the curves and into the V between thumb and remaining fingers. Apply Fray Chek® to seam where clipped. Let dry. Turn. Stuff arms, leaving the top inch or so unstuffed. Turn ¼" to the inside at the top of the arm. Whipstitch the opening closed. Whipstitch arms to body.

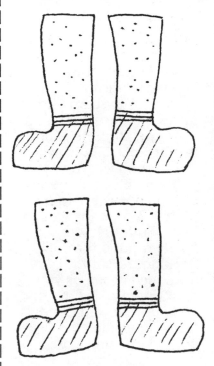

4. Legs: Lay the legs and shoes on a table, having the knees and toes pointing in the same direction. Right sides together, pin and stitch two shoes to two legs. Flip the remaining shoes and legs over. Stitch the two shoes to the two legs. Press the seams open. When wrong side up, they will appear as illustrated.

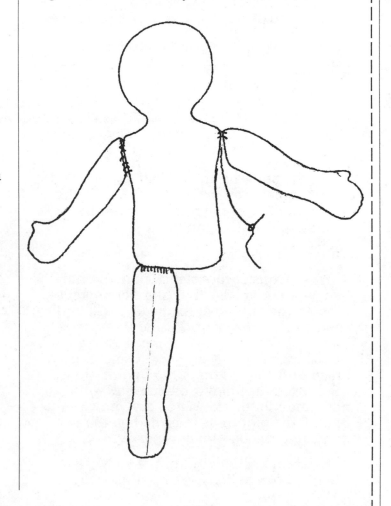

5. Hair: Cut two pieces of cardboard, each 1" x 14". Lay side by side. Tape across ends, leaving a small gap between the two pieces of cardboard. Starting 1" from one end, wind yarn loosely around the cardboard. Stop 1" from the other end. This will make a 12"-long string of wound yarn. Stitch down the center of the wound yarn, between the two pieces of cardboard. Remove the tape. Pull the cardboard out from inside the yarn, leaving the yarn in loops.

Place the center of the wound yarn at the center top of the doll's head, 1" below and in front of the top seam of the head. Stitch the yarn to the head, handsewing along the stitching, having the ends of the yarn meet at the bottom back of the head.

Repeat with a second, third, and fourth row of yarn, placing each of them about a 1/2" from the preceding row. Wind 10" of yarn on the cardboard for the second row, 8" for the third, and 6" for the last row.

6. Finishing the face: Sew buttons for eyes over the white eye patches, setting them toward the inner bottom corners of the eye patches to make the doll appear cross-eyed. Following the manufacturer's instructions, cover the button for the nose with red wool fabric, backing the wool with a smaller piece of muslin so the shiny button will not show through. Referring to the photo of the doll, sew in place on the face.

To make the clothing:

JACKET

1. Press under 1/4" on front opening edges of jacket. Repeat. Topstitch.

2. Stitch fronts to back at shoulders.

3. Press under 1/4" and 1/4" again on two short and one long edge of ruff. Topstitch. Gather along remaining long raw edge of neck ruff. Pin to neck edge of jacket, right side of ruff facing wrong side of jacket, matching finished front edges. Pull up on gathering threads to fit. Stitch neck ruff to neck of jacket. Press ruff to lie flat against right side of jacket.

4. Pin and stitch one short edge of sleeve to armhole. Repeat for other sleeve.

5. Pin and stitch underarm and side seams as one, right sides facing.

6. Press under 1/4" and then another 1/4" on bottom edges of sleeves and jacket hems. Topstitch.

7. Sew snaps to jacket front as indicated on pattern. Sew pompons to outside of jacket front over two bottom snaps. Sew two pompons to the front of ruff over snaps on jacket.

PANTS

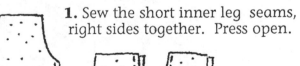
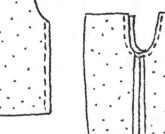
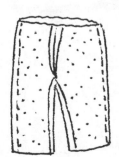

1. Sew the short inner leg seams, right sides together. Press open.

2. Pin and stitch the curved, crotch seam, right sides facing.

3. Match the long, outside leg seams. Pin and stitch.

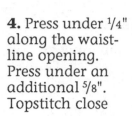

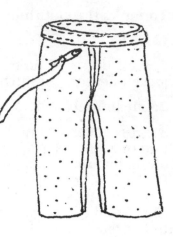

4. Press under ¼" along the waistline opening. Press under an additional ⅝". Topstitch close

to both folds, leaving a ½" opening in the stitching on the lower fold for inserting the elastic. Run a 7½" piece of elastic through the casing. Try the pants on the doll. Adjust the elastic, if necessary. Overlap and stitch the raw ends of the elastic. Stitch the gap in the casing closed.

5. Press under ¼" on the bottom edges of the pants legs. Press under another ¼". Topstitch.

ELF

This little elf wears all the expected accouterments: a lined green wool jacket; a matching, lined hat; knickers with elastic at legs and waist; pointed shoes which are stitched as one with the leg and topped with a jingle bell; and a belt buckled at the waist. Put a small hammer in one hand and a wooden toy in the other and this fellow will be right at home in Santa's workshop.

Red and white striped fabric is used for both the legs and the garment linings.

MATERIALS

For the doll:

⅓ yard muslin

Matching thread

Acrylic paints: red and white

Stencil brush

Heavy paper or stencil plastic

X-acto® knife

Black fine tip permanent marker, such as a Sharpie

One 6" piece of ¼" dowel

Fray Chek®

Polyester fiberfill stuffing

Large scrap of red and white striped fabric for legs

Two ½" black buttons for eyes

One ½" coverable button for nose

One skein dark carrot color yarn

Matching thread

Thin cardboard

For the clothing:

½ yard green wool for jacket, knickers, hat, and shoes

¼ yard red and white striped cotton fabric for lining

Matching thread

¼"-wide elastic

Five ½" gold jingle bells

½ yard of black 1"-wide belting

Matching thread

One 1" gold buckle

INSTRUCTIONS

Note: All seam allowances are ¼" unless otherwise instructed.

Make the patterns and cut out the doll and clothing pieces according to the instructions in chapter 1.

To make the doll:

1. Face: Transfer face stencil pattern onto heavy paper or stencil plastic. For reference, draw in the outline of the head, neck, and shoulders on the stencil. Using the X-acto® knife, cut out the face features. Lay the stencil over the muslin head, lining up the outline of the head and shoulders with the edges of the muslin. Using a dry brush and a small amount of paint, stencil the features as follows: eyes white, mouth red. When dry draw in the lines of the mouth as indicated on the pattern. Cover button with a scrap of red fabric as instructed on button package. Back the red fabric with a smaller piece of

muslin or the shiny button will show through. Sew in place for nose as indicated on pattern.

2. Head and body: Pin front of body (stenciled) to back of body (plain), right sides facing. Stitch, leaving an opening between the dots. Clip seam allowances along curves.

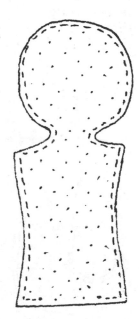

Turn. Stuff the head firmly. Insert a 6"-long dowel approximately three inches into the head. Stuff the neck firmly around the dowel, packing the stuffing as you go.

Continue stuffing the body. Handstitch the bottom opening closed.

3. Arms: Pin and stitch arms together, right sides facing. Clip the curves and into the V between thumb and remaining fingers.

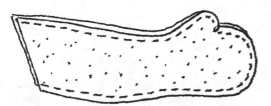

Apply Fray Chek® to seam where clipped. Let dry. Turn. Stuff arms, leaving the top inch unstuffed. Turn ¼" to inside at the top of the arm. Whipstitch the opening closed. Whipstitch arms to body.

4. Legs: Sew two shoes to two legs, making sure the shoes point in the direction of the knees. Flip the remaining legs and shoes. Stitch, checking to be sure shoes and knees point in the same direction. Press the seams open.

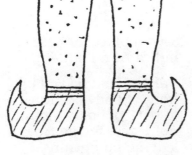

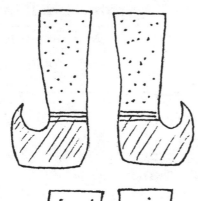

Right sides facing, match two leg/shoes. Pin. Sew the front and back seams, leaving the bottom of the shoes and the top of the legs open.

Matching the large dots to the seams at the front of the legs and the small dots to back leg seams, pin and stitch soles to bottom of shoes. Clip curved seams. Turn. Stuff firmly to within 1½" of the top of the leg.

Turn ¼" at top of legs to inside. Whipstitch openings closed. Whipstitch legs to bottom of body.

5. Hair: Cut two pieces of cardboard, each 1" x 14". Lay side by side. Tape across ends, leaving a small gap between the cardboard. Starting 1" from one end, wind yarn loosely around the cardboard. Stop 1" from the other end. This will make a 12"-long string of wound yarn. Stitch down the center of the wound yarn, between the two pieces of cardboard. Remove the tape. Pull the cardboard out from inside the yarn. The yarn will remain looped.

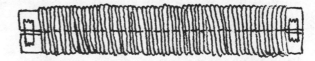

Place the center of the wound yarn at the center front of the doll's forehead, 1/4" below the top seam of the head. Stitch the yarn to the edge of the face, 1/4" from the seam, having the ends of the yarn meet at the top back of the neck.

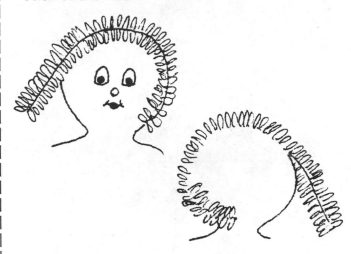

Repeat with a second row of wound yarn, this time having it go around the back of the head, 1/4" to the back of the seam.

Add a third row, this time winding only 10" of yarn on the cardboard. Stitch it to the back of the head, 1/2" to the inside of the second row. That's it — remember he's bald!

6. Finishing the face: Cover the button with two layers of muslin as directed in package instructions, cutting the inside layer smaller than directed. Stitch to face of doll as in photo. Handsew eyes over white patches.

7. Ears: Stitch two ears together, leaving a 1/2" gap along a straight side for turning. Turn. Stuff loosely. Whipstitch opening closed. Stitch through muslin and stuffing as marked. Pin to sides of head having middle of ears even with nose.

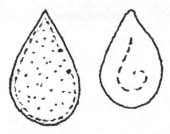

8. Stitch one bell to the tip of each shoe.

To make the clothing:

JACKET

1. Stitch fronts to back at shoulders and sides, for both jacket and jacket lining.

2. Pin lining to jacket, right sides facing. Stitch, leaving armhole edges open and leaving a 3" opening at the bottom of the back of the jacket for turning. Trim seams. Clip curves. Turn. Press. Handstitch opening closed.

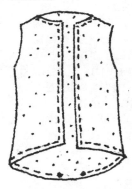

3. Stitch long, underarm seams in sleeves of jacket and jacket lining.

4. Pin sleeves of jacket and jacket lining together at bottom edges, right sides facing. Turn right sides out. Press.

5. Pin and stitch sleeve and sleeve linings to armholes treating the two layers as one.

6. Stitch jingle bells to jacket front as indicated on pattern.

7. Turn up sleeves 3/4" at bottom edge, showing lining.

BELT

1. Cut a piece of belting 14" long.

2. Put buckle on belt. Fold over 2" belting. Stitch close to raw edge.

PANTS

1. Sew the short inner leg seams, right sides together. Press open.

2. Pin and stitch the crotch seam, right sides facing.

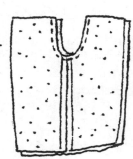

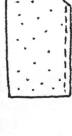

3. Match the long, outside leg seams. Pin Stitch.

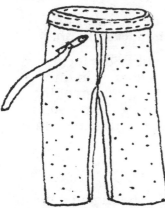

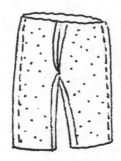

4. Press under ¼" along the waistline opening. Press under an additional ⅝". Topstitch close to both folds, leaving a ½" opening in the stitching on the lower fold for inserting the elastic. Run a 7½" piece of elastic through the casing. Try the pants on the doll. Adjust the elastic, if necessary. Overlap and stitch the raw ends of the elastic. Stitch the gap in the casing closed.

5. Press under ¼" on bottom edges of legs. Press under an additional ⅝". Topstitch close to both folds, leaving a ½" opening in the stitching on the upper fold for inserting the elastic. Run a 5½" piece of elastic through the casing of each leg. Try the pants on the doll. Adjust the elastic, if necessary. Overlap and stitch the raw ends of the elastic. Stitch the gaps in the casing closed.

HAT

1. Stitch hats together along two long side edges, right sides facing, leaving the bottom (head) edge open. Repeat for hat lining.

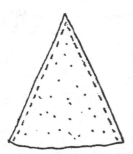

2. Turn hat lining right side out. Put inside hat. Match and pin bottom raw edges. Stitch, leaving an inch wide opening in the stitching for turning. Turn hat right side out. Press. Handstitch opening closed.

3. Turn up 1" on bottom edge of hat to show lining. Press. Tack to doll's head.

SANTA

With a slight alteration to the basic body pattern this jolly old elf's tummy will wiggle like a bowl full of jelly when Santa laughs. His red velvet suit is trimmed with fake shearling lamb's wool. Fill his burlap sack with small toys perhaps including the 25" doll's teddy bear and doll.

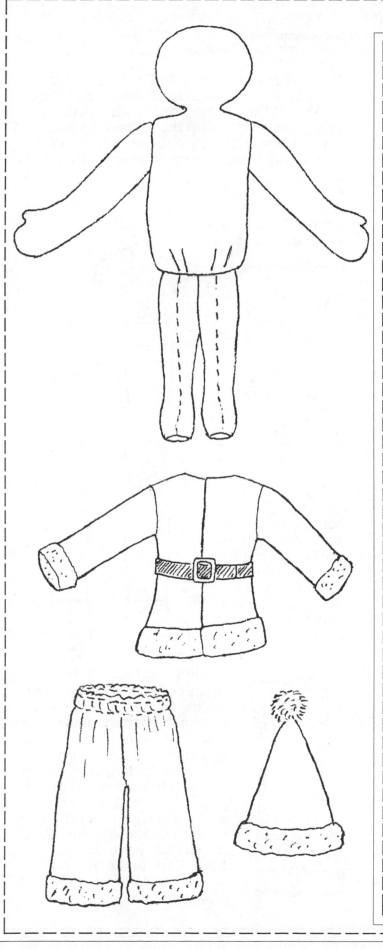

MATERIALS

For the doll:

⅓ yard muslin

Matching thread

Scrap of black wool fabric for boots

Scrap of red wool or velvet for gloves

Scrap of red and white striped fabric for the legs

Acrylic paints: red and white

Stencil brush

Heavy paper or stencil plastic

X-acto® knife

Black fine tip permanent marker, such as a Sharpie

One 6" piece of ¼" dowel

Fray Chek®

Polyester fiberfill stuffing

½" coverable button

One skein white yarn

Matching thread

Cardboard

For the clothing:

½ yard red velvet or wool

¼ yard red and white striped cotton fabric for lining

Matching thread

¼ yard imitation shearling lamb's wool

¼"-wide elastic

One white pompon

½ yard of 1"-wide black belting

One 1" gold buckle

¼ yard burlap for toy sack

Twine

Toys

INSTRUCTIONS

Note: All seam allowances are ¼" unless otherwise instructed.

Prepare patterns and cut out the doll and clothing pieces following the instructions in chapter 1.

To make the doll:

1. Face: Transfer face stencil pattern onto heavy paper or stencil plastic. For reference, draw in the outline of the head, neck, and shoulders on the stencil. Lay the stencil over one muslin body/head, matching the drawn outline with the edge of the head and shoulders. Using the X-acto® knife cut out the face features. With a dry brush and a small amount of paint, stencil the features as follows: Stencil eyes white, mouth red. When dry, draw in the lines of the mouth as indicated on the pattern.

2. Head and body: Make darts in body back and front. Pin front of body (stenciled) to back of body (plain), right sides facing. Stitch, leaving an opening between the darts as indicated on the pattern. Clip seam allowances along curves.

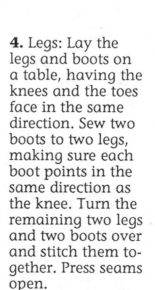

Turn. Stuff the head firmly. Poke a hole into the head stuffing using a pointed object. Insert a 6"-long dowel approximately 3" into the head. Stuff the neck firmly around the dowel, packing the stuffing as you go. Continue stuffing the body. Handstitch the bottom opening closed.

3. Arms: Sew four gloves to four arms, right sides together, making sure the thumb is on

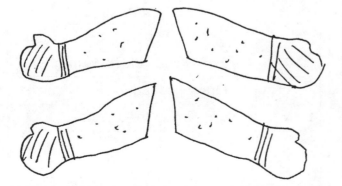

the inside curve of arm and that you have two sets of opposing arms. Press gloves open.

Pin and stitch two arm/hands together, right sides facing. Clip the curves and into the V between thumb and remaining fingers. Apply Fray Check® to seam where clipped. Let dry.

Turn. Stuff arms, leaving the top inch unstuffed. Turn ¼" to inside at the top of the arm. Whipstitch the opening closed. Whipstitch arms to body

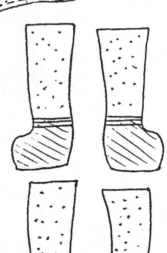

4. Legs: Lay the legs and boots on a table, having the knees and the toes face in the same direction. Sew two boots to two legs, making sure each boot points in the same direction as the knee. Turn the remaining two legs and two boots over and stitch them together. Press seams open.

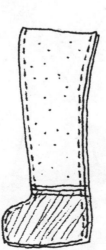

Right sides facing, match two opposing leg/boots as one. Sew the front and back seams, leaving the bottom of the boots and top of the leg open. Repeat for the remaining set.

Match the large dot on the shoe sole to the bottom of the front leg seam at the bottom edge of the shoe and the small dot to the back leg seam. Pin and stitch soles to bottom of shoes. Clip curved seams. Turn. Stuff leg firmly to within 1½" of top of leg.

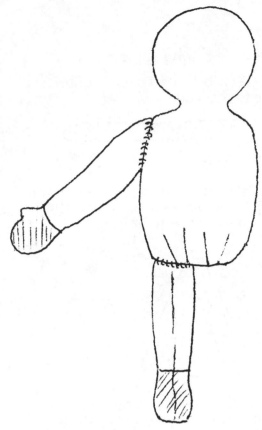

Turn under ¼" at the top of the legs. Whipstitch opening closed. Whipstitch legs to bottom of body.

5. Hair: For the beard, make 11 bundles of yarn, each containing 10 strands, 8" long, leaving the ends in loops. Starting with the middle bundle (#6 in illustration), stitch the center of each bundle to the face as illustrated.

For the mustache, make one bundle of yarn containing 20 strands, each 8" long. Stitch the center of the bunch to the face about ½" above the mouth.

To make the hair, form three bunches of yarn, each containing 50 continuous pieces

16" long. Stitch the first bundle to the center top of the head about ¼" in front of the seam on the front of the peak of the head. Sew the second batch to the center back of the head, about ¾" below the first bunch. Repeat for the third bundle. To keep hair from falling in the doll's face, tack front section to side of head just above top edge of beard.

6. Nose: Cover button with two layers of muslin following manufacturer's instructions, making the inner layer smaller than instructed. Sew to face just above the mustache.

To make the clothing:

JACKET

1. Stitch fronts to back at shoulders, for both jacket and jacket lining.

2. Pin lining to jacket, right sides facing. Stitch, leaving armhole and bottom edges open. Trim seams. Clip curves. Turn. Press.

Cut a piece of shearling 2½" x 19½" long. Fold in half lengthwise, right sides facing.

Stitch across short ends. Turn right side out. Pin one layer to bottom edge of jacket, treating jacket and jacket lining as one, right sides facing. Stitch. Turn under remaining edge of shearling ¼". Handstitch to inside of bottom edge of jacket.

3. Stitch long, underarm seams in sleeves of jacket and jacket lining.

4. Cut two pieces of shearling, each 2½" x 7½". Stitch short edges of one piece of shearling together, right sides facing. Fold in half lengthwise, wrong sides together. Pin both thicknesses to right side of bottom edge of sleeve. Stitch. Turn fur trim down. Repeat for other sleeve, using the second piece of shearling.

PANTS

1. Sew the short inner leg seams, right sides together. Press open.

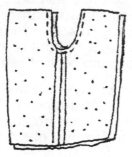

2. Pin and stitch the crotch seam, right sides facing.

3. Match the long, outside leg seams. Pin and stitch.

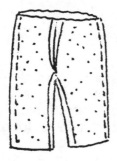

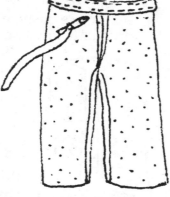

4. Press under ¼" along the waistline opening. Press under an additional ⅝". Topstitch close to both folds, leaving a ½" opening in the stitching on the lower fold for inserting the elastic. Run a 10" piece of elastic through the casing. Try the pants on the doll. Adjust the elastic, if necessary. Overlap and stitch the raw ends of the elastic. Stitch the gap in the casing closed.

5. Cut two pieces of shearling, each 2½" x 9½". Stitch short edges of one piece together, right sides facing. Repeat for other piece. Fold in half lengthwise, wrong sides together. Pin each through both thicknesses to the bottom edge of a leg, facing velvet. Stitch. Turn down.

BELT

1. Cut a piece of belting 18" long.

2. Put buckle on belt. Fold over 2" of belting. Stitch close to raw edge.

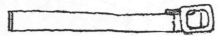

HAT

1. Stitch hats together along two long side edges, right sides facing, leaving the bottom (head) edge open. Repeat for hat lining.

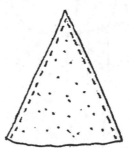

2. Turn hat right side out. Put lining inside hat. Pin and baste bottom raw edges of hat together. Cut a piece of fur 2½" x 14". Stitch short ends together, right sides facing. Fold in half lengthwise, wrong sides facing. Pin both layers to right side of hat. Stitch through all thicknesses. Turn fur down.

3. Tack hat to doll's head.

TOY SACK

1. Fold sack in half. Stitch two sides as illustrated. Turn right side out.

2. Stitch across corners 2" from seam as shown.

3. Cut a piece of twine 22" long. Tie a knot in the ends of the twine. Tack twine around top of sack as shown in illustration.

4. Fill the bottom with crumpled paper. Put toys in top.

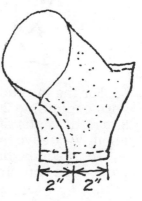

SCARECROW

Every garden needs a scarecrow, whether a large patch of land providing sustenance for an entire family or a lone potted plant.

After constructing this doll's body he is given a time-worn look with a paint brush and a weak tea solution. Then he is dressed in some "old" clothes, a hay string is tied around his waist, and he is crowned with a straw hat. Just don't expect this little guy to keep the crows away from your corn crop, as he will probably run from the noisy birds!

MATERIALS

For the doll:

⅓ yard muslin
Matching thread
Acrylic paints: red and white
Stencil brush
Heavy paper or stencil plastic
X-acto® knife
Black fine tip permanent marker, such as a Sharpie
One 6" piece of ¼" dowel
Fray Check®
Polyester fiberfill stuffing
Tea bags
Two ½" black buttons for eyes
One skein straw-colored yarn

Matching thread
Thin cardboard

For the clothing:

⅓ yard small flannel check, chambray, or other old looking fabric for shirt
⅓ yard osnaburg or other loosely woven, homespun-type fabric for pants
Scraps of old fabric for pants' patches
Scrap of fusible adhesive
Elastic thread, also called beading elastic
Jute or baling twine
7"-wide (brim edge to brim edge) straw hat
Jute or hay string to tie around waist and hat crown

INSTRUCTIONS

Note: All seam allowances are ¼" unless otherwise instructed.

Make the patterns and cut out the doll and clothing pieces following the instructions in chapter 1.

To make the doll:

1. Face: Transfer face stencil pattern onto heavy paper or stencil plastic. For reference, draw in the outline of the head, neck and shoulders on the stencil. Place the stencil over the muslin, lining up the edges of the muslin with the placement lines. With the X-acto® knife cut out the face features. Using a dry brush and a small amount of paint, stencil the features as follows: Eyes white, nose and mouth red. Allow to dry.

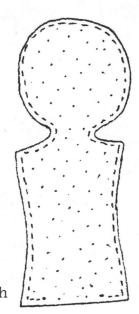

2. Head and body: Pin front of body (stenciled) to back of body (plain), right sides facing. Stitch, leaving an opening between the dots as indicated on the pattern. Clip seam allowances along curves.

Turn. Stuff the head, inserting a 6"-long dowel approximately 3" into the head. Stuff the neck firmly around the dowel, packing the stuffing as you go. Continue stuffing the body. Handstitch the bottom opening closed.

3. Arms: Pin and stitch arms together, right sides facing. Clip the curves and into the

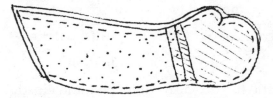

V between thumb and remaining fingers. Apply a drop of Fray Check to stitching at end of each clipping. Leave to dry.

Turn. Stuff arms, leaving the top inch unstuffed. Turn ¼" to the inside at the top of the arm. Whipstitch the opening closed. Repeat for second arm. Whipstitch arms to body.

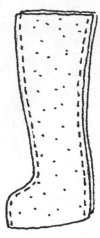

4. Legs: Stitch front and back leg seams, leaving bottom edges of the legs open.

Pin soles to bottom of legs matching large dots to front seams and small dots to back leg seams. Clip curves. Turn. Stuff legs to within 1½" of top.

Turn ¼" at top of legs to inside. Whipstitch opening closed. Whipstitch legs to bottom of body.

5. Tea-dying: Steep several tea bags in hot water. Allow to cool. With a paint brush "paint" the tea solution onto the doll, letting the fabric become blotchy, darker in some areas than others. Dye the entire doll. Set aside to dry. (Depending upon weather conditions and how wet the doll is, this may take one or more days.)

6. Hair: Cut one piece of cardboard measuring 2" x 14". Starting 1" from one end, wind yarn around the cardboard. Stop 1" from the other end. This will make a 12"-long string of wound yarn. Stitch down the center of the cardboard. Running the blades of a pair of scissors along the edge of the cardboard, cut the loops of the yarn on their outer, folded edges. Pull cardboard apart along stitching.

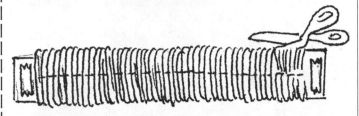

Place the middle of the wound yarn at the center front of the doll's forehead, just to the front of the seam at the top of the head, so that half of the yarn extends to either side. Stitch the yarn to the edge of the face, just in front of the seam, all the way around the head, having the ends of the yarn string meet at the back of the neck.

Repeat with a second row of wound yarn stitching it ½" inside the first row.

Add a third row in the same manner, this time winding only 10" of yarn on the cardboard. Stitch it to the back of the head, ½" to the inside of the second row.

Repeat for a fourth row, winding it just 8" long on the cardboard.

Fill in the remaining bare hole at the back of the head with two rows of yarn, each wound just 2" long. Stitch them straight across the back of the head, filling the empty hole.

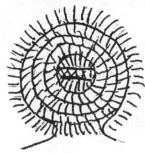

7. Finishing the face: Outline the whites of the eyes with the marker. Pencil in the lines for the mouth. When they are just right, add them with the permanent marker. Sew the two buttons over the whites of the eyes.

To make the clothing:

SHIRT

1. Stitch shoulder/top sleeve seams.

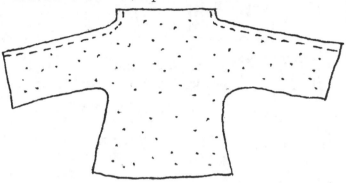

2. Stitch side/underarm seams.

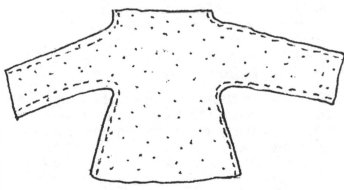

3. Press under ¼" on the bottom edge of the shirt. Turn under another ¼". Topstitch.

4. Press under ¾" on neck and sleeve edges. Lay the elastic thread on the inside of the turned over seam allowance of the neck edge, on the wrong side of the garment. Leave a tail of elastic 2" long to pull up later. Using a wide zigzag stitch, sew over the elastic, being careful not to stitch into the elastic. Repeat for sleeves.

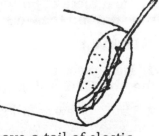

5. Put shirt on doll. Pull up elastic to fit. Tie elastic securely in a double knot.

PANTS

1. Sew the short inner leg seams, right sides together. Press seams open.

2. Pin and stitch the crotch seam, right sides facing.

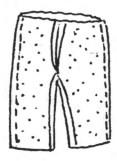

3. Match the long outside leg seams. Pin and stitch.

4. Cut several patches from scrap fabric, each about 1½" or 2" square or rectangle. Apply to pants with fusible adhesive, perhaps putting one at the seat of the pants.

5. Make a line of staystitching about ½" from bottom edges of pant legs and top waist opening of pants. Pull horizontal threads from fabric to outside of this stitching to make frayed edge.

6. As for the sleeves and neck of the shirt, lay the elastic on the inside of the staystitching at the waist, on the wrong side of the garment. Leave a tail of elastic 2" at both ends to pull up later. Using a wide zigzag stitch, sew over the elastic, being careful not to stitch into the elastic. Put the pants on the doll. Adjust the elastic. Knot.

7. Tie a piece of baling twine or other coarse rope around the waist of the doll.

STRAW HAT

1. Tie a piece of jute around the crown of the hat. Glue or tack in place.

2. Using a few small stitches in several places on the head, secure the straw hat to the scarecrow's head.

Interpretations of two old favorites, this duo are inseparable friends. These carrot tops wear red and white striped stockings and black boots, sewn as one with their legs.

Choose a calico, chambray, or a country print for the dress and shirt. Denim or a medium weight navy blue fabric is perfect for the boy's pants. You may wish to stencil, draw, or paint a heart or the traditional "I love you" on their chests.

One skein of yarn will complete the hair for both dolls.

MATERIALS

For each doll:

⅓ yard muslin

Matching thread

Scraps of red and white striped fabric for the legs

Scraps of black fabric for the boots

Acrylic paints: red and white

Stencil brush

Heavy paper or stencil plastic

X-acto® knife

Black fine tip permanent marker, such as a Sharpie

One 6" piece of ¼" dowel

Fray Check®

Polyester fiberfill stuffing

Two ½" buttons for eyes

Carrot-colored yarn

Matching thread

Cardboard

For the clothing:

Raggedy Ann

⅓ yard calico fabric for dress

½ yard natural color batiste for pantaloons and pinafore

Three ⅜" buttons for dress

¼"-wide elastic

Elastic thread, also called elastic beading

One red heart-shaped button

Raggedy Andy

¼ yard shirt fabric

⅓ yard denim for pants

Three ⅜" buttons for shirt

Two ⅝" buttons for suspenders

INSTRUCTIONS

Note: All seam allowances are ¼" unless otherwise instructed.

Make the patterns and cut out the doll and clothing pieces according to the instructions in chapter 1. For Raggedy Anne's skirt, cut a rectangle from the dress fabric measuring 9" x 27". Cut the following for Raggedy Ann's pinafore: one rectangle 10" x 24", one tie 1½" x 30", and two shoulder straps 1½" x 7". Cut two suspenders from pants fabric for Raggedy Andy, each 2" x 8½".

To make the dolls:

1. Face: Transfer face stencil pattern onto heavy paper or stencil plastic. For reference, draw in the outline of the head, neck, and shoulders on the stencil. Lay the stencil over one muslin head, matching reference lines with the raw edges of the head and shoulders. Using the X-acto® knife cut out the face features. Using a dry brush and a small amount of paint, stencil the features as follows: Stencil eyes white, nose and mouth red. When paint is dry draw in mouth, eyebrow, and eyelash lines.

2. Head and body: Pin front of body (stenciled) to back of body (plain), right sides facing. Stitch, leaving an opening between the dots as indicated on the pattern. Clip seam allowances along curves.

Turn. Stuff the head, inserting a 6"-long dowel approximately 3" into the head. Stuff the neck firmly around the dowel, packing the stuffing as you go. Finish stuffing the body. Handstitch the opening at the bottom closed.

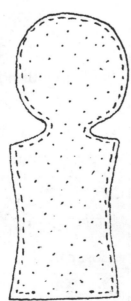

3. Arms: Sew two arms together, right sides facing, leaving the top of the arm open. Clip the curves. Clip into the V of hand. Apply a drop of Fray Check® to stitching at point of each clipping. Leave to dry.

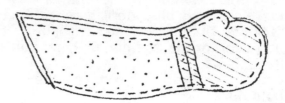

Turn. Repeat for second arm. Stuff arms, leaving the top inch unstuffed. Turn ¼" to inside at the top of the arm. Whipstitch the opening closed. Whipstitch arms to body.

4. Legs: Sew four shoes to four legs, making sure the shoes point toward the front of the leg (knee). Press the seam open.

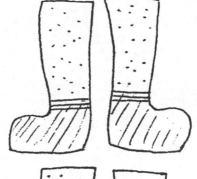

Right sides facing, match two leg/shoes. Sew the front and back seams, leaving the bottom of the shoes and the top of the legs open.

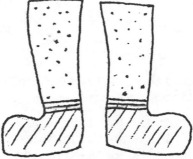

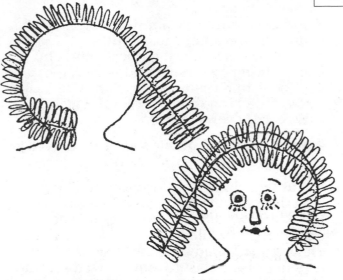

Matching dots to seams, pin and stitch soles to bottom of shoes, matching large dot to front seam and small dot to back seam. Clip curved seams. Turn. Stuff firmly to within 1½" of top of leg.

Turn ¼" at top of legs to inside. Whipstitch opening closed. Whipstitch legs to bottom of body.

5. Hair: Cut two pieces of cardboard, each 1" x 14". Lay side by side. Tape across ends, leaving a small gap between the cardboard. Starting 1" from one end, wind yarn loosely around the cardboard. Stop 1" from the other end. This will make a 12"-long string of wound yarn. Stitch down the center of the wound yarn, between the two pieces of cardboard. Remove the tape. Pull the cardboard out from inside the yarn. This will leave the yarn in loops.

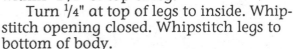

Place the center of the wound yarn at the center front of the top of the head, ¼" to the front of the seam. Stitch the yarn to the head, just in front of the seam, around the sides of the face and around the back of the head, having the ends of the yarn meet at the bottom back of the head.

Repeat with a second row of wound yarn, 12" long, stitching it ½" away from and inside the first row.

Add a third row in the same manner, this time winding only 10" of yarn on the cardboard. Stitch it to the back of the head, ¼" to the inside of the second row.

Repeat for a fourth row, winding it just 8" long on the cardboard.

Fill in the remaining bare hole at the back of the head with two rows of yarn each wound just 2" long. Stitch them straight across the back of the head, filling the empty hole.

6. Eyes: Stitch buttons to eye patches.

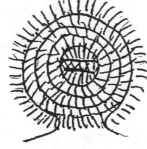

To make the clothing:

RAGGEDY ANN

Dress

1. Stitch front to back bodices at shoulders. Repeat for second (lining) set.

2. Fold neck ruffle in half lengthwise, right sides together. Stitch short ends. Trim seams. Turn. Press. Using a long machine stitch, gather the length of the neck ruffle.

3. Pin neck ruffle to right side of neck edge of bodice having short ends of ruffle ¼" in from back neck edge. Adjust gathers to fit. Pin bodice lining over ruffle and bodice, along neck edge and center backs, right side facing ruffle, matching shoulder seams. Stitch. Clip curves. Trim corners. Turn.

4. Press under ¼" at one short (bottom) edge of each sleeve. Repeat. Topstitch.

5. Cut two pieces of ¼"-wide elastic, each 4½" long. Holding the raw ends of the elastic at the side edges of the sleeve, zigzag stitch the elastic in place, along a line about 1" from the bottom, folded edge of the sleeve. Hold the ends of the elastic firmly and stretch the elastic as you sew.

6. Using a long machine stitch, gather the other short edge of the sleeves between the dots. Pin to armhole of bodice, matching dots. Pull up on gather stitches. Even out the fullness and pin. Stitch. Repeat for other sleeve.

7. Right sides together, sew the underarm and side seams as one.

8. Using a ½" seam allowance stitch center back seam of dress skirt, using a regular machine stitch from the bottom to 5" from the bottom, backstitching there to secure the stitching. Continue to the top with a basting stitch.

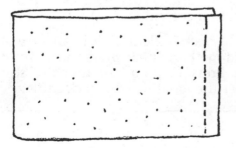

Press the seam open. turn under ¼" on each seam allowance. Topstitch a scant ¼" from either side of the seam. Remove basting stitches.

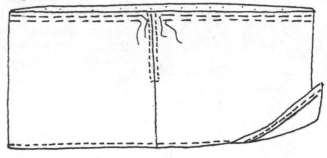

9. Turn under ¼" and then another ¼" on the bottom of the skirt. Topstitch.

10. Gather stitch along the top, raw, long edge of the skirt. Pin the bodice, right sides facing, having center back edges even. Adjust gathers. Pin. Stitch.

11. Make buttonholes on bodice. Try on doll. Mark positions for buttons. Sew on buttons.

BLOOMERS

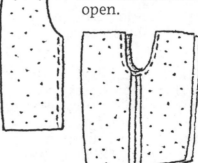

1. Stitch inside leg seams. Press open.

2. Stitch crotch seam.

3. Using a fine zigzag stitch, sew along the waist and leg edges ¼" from the raw edge. Trim to the stitching.

4. Stitch side leg seams.

5. Apply the elastic thread to the waist and legs by zigzag stitching over, but not through, it. Place the elastic about 1" from the finished edge of the legs and ½" from the top of the waist, leave a 2" tail at both ends to pull up later. Be careful not to stitch into the elastic. Put the bloomers on the doll. Adjust the elastic. Knot.

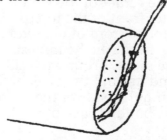

PINAFORE

1. Press under ¼" on two shorter edges (sides) and one longer (hem) edge of apron. Press under another ¼". Topstitch.

2. Press under ¼" and then ¾" on remaining long edge. Using a long gathering stitch, make two rows of stitching close together, barely 1" from the top folded edge of the pinafore.

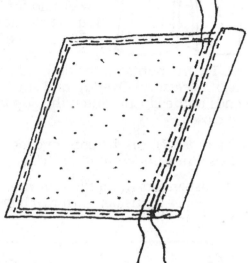

3. Press the long tie in half lengthwise. Unfold. Press long raw edges into center. Turn short ends to inside.

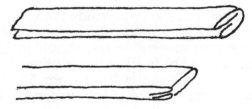

4. Lay pinafore face up on table. Find lengthwise center of tie. Pin it to center of pinafore, 1" down from the top. Pin right and left side of pinafore to tie, 5" from either side of the center of the tie. Adjust gathers to fit. Topstitch close to top and bottom edges of tie, through all layers of pinafore. Topstitch close to edges of remaining free extensions of tie.

5. Fold shoulder straps in half lengthwise. Unfold. Fold and press long raw edges to meet at center. Fold along first fold and press. Topstitch close to folded edges. Turn under ¼" on ends of shoulder straps. Handstitch one end of each strap to inside back of pinafore, one on each side of center back. Sew remaining ends to front of pinafore, about 3" to front of back ties.

6. Sew heart button to left front of pinafore band.

RAGGEDY ANDY

Shirt

1. Stitch fronts to backs at shoulders and sides. One set will be shirt, the other, shirt lining.

2. Apply interfacing to one of the collars. Pin and stitch collars, right sides together, leaving shorter, neck edge open. Trim corners. Turn. Press. Pin collar to neck edge of shirt, having collar edges start ¼" from the front edges of the shirt. Baste collar to shirt.

3. Pin lining to shirt, right sides facing, along neck, front, and bottom edges, sandwiching the collar between the two layers. Stitch. leaving armholes open and a gap in the stitch at bottom center back for turning. Turn right side out. Press.

4. Stitch two long sides of sleeves together, right sides facing.

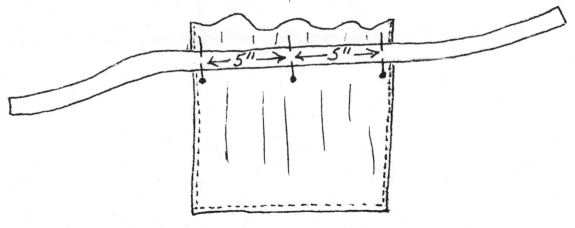

5. Press ¼" to inside on one short edge of both sleeves. Repeat. Topstitch.

6. Pin and stitch sleeve to armhole, treating shirt and shirt lining as one layer. Repeat for second sleeve.

7. Make button holes on left side of shirt front as indicated on pattern. Sew buttons in place.

8. Turn up sleeve edges to fit doll.

PANTS

1. Sew the short inner leg seams, right sides together. Press seams open.

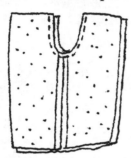

2. Pin and stitch the crotch seam, right sides facing.

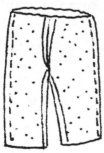

3. Match the long, outside leg seams. Pin and stitch.

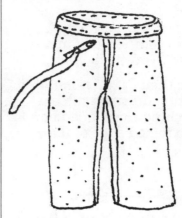

4. Press under ¼" along waistline opening. Press under an additional ⁵⁄₈". Topstitch close to both folds, leaving a ½" opening in the stitching on the lower fold for inserting the elastic. Run a 7½" piece of elastic through the casing. Try the pants on the doll. Adjust the elastic, if necessary. Overlap and stitch the raw ends of the elastic. Stitch the gap in the casing closed.

5. Press under ¼" on the bottom edges of the pant legs. Press under another ¼". Topstitch.

6. Press suspenders in half lengthwise. Press long raw edges to inside. Turn raw edges on one end to inside.

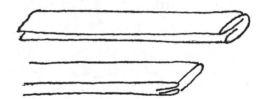

Stitch other end to inside back of pants about 1½" to the side of the center back seam. Run suspender over shoulder. Stitch finished end to front of pants about 1" to the side of the center front seam. Stitch a button over the end of the suspender. Repeat for other side.

P R U D E N C E

With her tea-dyed "skin" and torn muslin hair, this doll appears well-loved, as if handed down through the generations. Make your own Prudence, sign your name and date to her bottom, and she will become your own family heirloom.

Choose old-looking fabrics for the dress and pinafore, tea dying any that need a little extra aging. (See chapter 1.) Odd assortments of fabrics work well; perhaps an old-fashioned calico for the dress and a check for the pinafore. Or choose pillow ticking, matching it with a solid color, calico, or plaid for the dress. The shoes are painted after the legs are stitched and stuffed. The torn muslin hair gives this doll a homemade look, as in times past when someone sewing a doll would make due with what was available. Oftentimes this forced resourcefulness produced a finished item displaying the wonderful creative expression of the dollmaker.

MATERIALS

For the doll:

¹/₃ yard muslin

Matching thread

One 6" piece of ¹/₄" dowel

Fray Check®

Polyester fiberfill stuffing

Embroidery floss: medium brown, medium blue, dark red, dark brown

Black acrylic paint

Tea bags

1 yard muslin for the hair

⁷/₈ yard of ¹/₈"-wide black ribbon

For the clothing:

¹/₃ yard dress fabric

Matching thread

¹/₃ yard pinafore fabric

Matching thread

¹/₂ yard muslin for drawers and petticoat

Matching thread

1¹/₄ yards of 1³/₄"-wide natural color cluny lace to edge drawers and petticoat (see Sources)

¹/₄"-wide elastic

Elastic thread, also known as beading elastic

INSTRUCTIONS

Note: All seam allowances are ¼" unless otherwise instructed.

Make the patterns and cut out the doll and clothing pieces according to the instructions in chapter 1. Transfer markings for embroidery to face. For Prudence's petticoat, cut a rectangle from the dress fabric measuring 9" x 27". For Prudence's hair tie, cut a piece of dress or pinafore fabric 2" x 12".

To make the doll:

1. Head and body: Pin front of body (stenciled) to back of body (plain), right sides facing. Stitch, leaving an opening between the dots as indicated on the pattern. Clip seam allowances along curves.

Turn. Stuff the head firmly, inserting a 6"-long dowel approximately 3" into the head. Stuff the neck firmly around the dowel, packing the stuffing as you go. Continue stuffing the body, not quite as firmly as the neck. Handstitch the bottom opening closed.

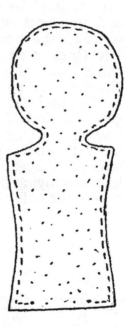

2. Arms: Sew two arms together, right sides facing, leaving the top of the arm open for turning. Clip curves. Clip into V of hand. Apply a drop of Fray Check® to stitching at end of each clipping. Leave to dry.

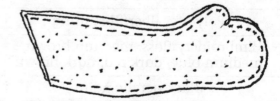

Turn. Stuff arms, leaving the top inch unstuffed. Turn ¼" to inside at the top of the arm. Whipstitch the opening closed. Whipstitch arms to body.

3. Legs: Stitch front and back leg seams, leaving bottom edges of the foot open.

Pin soles to bottom of legs, matching large dots on soles to front seams and small dots to back leg seams. Clip curves. Turn. Stuff legs to within 1½" of top.

Turn ¼" at top of legs to inside. Whipstitch opening closed. Whipstitch legs to bottom of body.

4. Finishing the face: With a soft pencil, make a dot at the center of the front top of the head. Put another dot at the center front bottom of the body. Connect the dots with a light pencil line. Using two strands of the medium brown floss make small cross stitches down the line. Don't worry if the stitches are uneven; this is a homemade doll!

Using four strands of floss, embroider eyes, nose, and mouth according to markings.

5. Shoes: From the mark down, paint shoes black, including soles. When dry, apply laces as shown. Push pins into the foot to mark the dots, making the dots ⅝" apart horizontally and about ⅜" apart vertically. Tie in bow at the top.

6. Tea-dying: Steep several tea bags in hot water. With a paint brush, apply the tea solution to the doll, letting the color overlap and become blotchy, darker in some areas than others. Do cover embroidery, too, as this gives it the appearance of age. Set aside to dry. This may take a day or more, depending upon the weather conditions and just how wet the doll is.

7. Hair: Tea-dye the muslin for the hair by wetting it and immersing it in a hot solution of strong tea, as instructed in chapter 1. Drip dry or toss in the dryer separate from clothing.

Tear six strips of the tea-dyed muslin, each 14" x ⅜" or 14" x ½", along the grainline of the muslin. Repeat until you have twelve bunches of six 18" strips.

Fold a batch of strips in half to find the middle. Unfold. Starting at one side of head, about even with the nose, stitch the center of the bunch to the head along the seam. Repeat for the next bunch of strips, and so on until you reach the opposite side of the head and have used all twelve bunches. Fold the strips that are falling over the face to the back of the head.

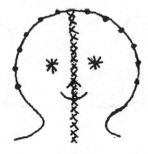

Tear six strips from the muslin, each 18" x ¹⁄₂". Cut these strips in half, and in half again. Divide them into six bunches of four strips each.

Approximately 1¹⁄₂" to one side of the head's center front top, sew a bunch of the short muslin strips close to the point where the long hair strips are stitched. Continue adding batches of short strips, placing the last bunch about 1¹⁄₂" to the opposite side of the head.

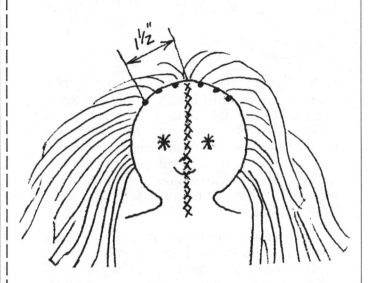

Take five or six strips of hair from each side of the head, just below the bangs. Pull them together to meet at the top back of the head. Tie with the hair tie.

To make the clothing:

DRESS

1. Stitch shoulder and side/underarm seams, right sides facing.

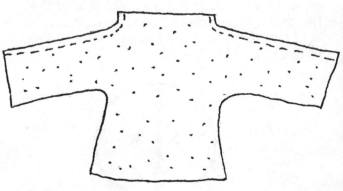

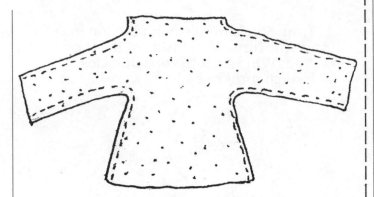

2. Press under ¹⁄₄" on the bottom edge of the dress. Turn under another ¹⁄₄". Topstitch.

3. Press under ³⁄₄" on neck and sleeve edges. Lay the elastic thread on the inside of the turned-over seam allowance of the neck edge, on the wrong side of the garment. Leave a tail of elastic 2" long to pull up later. Using a wide zigzag stitch, sew over elastic, being careful not to stitch into the elastic. Repeat for sleeves.

4. Put dress on doll. Pull up elastic to fit. Tie elastic securely in double knots.

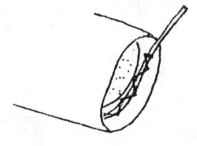

PETTICOAT

1. Turn under ¹⁄₄" on one long raw edge (to become bottom hem) of petticoat. Press under another ¹⁄₄". Pin lace to underside of hem, right side facing hem. Topstitch, including lace in the stitching.

2. Stitch short ends of petticoat together, right sides facing, including raw edges of lace in seam. Press seam open.

3. Turn under ¹⁄₄" on remaining long raw edge. Turn under ⁵⁄₈". Topstitch close to both folded edges, leaving a ¹⁄₂"-wide opening in the bottom stitching for inserting the elastic. Cut a piece of ¹⁄₄"-wide elastic 7¹⁄₂" long. Insert elastic into casing as instructed in chapter one. Stitch ends of elastic together. Stitch gap in casing closed.

BLOOMERS

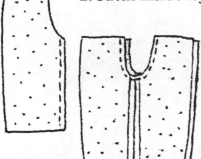

1. Stitch inside leg seams.

2. Turn under ¼" on bottom leg edges. Turn under another ¼". Pin and top-stitch lace to leg hems.

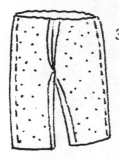

3. Stitch crotch seams.

4. Stitch leg side seams.

5. Press under ¼" on waist. Press under an additional ⅝". Topstitch close to both folded edges, leaving an opening in the bottom edge for inserting elastic. Cut a piece of ¼" elastic 7½" long. Insert elastic. Stitch the raw ends of the elastic together. Sew opening closed.

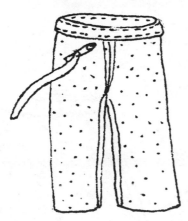

PINAFORE

1. Press under ¼" twice on armhole edges, which are cut at an angle. Topstitch.

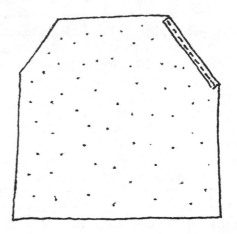

2. Stitch side seams. Press seams open.

3. Press under ¼" for hem. Press under another ¼". Topstitch.

4. Gather top edges of pinafore front and back between dots.

5. Right sides facing, fold bands along fold-line. Pin and stitch short side edges of bands. Press under ¼" on one long edge of each band.

6. Pin pinafore front to one band, along long unturned edge, with right sides facing. Pull up on gathering stitches. Adjust gathers evenly. Pin. Stitch. Repeat for second band. Turn band right sides out.

7. Slipstitch folded edge of band to inside along stitching.

8. Fold ties in half lengthwise, right sides together. Stitch across one short edge and down the long raw edge. Turn. Press. Turn under ¼" on remaining short raw edge with the turned under edge facing the inside of the top corner edge of one band, slipstitch tie to band. Repeat for other three ties.

FANCY DRESS–UP LADY

Beaming with pride at her fancy ensemble this little girl has turned a rainy afternoon into a bright game of dress-up.

Her shoes, stockings, and gloves are stitched as one with her legs and arms, easing construction and saving a few steps. Her hat is a store-bought crocheted doily dyed black, formed with fabric stiffener, and adorned with silk flowers. Her dress is a bold polka dot taffeta-type fabric. Underneath she wears fancy black lace-edged drawers and several layers of white netting petticoats which give her dress extra fullness. Her hair, a highly textured yarn purchased at a yarn shop, is curled in the oven. Glue a bunch of silk flowers to her hat, wrap a feather boa around her neck, and bedeck her with a few pieces of costume jewelry — you've brought to life any young girl's dress-up dream.

MATERIALS

For the doll:

1/3 yard muslin	1/4"-wide elastic
Matching thread	Three 3/8" buttons
Acrylic paints: red and white	1/2 yard black netting
Stencil brush	1/2 yard white netting
Heavy paper or stencil plastic	Matching thread
X-acto® knife	1/4 yard black fabric for panties
Black fine tip permanent marker, such as a Sharpie	Matching thread
One 6" piece of 1/4" dowel	Elastic thread
Fray Check®	1/2 yard black lace to trim panties, 1/2" to 1"-wide
Polyester fiberfill stuffing	Feather boa (See Sources)
Two 3/8" buttons for eyes	Costume jewelry: necklace and post earrings
One skein variegated yellow yarn for hair	Crocheted doily, approximately 12" in diameter
Matching thread	Black dye
Metal knitting needles or shish kebab skewers	Fabric stiffener
Scotch tape	Waxed paper

For the clothing:

	Elastic band
1/3 yard fancy dress fabric	Silk flowers
Matching thread	Hot glue gun or glue

INSTRUCTIONS

Note: All seam allowances are 1/4" unless otherwise instructed.

Make the patterns and cut out the doll and clothing pieces according to the instructions in chapter 1. Cut the dress skirt 9" x 27". For the petticoats, cut one rectangle from the white netting measuring 16" x 28".

To make the doll:

1. Face: Transfer face stencil pattern onto heavy paper or stencil plastic. For reference, draw in the outline of the head, neck, and shoulders on the stencil. Place the stencil over the head of one of the muslin bodies, lining up the drawn reference line with the edges of the head and shoulders. Using the X-acto® knife, cut out the face features. Using a dry brush and a small amount of paint, stencil the features as follows: Stencil eyes white and mouth red. When paint is dry, draw in the eyebrows, nose, and mouth lines with the permanent marker.

2. Head and body: Pin front of body (stenciled) to back of body (plain), right sides facing. Stitch, leaving an opening between

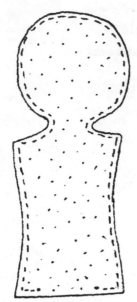

the dots as indicated on the pattern. Clip seam allowances along curves.

Turn. Stuff the head and neck firmly, inserting a 6"-long dowel approximately 3" into the head. Finish stuffing the body until it is full and firm. Handstitch the bottom opening closed.

3. Arms: Pin black netting arm over muslin arms, having two thumbs facing right and two facing left. Baste inside seam lines. Treat as one according to the following instructions. Sew two arms together, netting sides facing, leaving the top open. Clip curves. Clip into V of hand. Apply a drop of Fray Check® to stitching at end of clipping. Leave to dry. Repeat for two remaining arms.

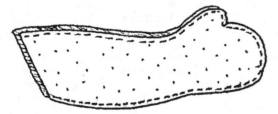

Turn. Stuff arms, leaving the top inch unstuffed. Turn 1/4" of top of arm to inside. Whipstitch the top opening closed. Whipstitch arms to body.

4. Legs: Lay black netting legs over muslin legs. Check to be sure there are two right pointing and two left pointing legs. Pin. Baste inside seam line. Lay the legs down, netting sides up. Pin shoes over legs, matching raw edges. Using a small zigzag stitch, applique top edge of shoe to leg, covering the raw edge of the shoe with stitches. Baste remaining raw edges of shoes to legs just inside the seam lines.

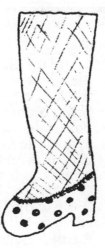

Right sides facing, stitch legs together. Clip curves. Turn. Stuff legs to within 1 1/2" of top.

Turn 1/4" at top of legs to inside. Whipstitch opening closed. Whipstitch legs to bottom of body.

5. Finishing the face: Sew the buttons in place for the eyes. Rub a little powder blush on a tissue. Dab gently on the doll's checks, building the color slowly. Rub gently with a fresh tissue to smooth the color.

6. Hair: Preheat oven to 275 degrees F. Tape the end of the yarn to one end of a metal shish kebab skewer or knitting needle. Wind the yarn tightly around the skewer. Tape the end.

Soak the skewered yarn under running water. Place the skewer on the oven rack. Bake the yarn for approximately fifteen minutes, or until the yarn is completely dry. Remove from oven. Allow to cool. Remove from skewer. Repeat until you have enough yarn for the hair.

Starting about 1 1/2" to one side of the forehead, stitch the curled yarn to the doll's head just in front of the seam. Add strands of yarn until the bangs are complete. Make the loops of varying lengths, about 1 1/2" long. Make the side loops slightly longer, perhaps 2" long.

To form the hair, start at the center top of the head, along the seam. Stitch loops measuring 7" or 8" in length along the seam, continuing down one side for about 3". Add strands of yarn as you go to keep the hair looking full. Repeat for the other side of the head.

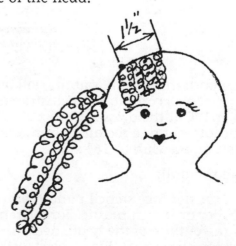

To make the clothing:

DRESS

1. Stitch front to back bodices at shoulders. Repeat for the lining set.

2. Pin bodice to bodice lining at neck and back edges, right sides facing. Stitch. Clip corners. Turn.

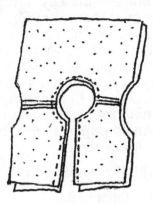

3. Press under 1" at one long (bottom) edge of each sleeve. Cut two pieces of ¼"-wide elastic, each 4½" long. Holding the raw ends of the elastic at the side edges of the sleeve, zigzag stitch the elastic to the wrong side of the sleeve, over the turned under raw edge of the sleeve edge. Hold the ends of the elastic firmly and stretch the elastic as you sew. Repeat for second sleeve.

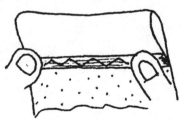

4. Using a long machine stitch, gather the other long edge of the sleeves between the dots. Pin to armhole of bodice, matching dots. Pull up on gathering stitches. Even out the fullness and pin. Stitch. Repeat for other sleeve.

5. Right sides together, sew the underarm and bodice side seams as one.

6. Using a ½" seam allowance stitch center back seam of dress skirt, using a regular machine stitch from the bottom to 5" from the bottom, backstitching there to secure the stitching. Continue to the top with a basting stitch. Press the seam open. Turn under ¼"

on each seam allowance. Topstitch a scant ¼" from either side of the seam. Remove basting.

7. Turn under ¼" and then another ¼" on the bottom of the skirt. Topstitch.

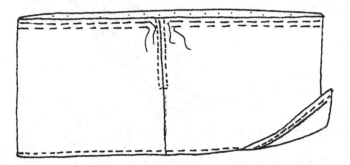

8. Pin skirt to bottom raw edges of bodice, matching finished edges of center back bodice and skirt. Adjust gathers. Pin. Stitch.

9. Make buttonholes on bodice. Try on doll. Mark positions for buttons. Sew buttons on.

PANTIES

1. Stitch inside leg seams. Press open.

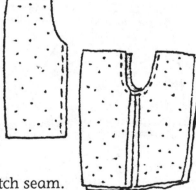

2. Stitch crotch seam.

3. Press under ¼" and another ¼" on bottom edges of legs. Pin black lace trim to underside of hem. Topstitch.

4. Stitch side leg seams.

5. Press under ¼" on raw edge at waist. Repeat. Topstitch.

6. Apply the elastic thread to the waist by zigzag stitching over it. Place the elastic about ½" from the finished edge, leaving a 2" tail at both ends to pull up later. Be careful not to stitch into the elastic. Put the panties on the doll. Adjust the elastic. Knot.

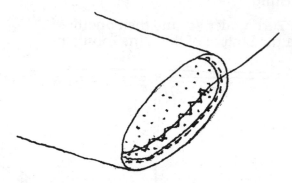

PETTICOAT

1. Using a small zigzag stitch, sew ¼" from edge on both long raw edges of petticoat. Trim extra netting that extends beyond stitching back to the stitching.

2. With the small zigzag stitch, sew short (16") ends together. Trim the seam allowances to the stitching. Fold the petticoat in half lengthwise. Zigzag stitch about ½" from the folded edge, leaving a ½" opening in the stitching.

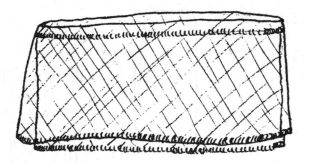

3. Cut a piece of ¼" elastic 7½" long. Insert into casing. Stitch ends of elastic together. Stitch opening in casing closed.

HAT

1. Dye the doily according to manufacturer's instructions. Use a strong concentration of the black dye. Allow to dry.

2. Find a margarine or other plastic container that fits the doll's head. Lay a large piece of waxed paper over the container. Moisten the doily with fabric stiffener; do not saturate. Drape the doily over the waxed paper and margarine container. Mold the doily to the container and secure with a large rubber band. Adjust doily to fit smoothly. Put wadded paper under the outer edges of the doily (under the waxed paper) to give the hat brim some waves. Allow to dry.

3. Hot glue silk flowers around hat.

4. Tack hat to doll's head.

FINISHING

1. Cut posts from costume earrings. Glue earrings to top front of shoes. Put necklace on doll. Wrap boa around her neck.

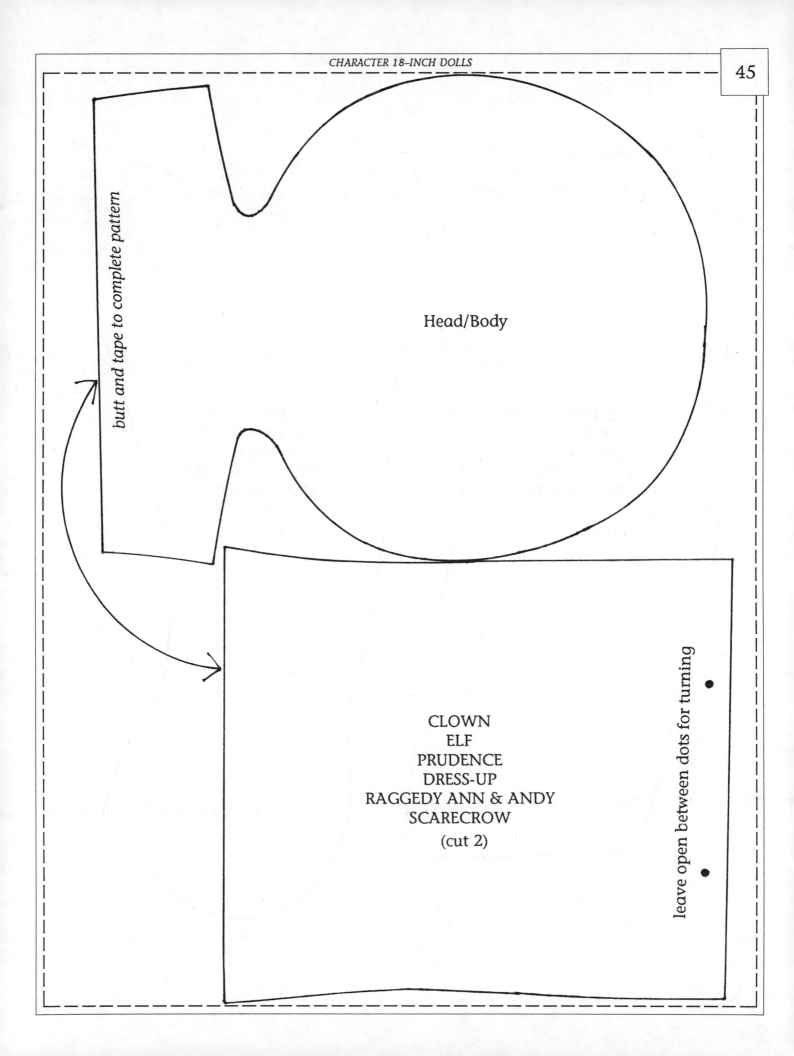

butt and tape to complete pattern

Head/Body

CLOWN
ELF
PRUDENCE
DRESS-UP
RAGGEDY ANN & ANDY
SCARECROW

(cut 2)

leave open between dots for turning

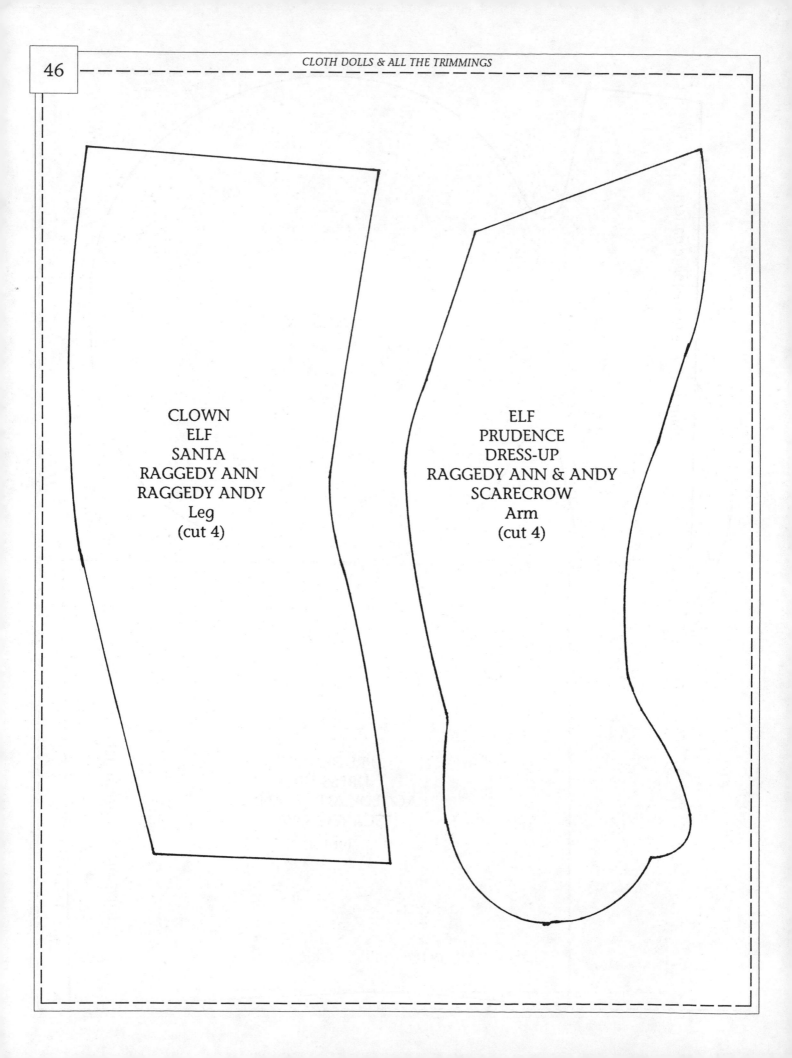

CLOWN
ELF
SANTA
RAGGEDY ANN
RAGGEDY ANDY
Leg
(cut 4)

ELF
PRUDENCE
DRESS-UP
RAGGEDY ANN & ANDY
SCARECROW
Arm
(cut 4)

CLOWN
Face diagram/stencil

CLOWN
ELF
Sleeve
(cut 2 of fabric)
(cut 2 of lining)

place on fold of pattern paper and cut out

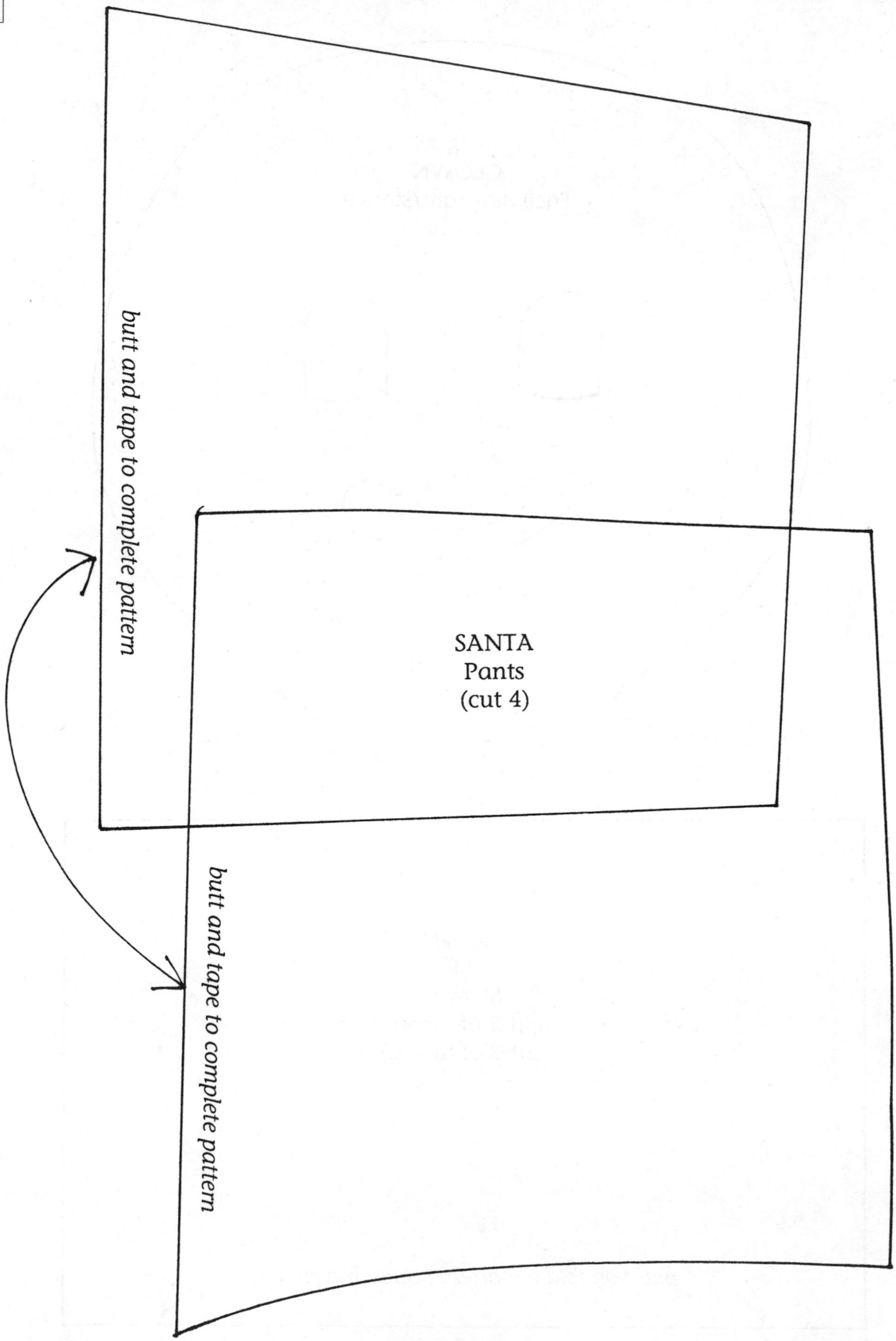

butt and tape to complete pattern

SANTA
Pants
(cut 4)

butt and tape to complete pattern

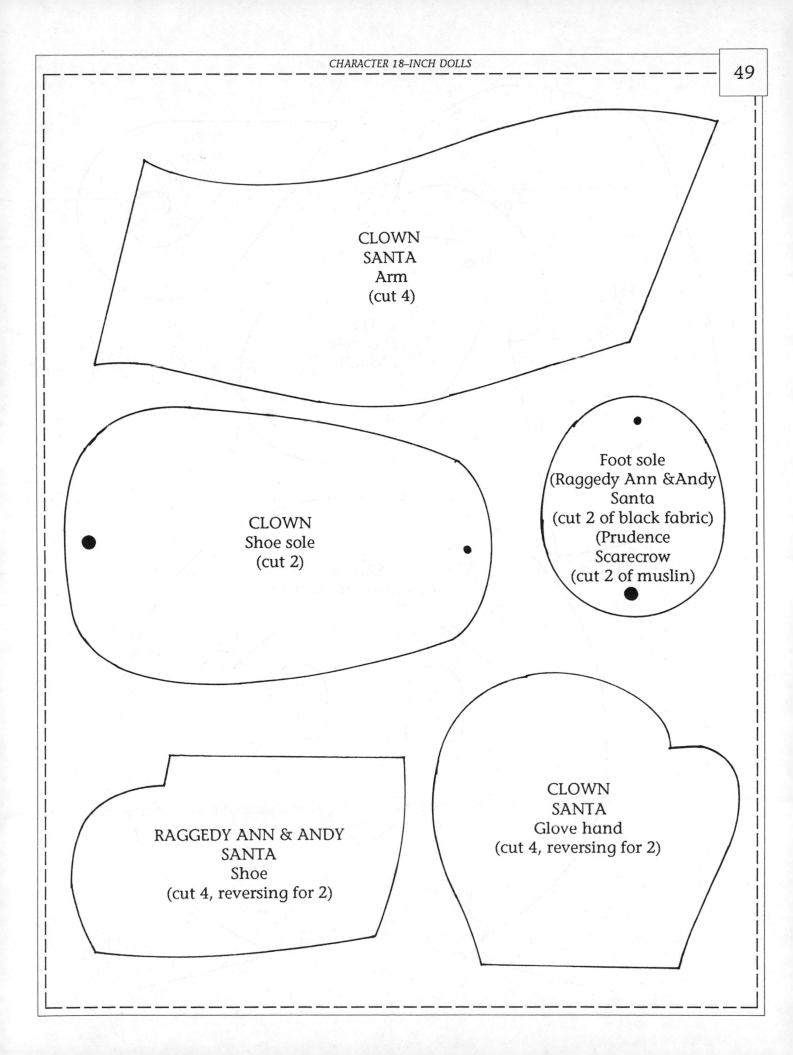

CLOWN
SANTA
Arm
(cut 4)

CLOWN
Shoe sole
(cut 2)

Foot sole
(Raggedy Ann &Andy
Santa
(cut 2 of black fabric)
(Prudence
Scarecrow
(cut 2 of muslin)

RAGGEDY ANN & ANDY
SANTA
Shoe
(cut 4, reversing for 2)

CLOWN
SANTA
Glove hand
(cut 4, reversing for 2)

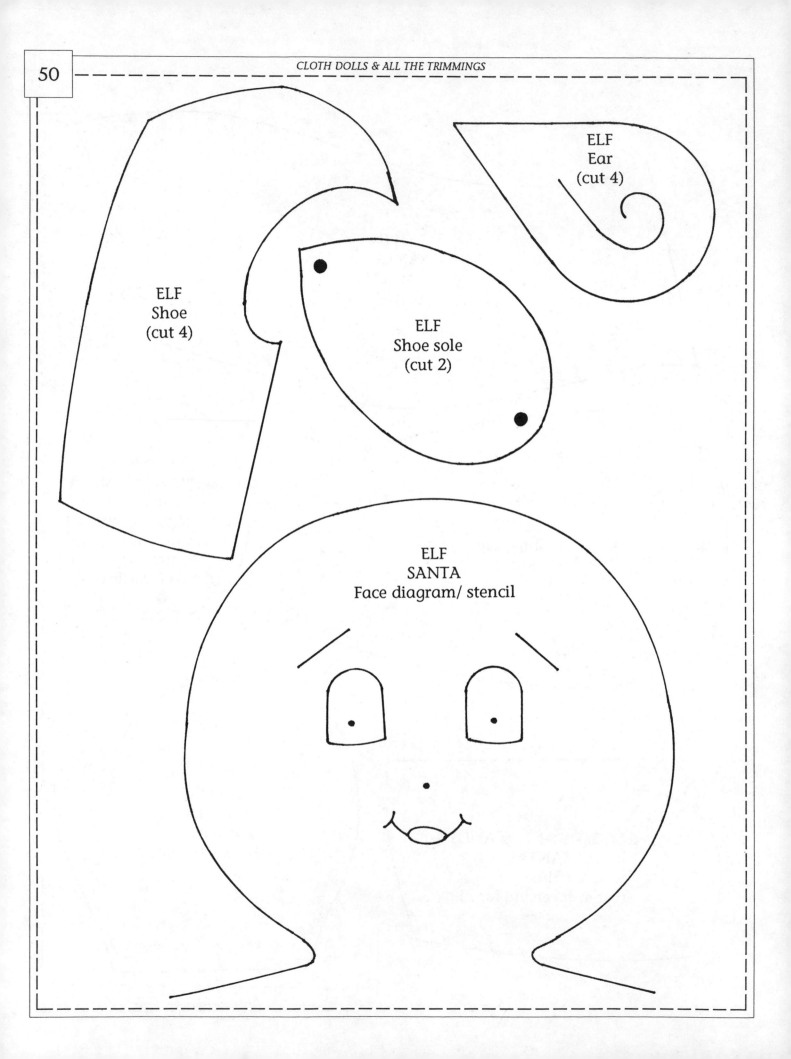

ELF
Ear
(cut 4)

ELF
Shoe
(cut 4)

ELF
Shoe sole
(cut 2)

ELF
SANTA
Face diagram/ stencil

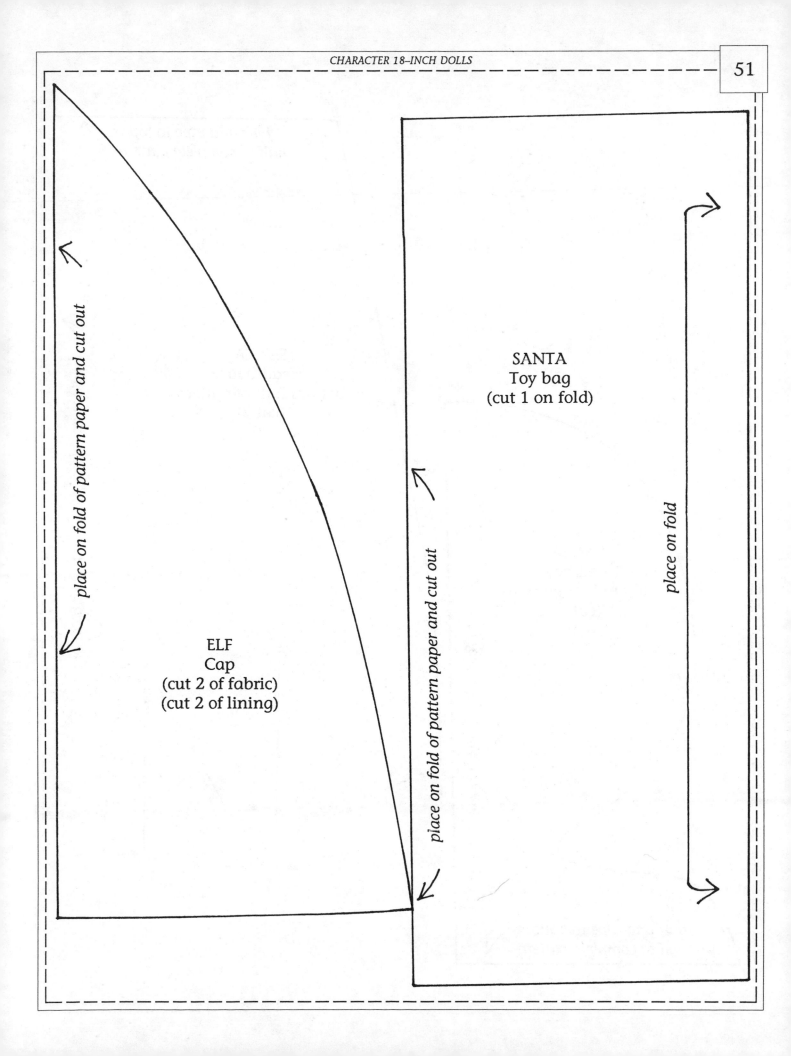

place on fold of pattern paper and cut out

ELF
Cap
(cut 2 of fabric)
(cut 2 of lining)

SANTA
Toy bag
(cut 1 on fold)

place on fold of pattern paper and cut out

place on fold

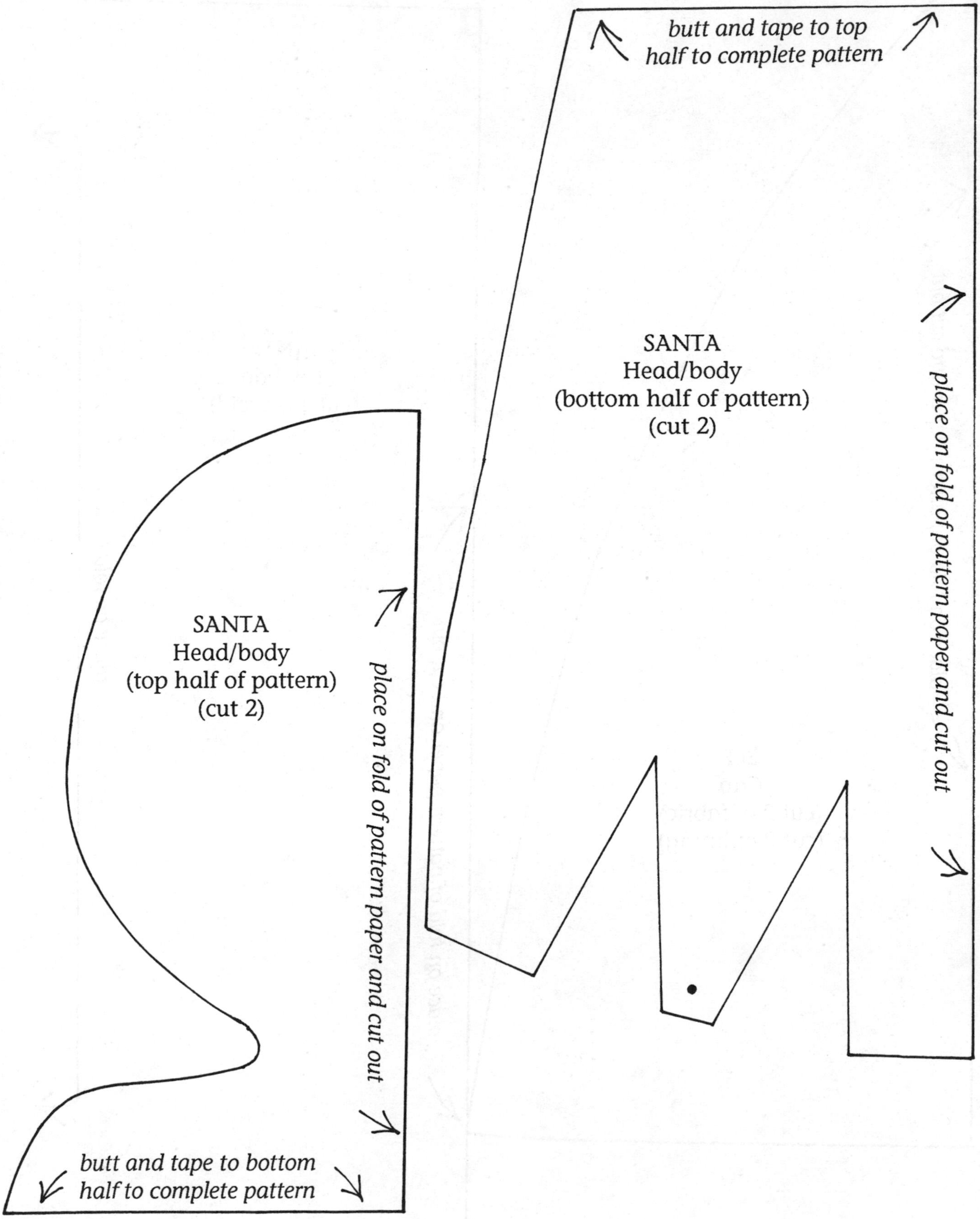

*butt and tape to top
half to complete pattern*

SANTA
Head/body
(bottom half of pattern)
(cut 2)

place on fold of pattern paper and cut out

SANTA
Head/body
(top half of pattern)
(cut 2)

place on fold of pattern paper and cut out

*butt and tape to bottom
half to complete pattern*

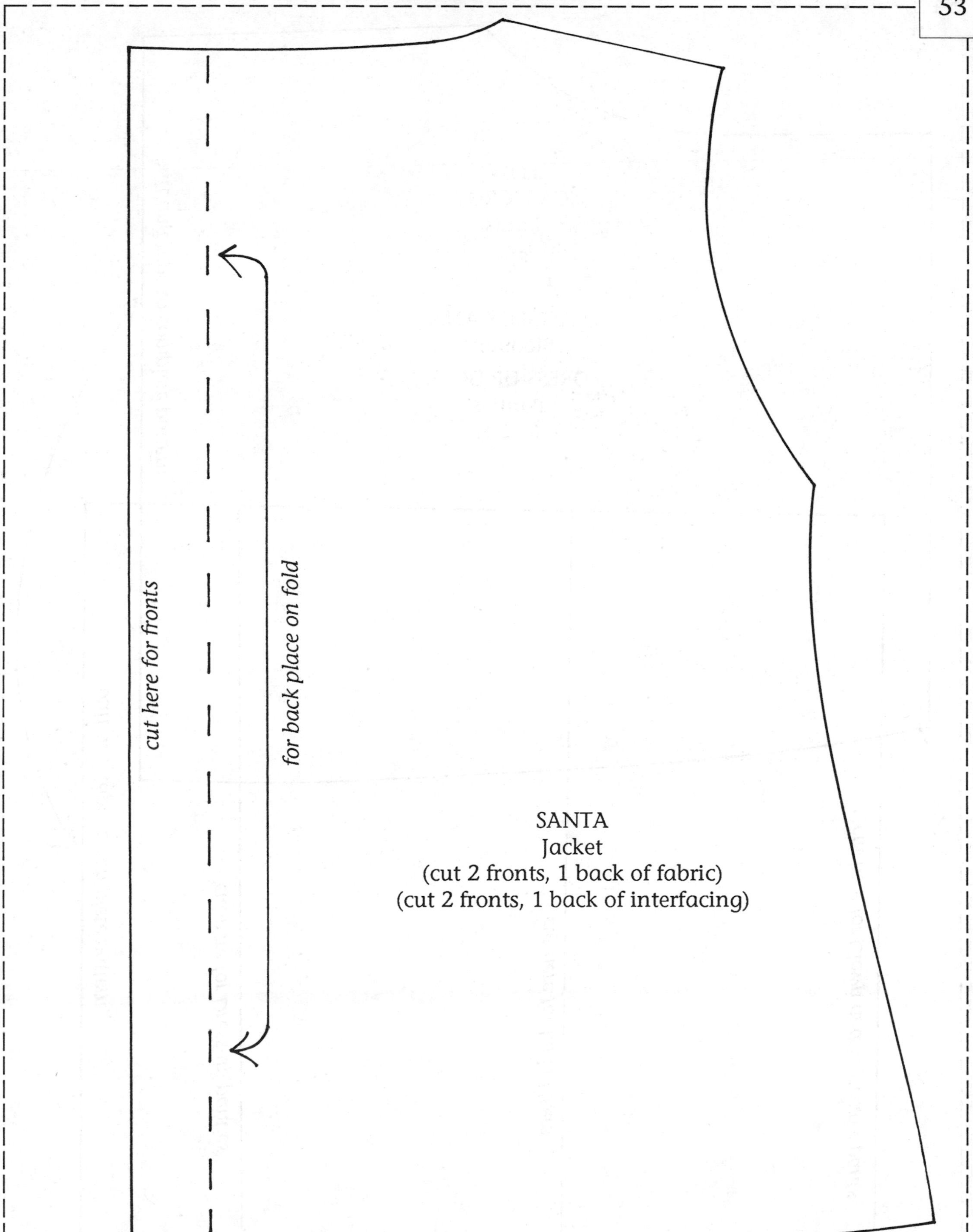

cut here for fronts

for back place on fold

SANTA
Jacket
(cut 2 fronts, 1 back of fabric)
(cut 2 fronts, 1 back of interfacing)

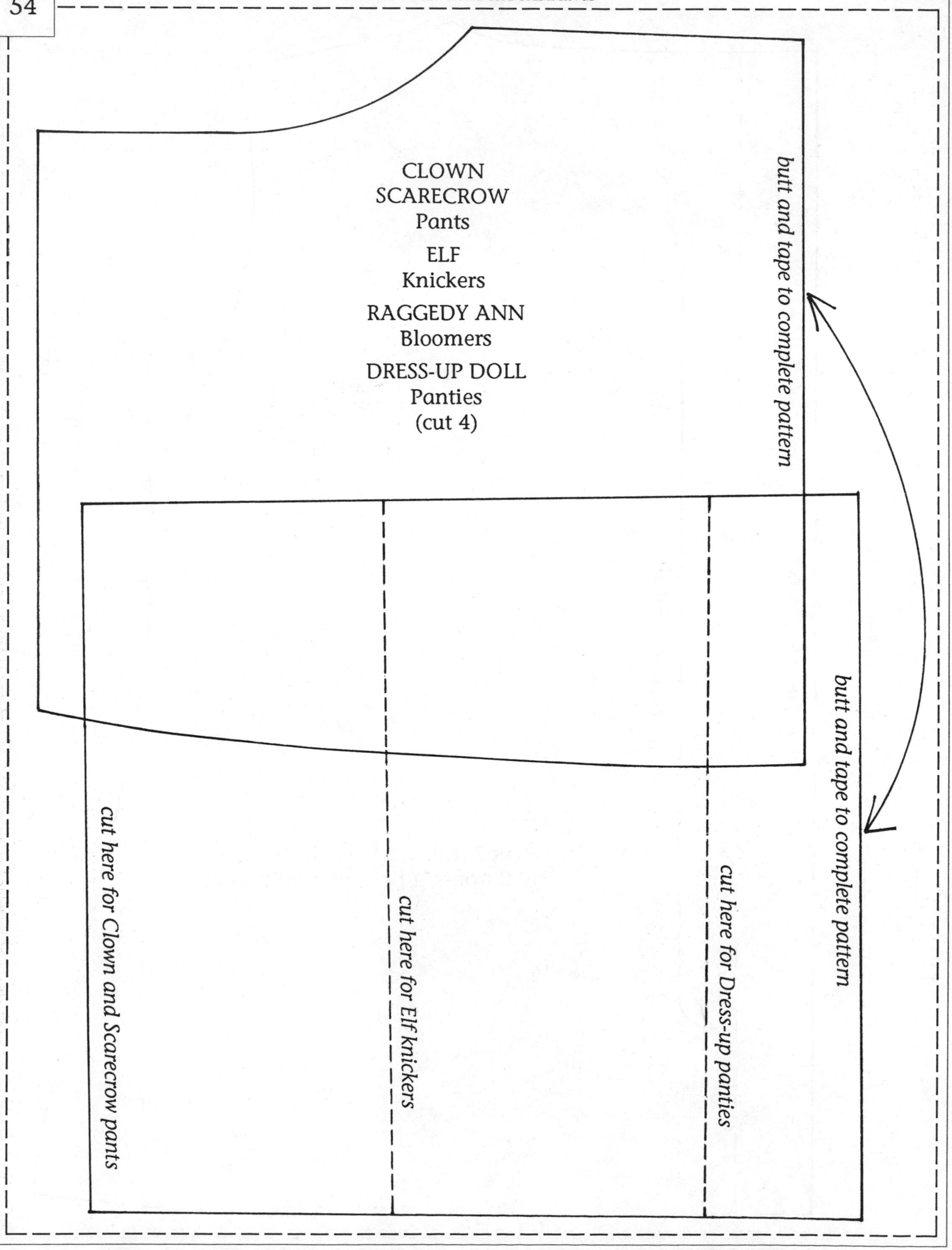

CLOWN
SCARECROW
Pants

ELF
Knickers

RAGGEDY ANN
Bloomers

DRESS-UP DOLL
Panties
(cut 4)

butt and tape to complete pattern

butt and tape to complete pattern

cut here for Clown and Scarecrow pants

cut here for Elf Knickers

cut here for Dress-up panties

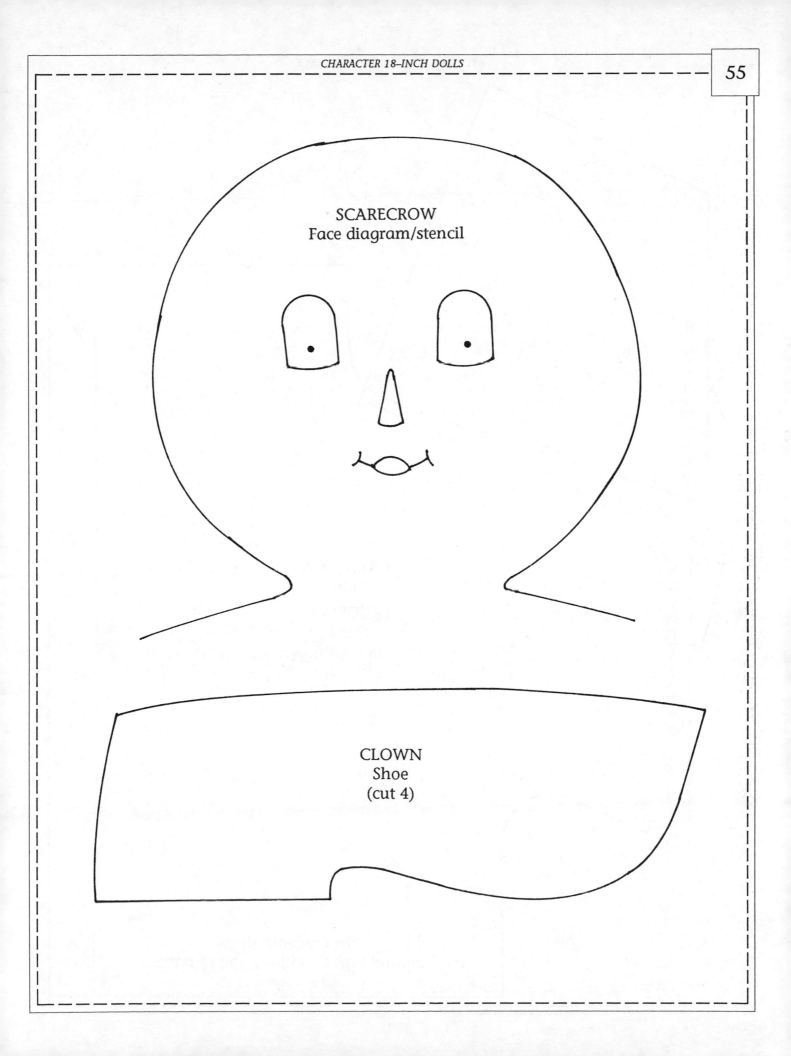

SCARECROW
Face diagram/stencil

CLOWN
Shoe
(cut 4)

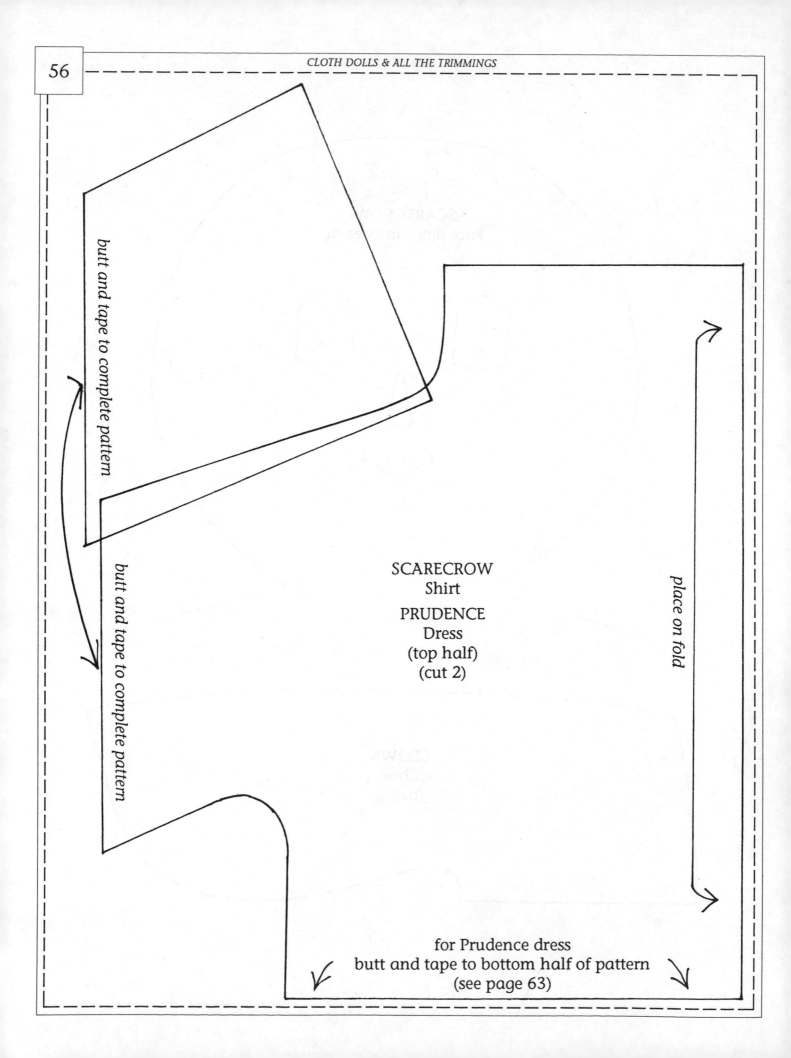

butt and tape to complete pattern

butt and tape to complete pattern

SCARECROW
Shirt
PRUDENCE
Dress
(top half)
(cut 2)

place on fold

for Prudence dress
butt and tape to bottom half of pattern
(see page 63)

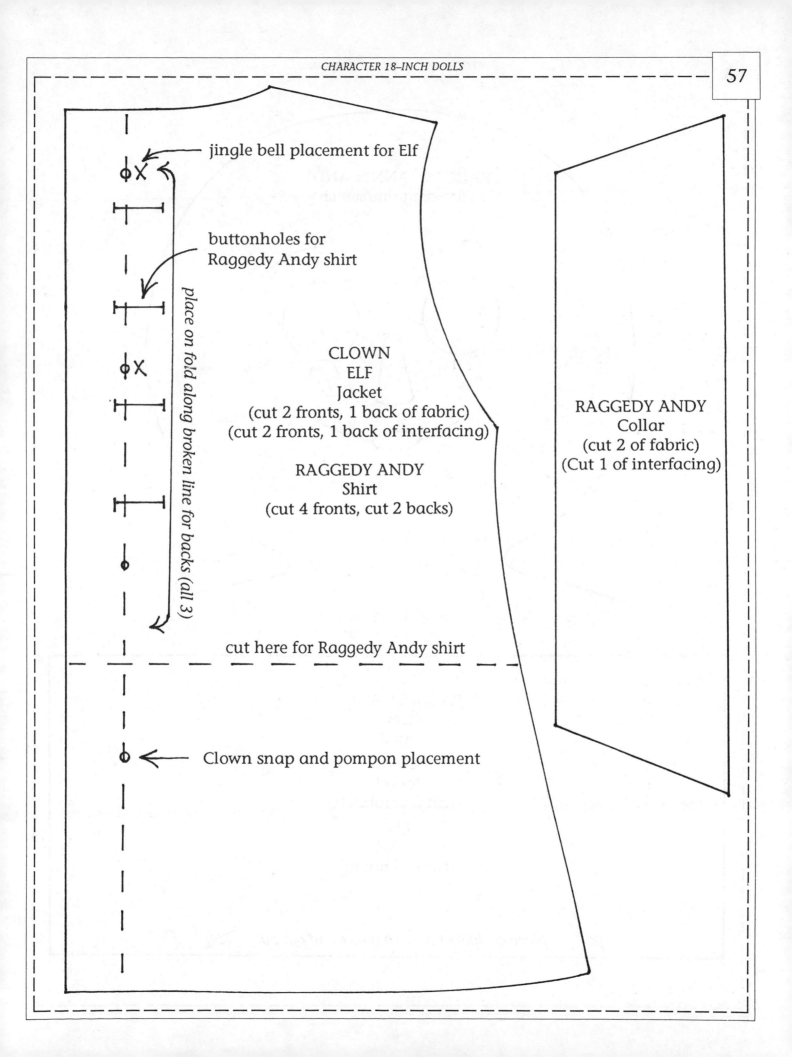

jingle bell placement for Elf

buttonholes for
Raggedy Andy shirt

place on fold along broken line for backs (all 3)

CLOWN
ELF
Jacket
(cut 2 fronts, 1 back of fabric)
(cut 2 fronts, 1 back of interfacing)

RAGGEDY ANDY
Shirt
(cut 4 fronts, cut 2 backs)

RAGGEDY ANDY
Collar
(cut 2 of fabric)
(Cut 1 of interfacing)

cut here for Raggedy Andy shirt

Clown snap and pompon placement

RAGGEDY ANN & ANDY
Face diagram/stencil

RAGGEDY ANDY
Sleeve
(cut 2)

CLOWN
Jacket
(cut 2 of fabric)

ELF
Jacket
(cut 2 of lining)

 place on fold of pattern paper and cut out

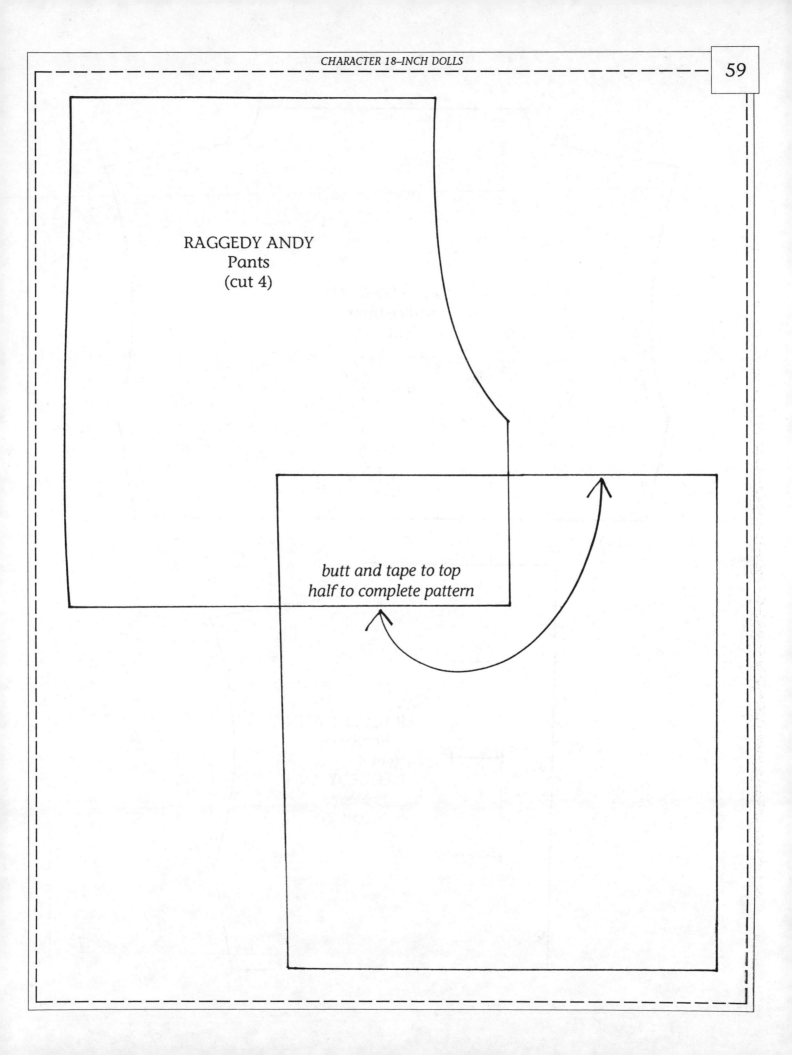

RAGGEDY ANDY
Pants
(cut 4)

butt and tape to top
half to complete pattern

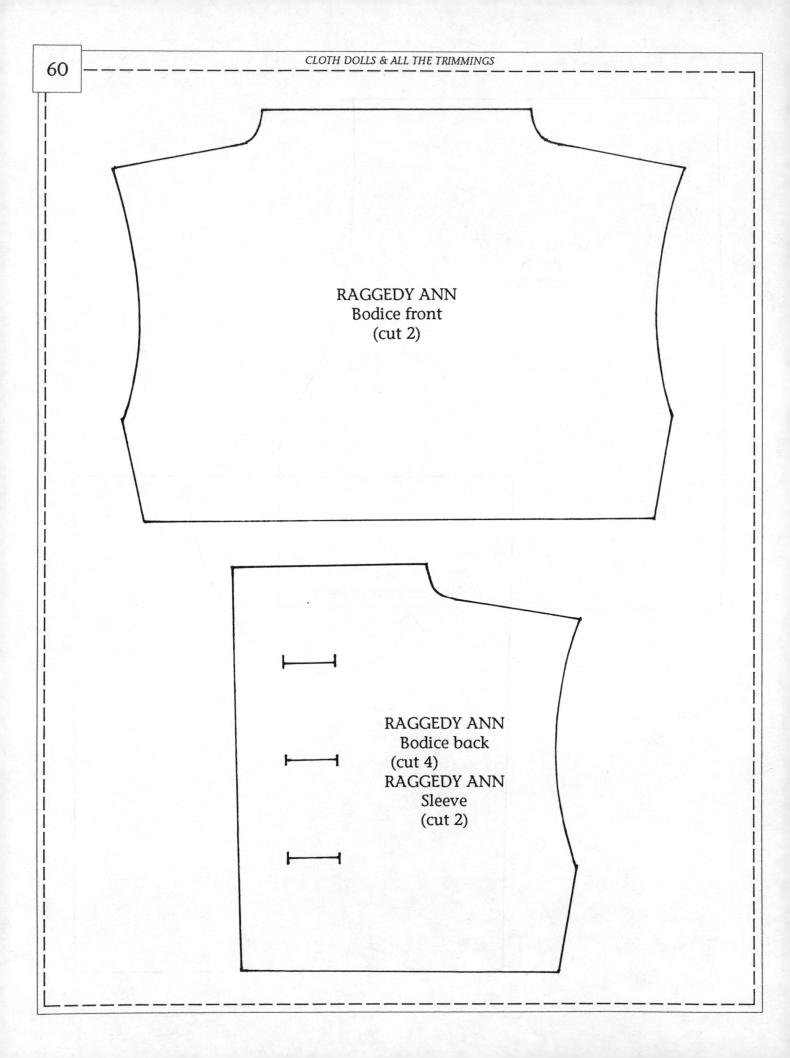

RAGGEDY ANN
Bodice front
(cut 2)

RAGGEDY ANN
Bodice back
(cut 4)
RAGGEDY ANN
Sleeve
(cut 2)

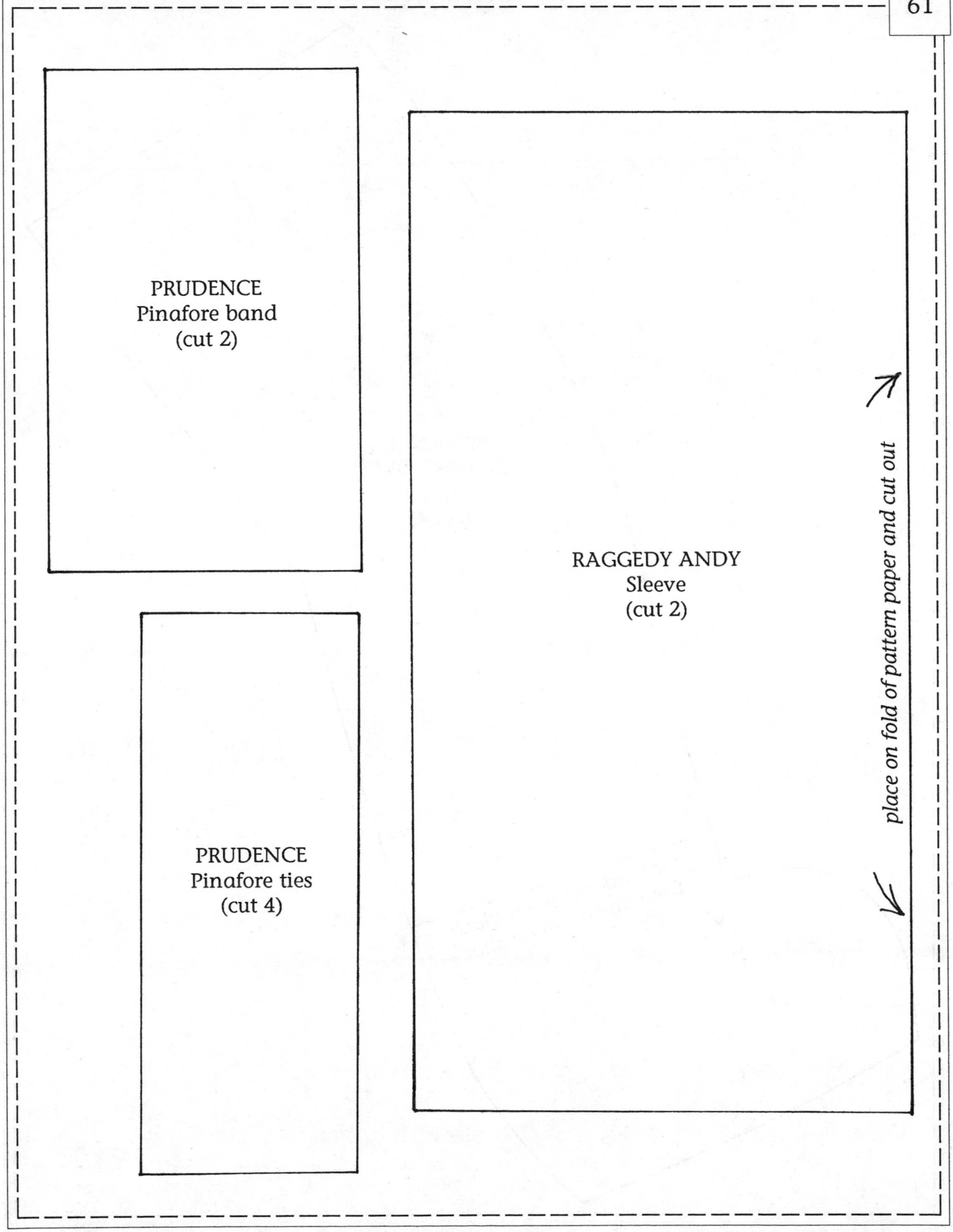

PRUDENCE
Pinafore band
(cut 2)

PRUDENCE
Pinafore ties
(cut 4)

RAGGEDY ANDY
Sleeve
(cut 2)

place on fold of pattern paper and cut out

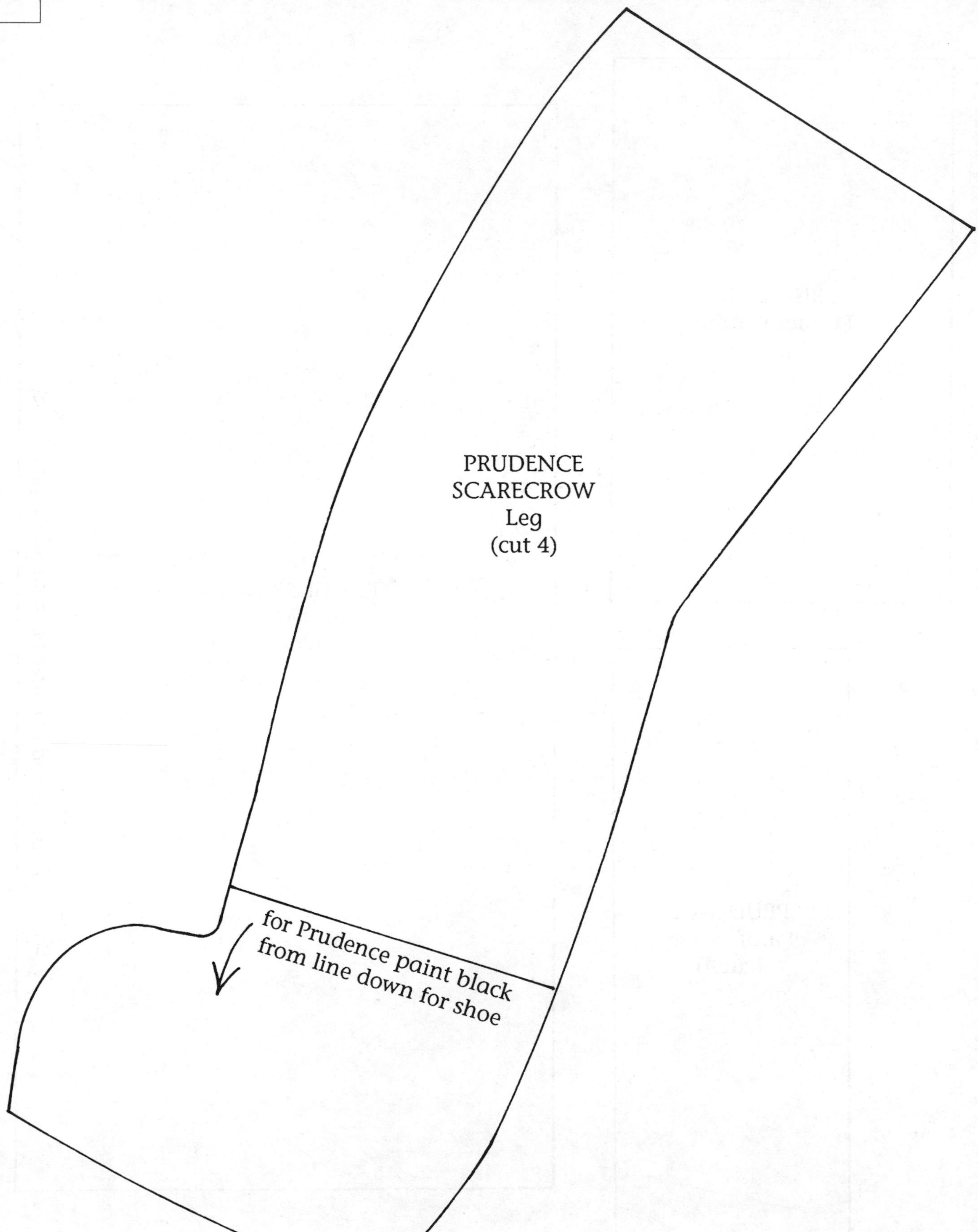

PRUDENCE
SCARECROW
Leg
(cut 4)

for Prudence paint black
from line down for shoe

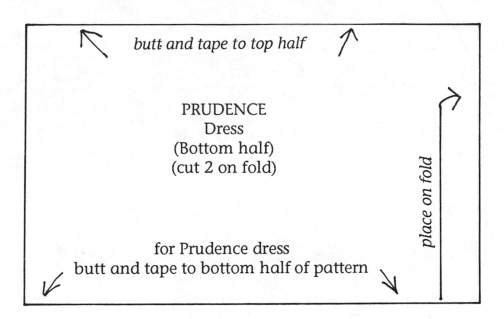

butt and tape to top half

PRUDENCE
Dress
(Bottom half)
(cut 2 on fold)

for Prudence dress
butt and tape to bottom half of pattern

place on fold

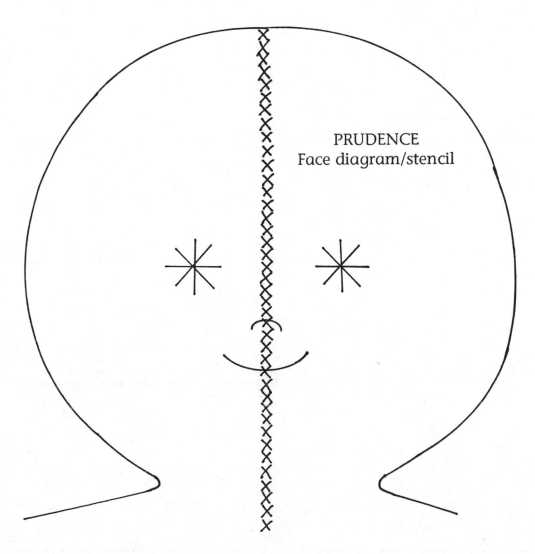

PRUDENCE
Face diagram/stencil

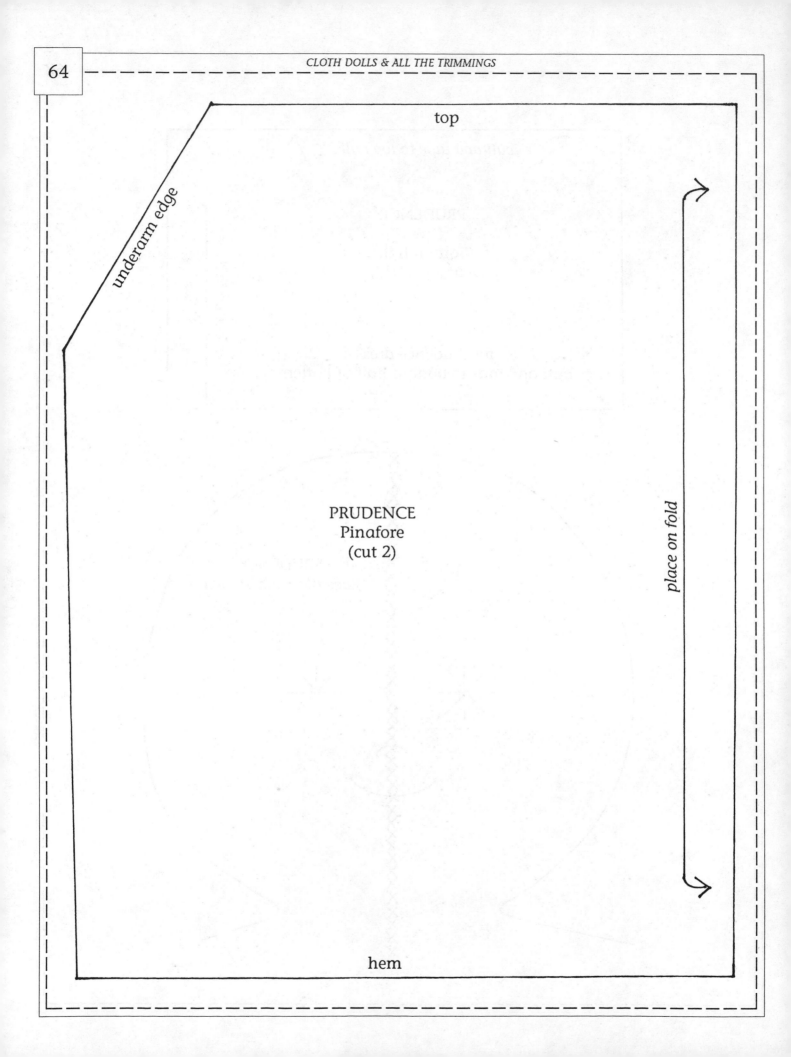

top

underarm edge

place on fold

PRUDENCE
Pinafore
(cut 2)

hem

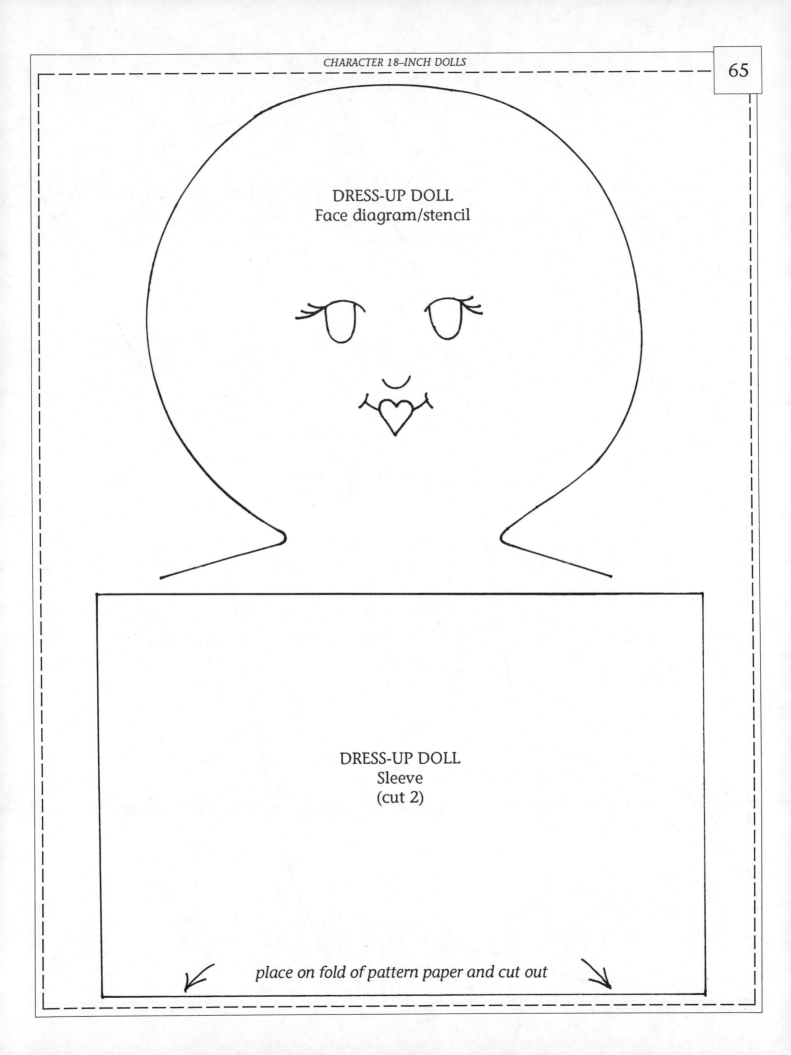

DRESS-UP DOLL
Face diagram/stencil

DRESS-UP DOLL
Sleeve
(cut 2)

place on fold of pattern paper and cut out

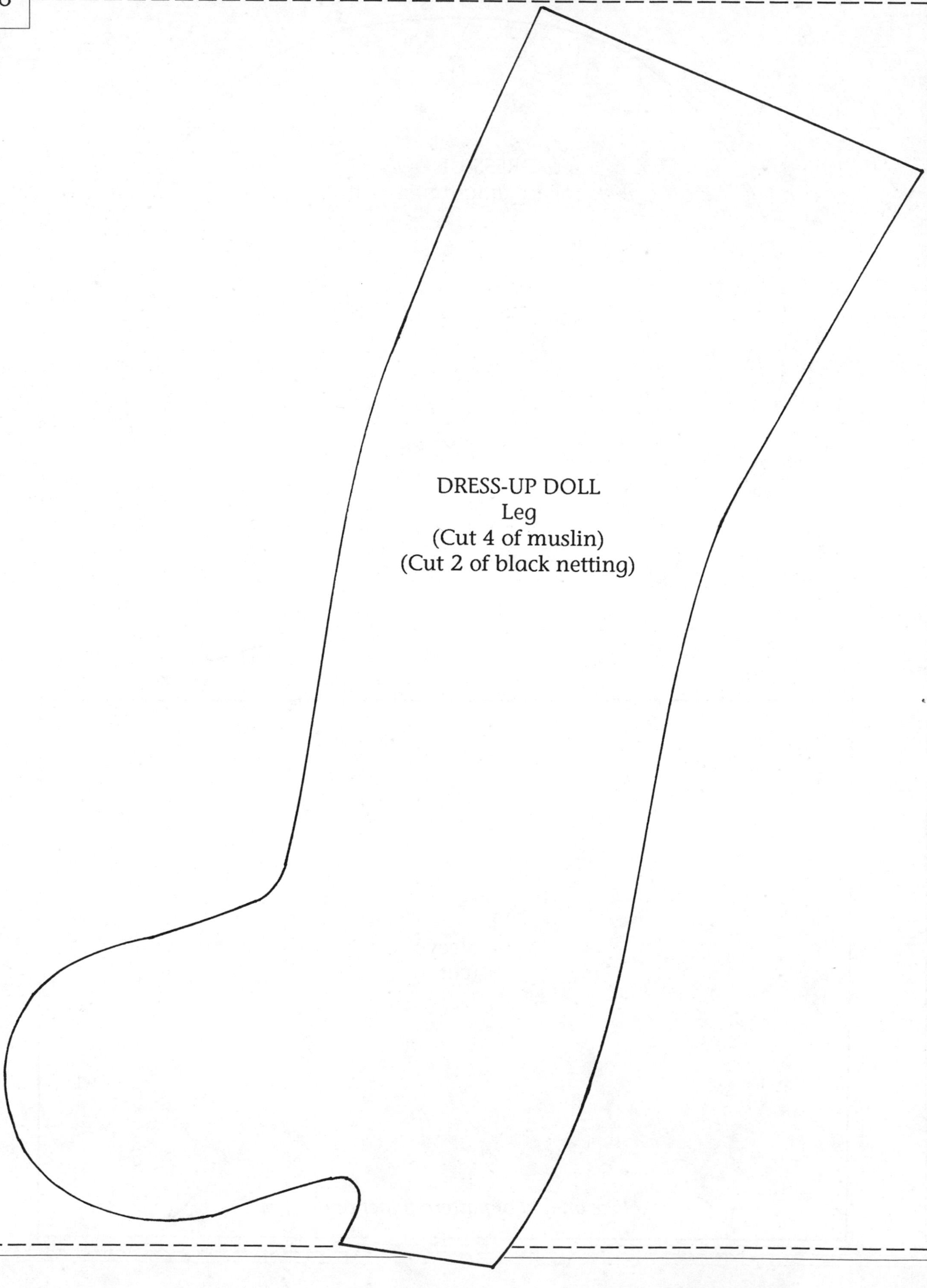

DRESS-UP DOLL
Leg
(Cut 4 of muslin)
(Cut 2 of black netting)

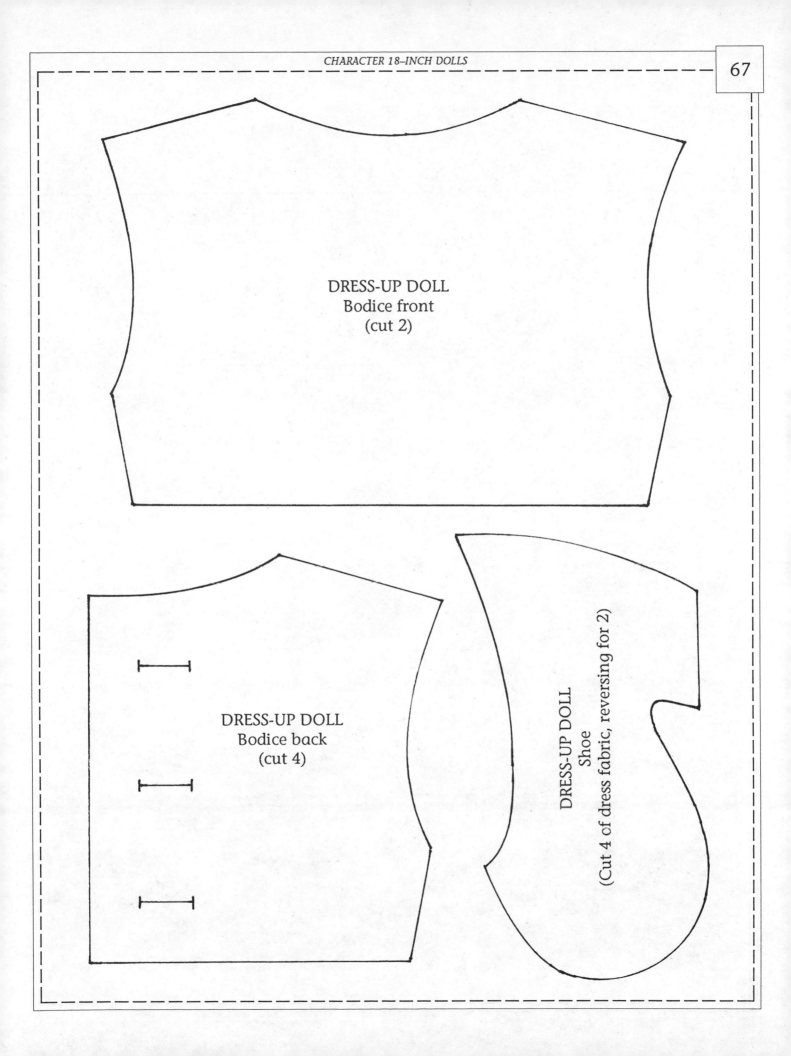

DRESS-UP DOLL
Bodice front
(cut 2)

DRESS-UP DOLL
Bodice back
(cut 4)

DRESS-UP DOLL
Shoe
(Cut 4 of dress fabric, reversing for 2)

CHAPTER ♥ 3

COTTON 20-INCH BABY DOLL & WARDROBE

*A*ll twenty inches of this cuddly doll ask to be held. And you're in for a surprise! When you pick up this baby, the beads inside the body make it feel almost like you are holding a real one. Cotton flannel gives the doll's skin a softer texture.

Included are patterns for a diaper, romper and T-shirt, a ruffled dress and panties, and a gorgeous christening gown with panties and cap. When completed, your new baby doll will fit into infant-sized clothing.

BABY DOLL

This sweet little baby doll will always be a special little sweetheart for the lucky recipient of this treasure.

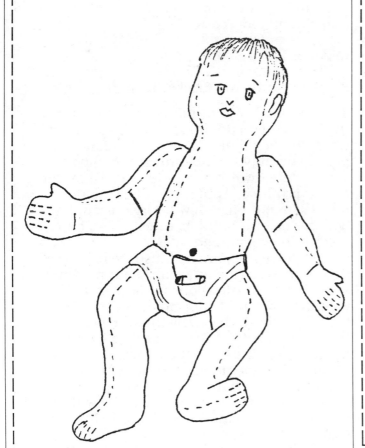

MATERIALS

To make the doll:

¾ yard pale pink flannel*

Matching thread

Embroidery floss: baby blue, medium brown, and red

Polyester fiberfill

Plastic beads (see Sources)

Funnel

Two pairs of 55 mm doll joints (see Sources)

Beige Pretty Hair® for hair (see Sources)

Matching thread

Glue

One ½" button to cover

Fray Check®

If you are unable to obtain a light pink flannel, dye white flannel with a dilute solution of light pink or peach dye.

INSTRUCTIONS

Note: All seam allowances are ¼" unless otherwise instructed.

As instructed in chapter 1, prewash and press all fabrics and trace the patterns from the book onto heavy paper. Transfer all markings from patterns to fabric.

1. Body: Lay one body side right side up on a flat surface, so that front edge faces right. Lay body front right side down over side. Match and pin side front edge. Stitch.

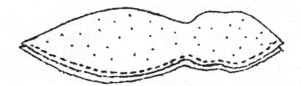

Lay body back right side up on table, front edge facing right. Lay remaining body side, right side down over body side. Match side back edges. Pin. Stitch.

Stitch these two sections together, matching seams and curved edges, leaving an opening for turning between the dots at one side back.

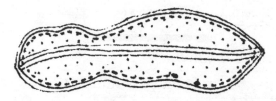

Clip curves. Reinforce clipped curves and raw edges of stuffing opening with Fray Check®. Turn body right side out.

2. Arms: To form two underarms, stitch darts in two opposing arm pieces.

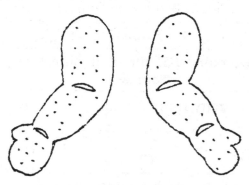

Pin underarms to (undarted) arms. Stitch, leaving an opening in the stitching between the dots.

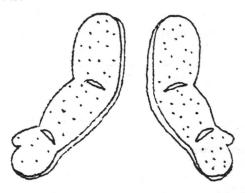

Clip curves. Reinforce clipped curves and raw edges of opening with Fray Check® Turn right side out.

3. Legs: Stitch two legs together, leaving the bottom V unstitched and leaving an opening between the dots on the back thigh for turning, as indicated. Repeat for other leg.

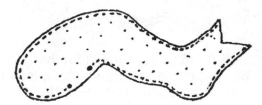

Fold feet at inside point of V so that top and bottom foot seams meet. Stitch from dot to dot as illustrated.

Trim seam to ⅛". Clip curves of legs. Reinforce with Fray Chek®. Turn.

4. Jointing: For joint holes, fold the fabric at the dot and fold again, so that the dot is at the tip of the point. Cut across the folded point. You may wish to practice on a piece of scrap fabric since it is easy to mistakenly cut too large a hole. Apply Fray Chek® to the hole to strength it. Allow to dry. Repeat for both inside arm holes, both leg holes, and for dots on the body/head sides.

Assemble the joint as illustrated. The stationary disk (the one with the threaded screw-like protrusion) always goes in the limb with the screw part sticking out of the hole in the fabric. Push the screw into the hole in the body side of the doll. Check to be sure the limb is pointing in the correct direction (thumbs and toes up and to front of doll). From the inside of the doll's body, place the washer (large flat disk) on the screw with the rounded edge facing the stationary disk. Push the flat side of the locking disk onto the screw. Use an empty thread spool to press and lock the disk firmly in place, perhaps placing the assembly on a table and using your weight to get a tight fit.

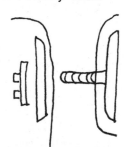

5. Stuffing: Line the inside of the doll's face and top of head evenly with about an inch thick layer of polyester fiberfill. Insert the pointed end of the funnel through the body opening into the neck. Pour pellets into the head, stirring and tapping or gently shaking the head to settle them. Fill up to the neck. Stuff the neck tightly with fiberfill. Make sure the head is stuffed firmly so it will hold its shape.

Line the bottom of the doll from the fanny to about 2" below the belly button area with a 1"-thick layer of fiberfill. Funnel the pellets into the body, stirring frequently to settle the plastic beads. When the body is almost full, lay the doll down so that the body opening is facing up. Fill as full as possible with the pellets. Pull up on the fabric at the body opening and fill the space created. Line the inside of the opening with fiberfill to keep the beads inside. Handstitch the opening closed.

Stuff and fill the arms and legs in the same manner. Fill the hands, starting with the thumb, and the toes, half way up the foot, with fiberfill. Line the top of the legs and arms with fiberfill. Add the pellets, taking time to stir and add beads as you go until no more will fit. Stuff the openings with fiberfill and stitch the openings closed.

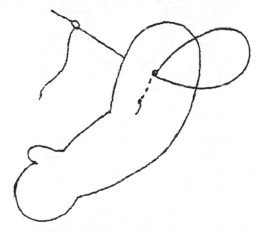

6. Ears: Stitch two ears together leaving an opening between the dots. Stuff lightly. Close opening. Topstitch along curlicue marked on pattern. Whipstitch to head as marked on head side.

7. Navel: Cover the button with a piece of the flannel as instructed on the button manufacturer's package. Sew to dot on body front.

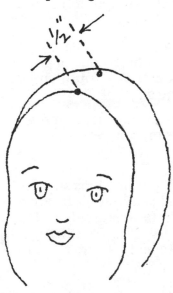

8. Hair: Cut two lengths of hair material each 7" long. Divide the bunches in half. Wrap the bunches with thread around their middles. Sew to head as shown.

Cut one length of hair 8" long. Wrap with thread and stitch to head as shown.

Comb the hair to fluff it and distribute it around head. Combing will remove some of the hair, giving it a softer, less clumpy look. Trim the ends as needed.

To hold the hair in place lift sections of hair and apply small dabs of glue diluted with water to the head. Press the hair to the head.

To make the clothing:

DIAPER

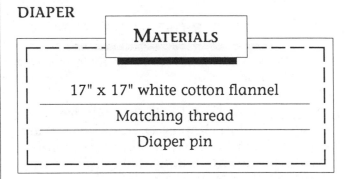

MATERIALS
17" x 17" white cotton flannel
Matching thread
Diaper pin

INSTRUCTIONS

1. Use a wide zigzag stitch to finish raw edges of diaper.

2. Fold diaper crosswise to form a triangle. Place baby on the center of the diaper, point of triangle facing down, the long folded edge under the baby's waist. Fold the bottom point up to the belly button, one side over, and then the other. Secure the diaper pin through all layers of the diaper at the middle center front.

ROMPER AND T-SHIRT

Playtime calls for fun clothing. This set starts with a red T-shirt. Over it, the baby wears a romper buttoned with colorful buttons shaped as toys and animals. Make the romper out of one fabric or choose separate, matching fabrics for the top and bottom. The T-shirt is trimmed with fabric from the romper.

MATERIALS

½ yard fabric for bottom of romper

¼ yard fabric for top

¼ yard fabric for top lining

Matching thread

⅓ yard matching T-shirt fabric

Matching thread

Four ⅝" buttons

INSTRUCTIONS

Note: All seam allowances are ¼" unless instructed otherwise.

Trace patterns from book onto pattern paper as instructed in chapter 1. Transfer all markings to the pattern paper. Pin and cut patterns from fabric as indicated on patterns. Transfer all markings. Cut two pieces of romper fabric for T-shirt trim, each 12" long. On bias (diagonal of fabric), cut two strips of romper fabric for the neck/shoulder edges of T-shirt, each 1" x 14".

Romper

1. Stitch sides of top back to top front. Repeat for top lining front and back. Press seams open.

2. Right sides facing, pin lining to romper top at neck, tab, and armhole edges, matching side seams. Stitch, leaving straight, bottom edges open.

Trim corners. Clip curves. Turn. Press.

3. Pin curved crotch seams in two pant legs together, right sides facing. Stitch. Repeat for second set of pant legs.

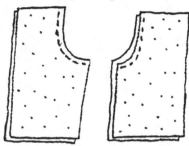

Open pants. Pin and stitch side seams. Pin and stitch inseam.

4. To gather the top of the pants, stitch two separate rows of long machine stitches in each of the four sections of the top of the pants, the first row just inside the seam allowance and the second row close to the first. Pin pants to romper top, right sides together, matching side seams and matching front and back seams to dots. Treat the romper top and facing as one. Pull up on gathering stitches to fit. Stitch.

5. Press under ¼" on bottom edge of pant legs. Turn under another ¼". Topstitch just less than ¼" from the edge.

6. Make buttonholes as indicated on the pattern. Sew buttons on romper.

T-Shirt

1. Right sides facing, pin one bias strip to shoulder and neck edge of one T-shirt body. Stitch. Turn bias strip to wrong side of T-shirt, turning under ¼". Pin. Topstitch through all layers. Repeat for other T-shirt body.

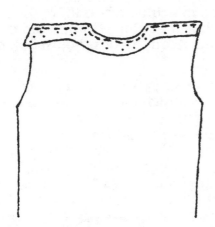

Overlap shoulders of T-shirt front and back so that inside edges of bias strips touch. Baste in place.

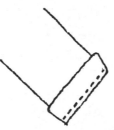

2. Right sides together, stitch side seams.

3. Press under ¹/₄" along hem of T-shirt. Repeat. Topstitch.

4. Right sides facing, stitch underarm seams of sleeves.

5. Stitch short ends of sleeve bands together, right sides facing.

Fold and press in half lengthwise, wrong sides facing. Pin to right side of bottom of sleeve edge. Stitch. Trim seam. Press band downward.

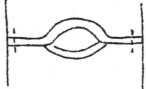

DRESS AND PANTIES

This versatile dress combo can be made from a calico, juvenile print, or, as on the pictured doll, from a seersucker check. Or try velvet or satin for special occasions. Trim the dress with lace and pretty appliques. The legs of the panties are edged with lace.

MATERIALS

¹/₄ yards fabric
Matching thread
¹/₄"-wide elastic
4 yards of 1"-wide eyelet
One applique (optional)

INSTRUCTIONS

Note: All seam allowances are ¹/₄" unless instructed otherwise.

Prepare fabric and patterns as instructed in chapter 1. Cut the fabric according to the information written on the patterns. Transfer all markings. Cut the dress skirt 7¹/₂" x 45". Cut a ruffle for the bottom of the dress skirt 4¹/₂" x 90".

DRESS

1. Pin two bodice fronts to four backs at side and shoulder seams, right sides facing. Stitch.
Press seams open.

2. Pin bodice tops together at neck and back edges, right sides facing. Stitch.

Trim corners and clip curves. Turn. Press.

3. Cut a piece of lace 19¹/₂" long. Turn under ¹/₄" on both short ends of lace. Turn under another ¹/₄". Stitch to secure. Pin lace to the bottom raw edge of the bodice, right sides facing. Baste in place.

4. Right sides facing, pin and baste lace to one long edge of skirt.

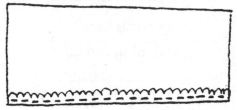

5. Match and pin the two short sides of the dress skirt, right sides facing. Using a basting stitch, sew half way down the center back seam of the dress skirt. Change to a regular sewing stitch. Sew to the lace-edged bottom of the skirt.

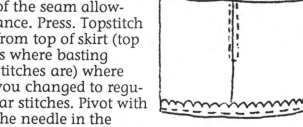

Press the seam open. Turn under ¼" of the seam allowance. Press. Topstitch from top of skirt (top is where basting stitches are) where you changed to regular stitches. Pivot with the needle in the fabric, turn across the seam, and continue topstitching up the other side.

Remove basting stitches.

6. Gather top edge of skirt with two rows of gathering stitches, as instructed in chapter 1. Pin to bottom edge of bodice, pulling up on gathering stitches evenly, leaving bodice lining free. Stitch. Turn under ¼" at bottom edge of bodice lining to wrong side. Pin and handstitch over seam allowances.

7. Sew two short ends of ruffle together, right sides facing. Press ruffle in half lengthwise. To divide ruffle into quarters, fold ruffle in half and in half again and put pins at folds. One pin will be at seam. Gather stitch between the pins in four section, stopping and starting at the pins.

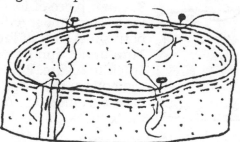

Divide the bottom edge of the skirt in the same manner. Pin the ruffle to the bottom of the skirt, matching the seam of the ruffle to the back seam of the skirt and matching the pins. Pull up on threads. Adjust gathers. Pin. Stitch.

8. Press under ¼" at bottom edges of sleeves. Repeat. Topstitch lace to wrong side of hem. Lay a 6"-long piece of elastic on the wrong side of the sleeve, ¾" from the hem's edge. As instructed in chapter 1, zigzag stitch the elastic to the sleeve, holding the ends of the elastic firmly and stretching the elastic as you sew.

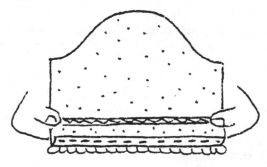

9. Right sides together, sew the sleeve underarm seams.

10. Using a long machine stitch, gather the long curved edge of a sleeve between dots. Match dots to dots on bodice. Pin sleeve to bodice, leaving bodice lining free, right side of sleeve facing right side of bodice. Pull up on gather stitches. Even out the fullness and pin. Stitch. Turn ¼" along raw edge of armhole of bodice lining. Pin over seam allowances. Handstitch. Repeat for other sleeve.

11. Make buttonholes on back of bodice as marked. Try dress on doll. Mark positions for buttons. Sew buttons in place.

12. Apply applique to center front of bodice.

Panties

1. Turn under ¼" along bottom edges of both panties' legs. Repeat.

2. Pin lace to underside of turned under edge. Topstitch in place.

3. Cut two pieces of elastic, each 8" long. On wrong side, zigzag elastic to panties' legs about ½" from lace, stretching elastic to fit across leg as you sew. Repeat for other leg.

4. Right sides facing, stitch short inside leg seams.

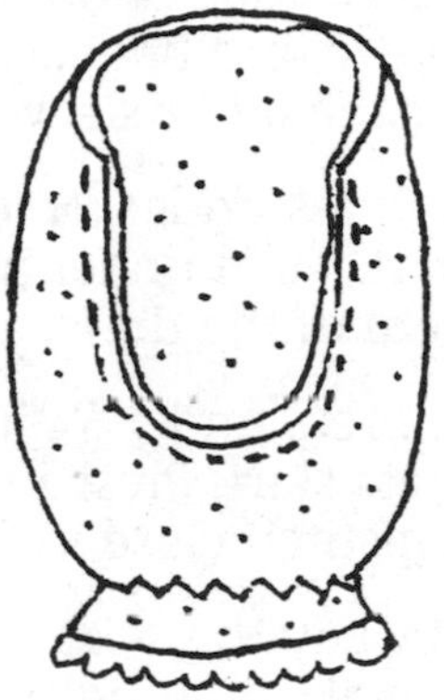

5. Turn one panties' leg right side out. Put inside other panties' leg, right sides facing. Match and pin crotch seam. Stitch. Turn wrong side out.

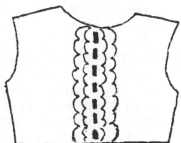

6. Press under ¼" along top, waist edge. Press under another ⅝". Topstitch close to both folded edges, leaving a ½" gap in the bottom stitching for inserting elastic. Insert a 15"-long piece of elastic into the casing. Overlap the ends ½". Stitch to secure. Sew gap in casing closed.

CHRISTENING GOWN, CAP, & PANTIES

Make this elegant dress of a polyester/cotton blend batiste or splurge on a fine, all cotton Swiss batiste. The bottom of the skirt is flounced with three rows of wide eyelet and topped with ribbon. The cap is made simply, with eyelet for the top and batiste forming the back. When finished you will proudly display this heirloom quality gown, cap, and panties on your baby doll — either the one you constructed above or a real one!

MATERIALS

1¾ yards cotton batiste
Matching thread
1½ yards of ¾"-wide ungathered edging eyelet
1¾ yards of 4½"-wide gathered eyelet
⅛ yard beading lace (has holes to run ribbon through) for front of bodice
⅔ yard of ¼"-wide baby blue, pale pink, or ecru ribbon
3½ yards of ⅞"- or 1"-wide ribbon to match above
Matching thread
Thirteen ¼" buttons
¼"-wide elastic

INSTRUCTIONS

Note: All seam allowances are ¼" unless instructed otherwise.

As instructed in chapter 1, prepare patterns, prewash, press, and cut and mark fabrics. Cut the skirt for the christening gown 24" by the width of your fabric (44" or 45" wide) and one piece of 4½"-wide eyelet 19" long for the christening cap.

1. Fold one front of the bodice in half and finger press to form a center line mark. Cut two pieces of ¾"-wide ungathered edging eyelet, each 4½" long. Lay two pieces of edging eyelet along the center fold, raw edges meeting at fold. Pin or use a bit of fabric glue to hold the lace in place.

Run a 4½"-long piece of ¼"-wide ribbon through the beading. Lay the beading over the raw edges of the edging eyelet, centering it over the folded center line. Topstitch close to the edge of the beading.

2. Pin and stitch bodice front to two bodice backs at shoulders and sides. Repeat for second set to make bodice linings. Press seams open.

3. Pin bodice and bodice lining together at neck and back edges, right sides facing. Stitch.

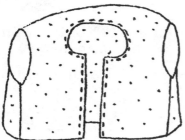

Trim corners and clip curves. Turn. Press.

4. Cut two pieces of 4½"-wide eyelet, each 9¾". Stitch short raw edges together, right sides facing. Pin to armhole of bodice, leaving bodice lining free. Baste.

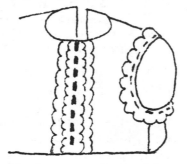

5. Press under ¼" on the bottom edges of the sleeves. Press under another ¼". Topstitch a row of lace to the wrong side of the turned under hem.

Cut two pieces of elastic, each 6" long. Lay the elastic on the wrong side of the sleeve, 1" from the finished edge. Pin one end of the elastic to the top raw edge, with the end of the elastic even with the side edge of the sleeve. Repeat for the other end of the elastic, pinning the raw end of the elastic to the opposite raw side edge of the sleeve. Zigzag stitch the elastic in place, holding the ends of the elastic firmly. Stretch the elastic as you sew. Repeat for the second sleeve.

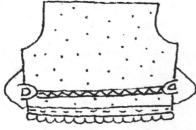

6. Stitch underarm seams, right sides facing.

7. Using a long machine stitch, gather the top edge of the sleeves between dots. Match dots on sleeves to dots on bodice. Pin sleeve to bodice leaving bodice lining free, with right side of sleeve facing right side of bodice. Pull up on gather stitches. Even out the fullness and pin. Stitch. Turn under ¼" on sleeve edge of bodice lining. Handstitch over sleeve and bodice seam allowances. Repeat for the other sleeve.

8. Press under ¼" on one long edge of dress skirt. Turn under another ¼". This will be the hem of the dress.

9. Press under ¼" on the two short edges of dress skirt. Press under an additional inch. Topstitch close to first folded edge.

10. Lay the skirt on a flat surface. With a pencil and a light touch measure up 2½" from the bottom edge of the skirt and make a dot. Repeat all along the skirt bottom. Connect the dots. Make two more pencil lines above this first one, each 2½" above the previous line.

Cut three pieces of 4½"-wide eyelet, each 46" wide. Turn ¼" on short raw ends to wrong side. Repeat. Topstitch.

Pin one length of eyelet over folded hem, matching edges of dress and short, finished edges of skirt. Topstitch.

Pin and topstitch second row of eyelet to middle pencil line.

Repeat for the third line of eyelet.

Cut a piece of the wide ribbon 46" long. Pin the bottom of the ribbon over the top edge of the top row of eyelet, turning under the short raw edges at ends (back of skirt) ½" to wrong side of ribbon. Topstitch close to all edges of ribbon.

11. Gather top edge of skirt with two rows of gathering stitches, as instructed in chapter 1. Pin to bottom edge of bodice, leaving the bodice lining free. Pull up on gathering stitches and adjust to fit. Pin. Stitch.

12. Turn under ¼" on bottom of bodice lining. Pin over seam allowances and hand-stitch in place.

13. Lay a piece of paper over buttonhole markings on bodice. Trace markings and edge of bodice. Move paper down two button-holes so that tracing for first buttonhole is over bottom buttonhole. Keep edge marking even with edge of dress skirt. Transfer the next two buttonhole markings. Repeat until you have marked thirteen buttonholes. Make buttonholes as marked. Try dress on doll. Mark positions for buttons. Sew buttons in place.

14. Cut a piece of the wide ribbon 50" long. Tie a bow in the center. Tack to the front of the bodice at the bottom of the beading. Trim ends of ribbon on an angle.

15. Cut two pieces of the ¼"-wide ribbon, each 12" wide. Tie them both into bows. Tack over sleeve elastic at top sides of arms. Trim ends at an angle.

Panties

Follow instructions for dress panties above.

Christening Cap

1. Cut a piece of 4½"-wide eyelet lace 19" long.

2. Right sides together, stitch the short, raw edges of the lace together. Turn right sides out. Press. Fold lace in half to find center. Mark with a pin.

3. Cut two pieces of ribbon, each 14" long. Pin one raw end of each piece of ribbon to the edges of the lace as shown, wrong side of ribbon facing right (to the outside) side of lace. Baste. Topstitch edges of ribbon with bottom edge even with folded edge of cap.

4. Gather one long curved edge of back of cap between dots. Fold cap in half vertically to find center. Mark with a pin. Pin ribbon side of lace, matching pins marking centers and edges of lace to dots. Pin. Stitch.

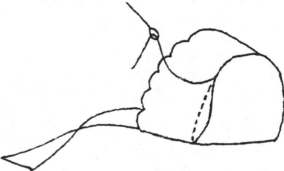

5. Turn ¼" to inside on remaining long curved edge of cap back. Pin as shown. Handstitch in place.

6. Pinch together ¼" of fabric at center bottom back of cap back. Tack together. Make a bow from the remaining ribbon. Tack over tuck.

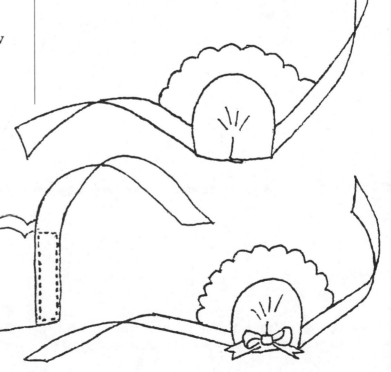

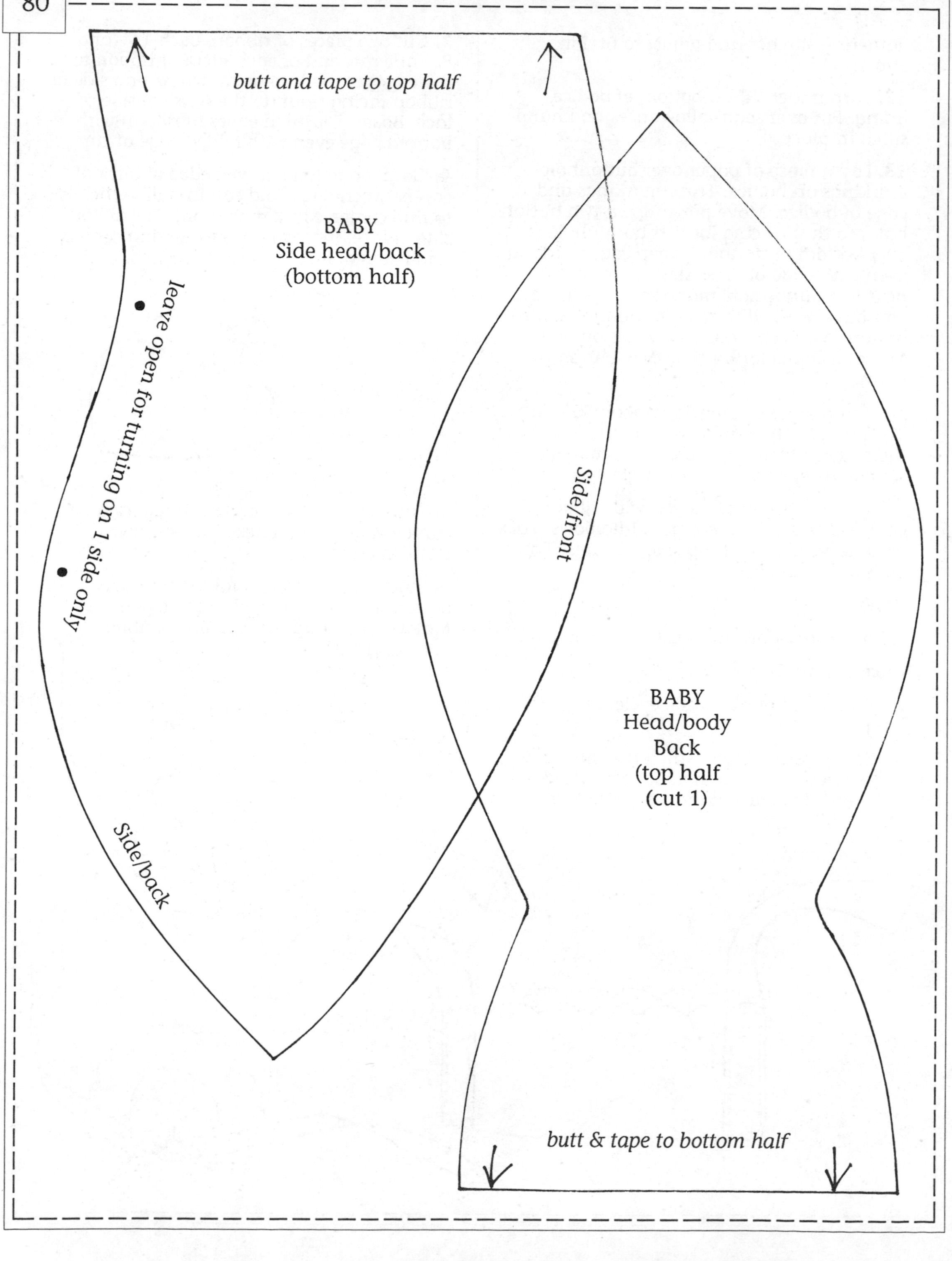

butt and tape to top half

BABY
Side head/back
(bottom half)

leave open for turning on 1 side only

Side/back

Side/front

BABY
Head/body
Back
(top half
(cut 1)

butt & tape to bottom half

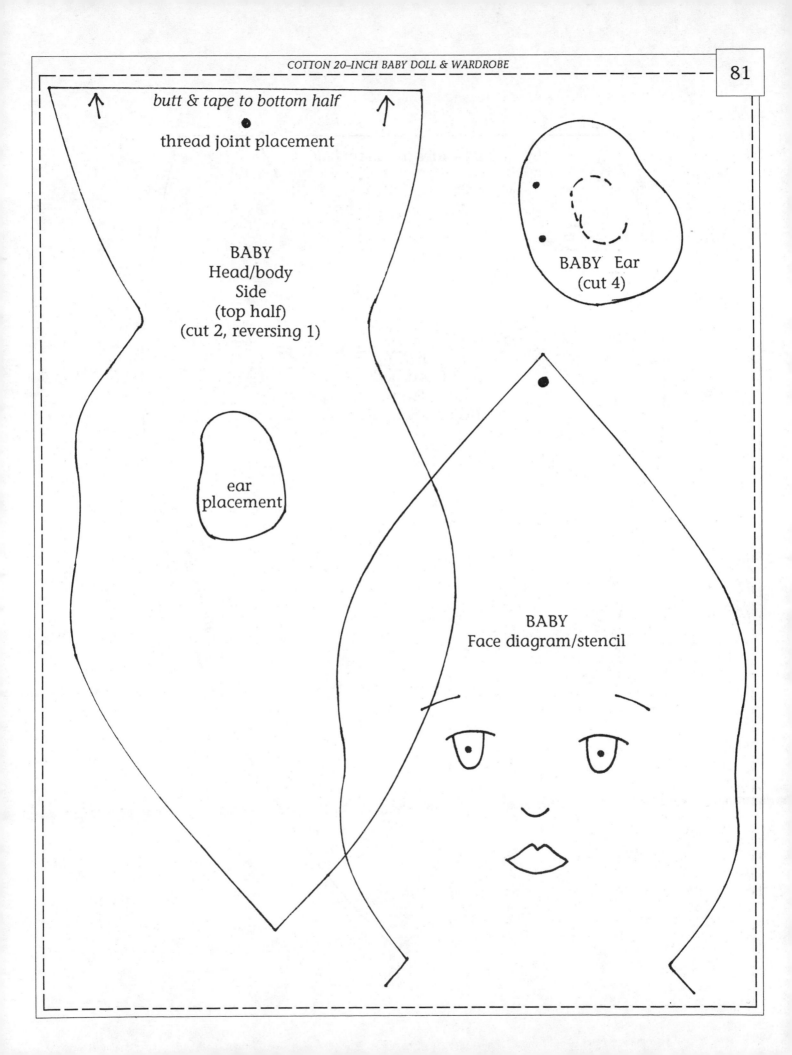

butt & tape to bottom half

thread joint placement

BABY
Head/body
Side
(top half)
(cut 2, reversing 1)

ear
placement

BABY   Ear
(cut 4)

BABY
Face diagram/stencil

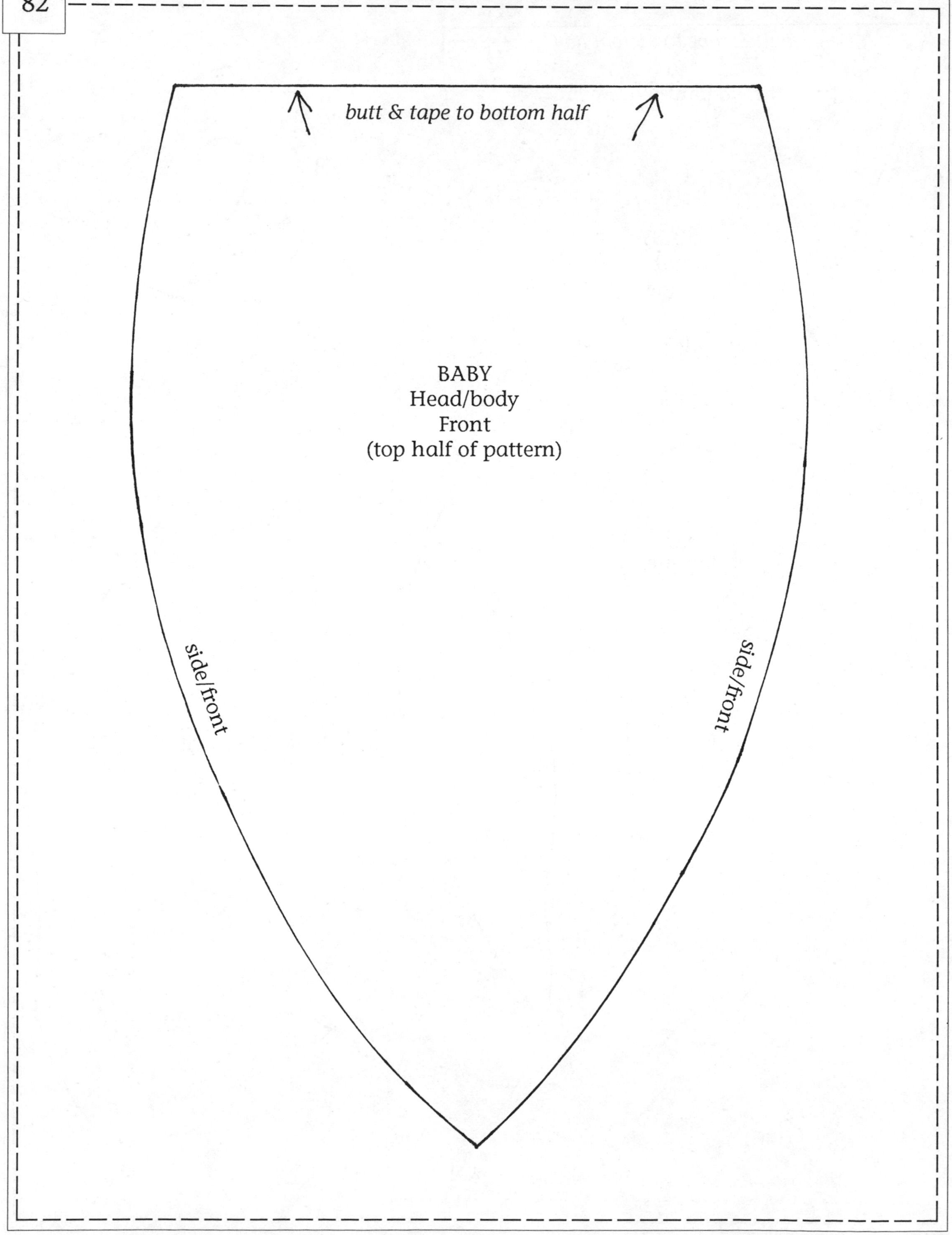

butt & tape to bottom half

BABY
Head/body
Front
(top half of pattern)

side/front

side/front

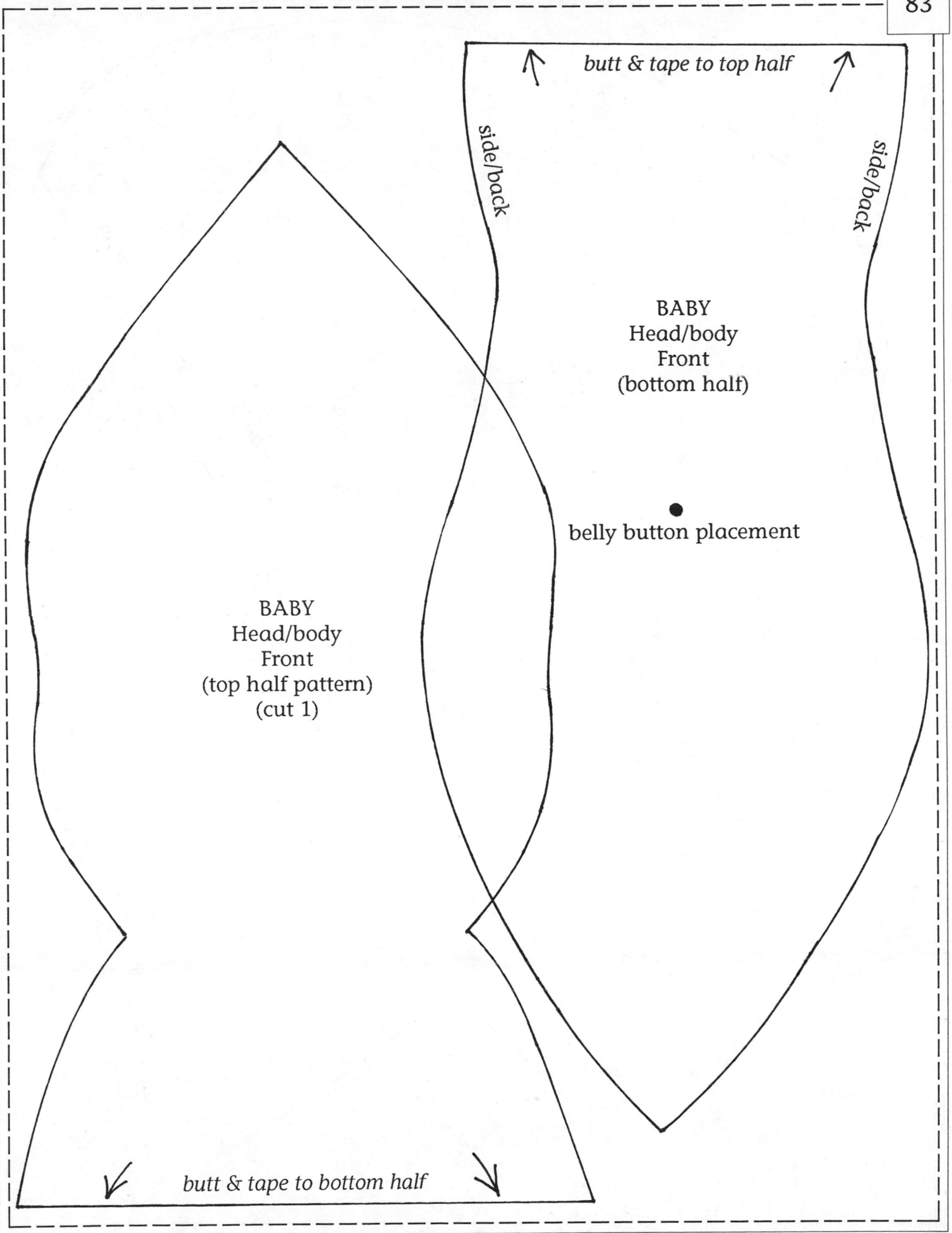

butt & tape to top half

side/back

side/back

BABY
Head/body
Front
(bottom half)

● belly button placement

BABY
Head/body
Front
(top half pattern)
(cut 1)

butt & tape to bottom half

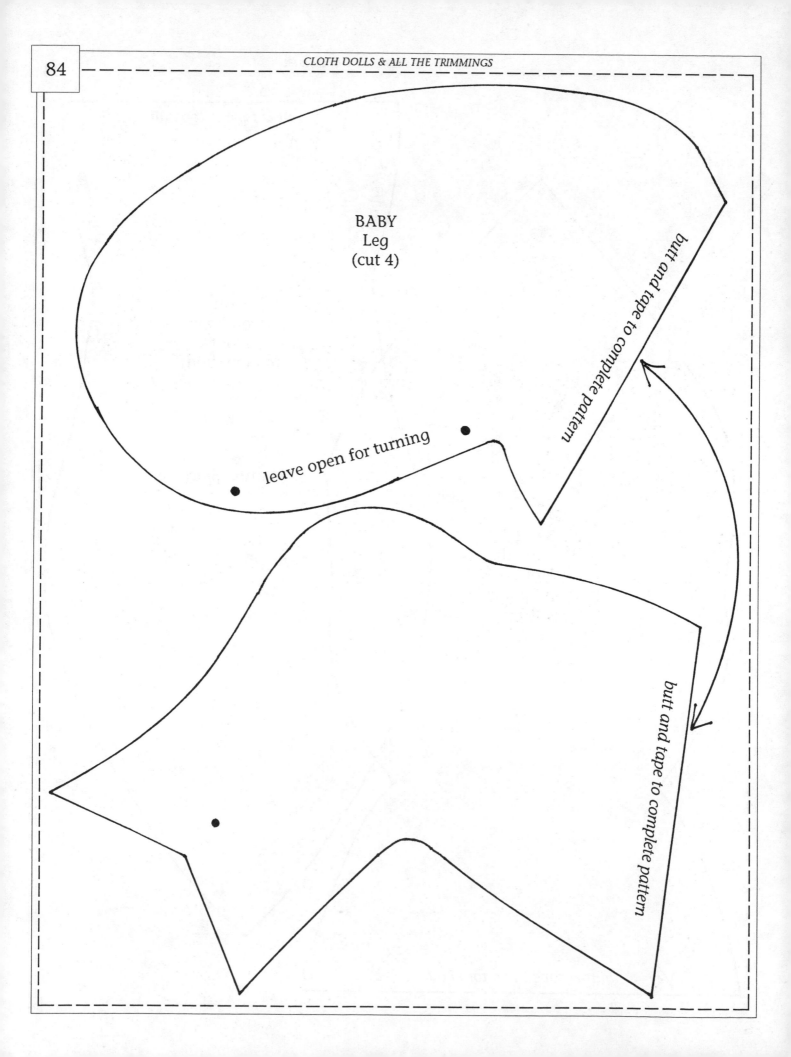

BABY
Leg
(cut 4)

leave open for turning

butt and tape to complete pattern

butt and tape to complete pattern

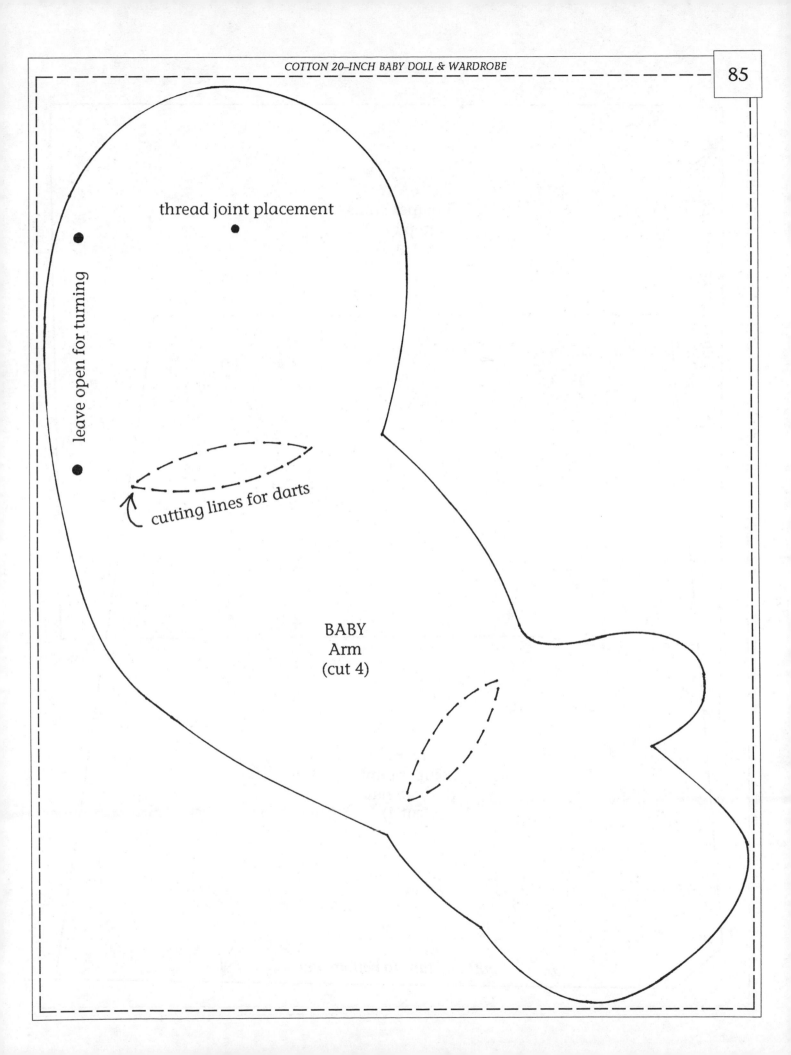

thread joint placement

leave open for turning

cutting lines for darts

BABY
Arm
(cut 4)

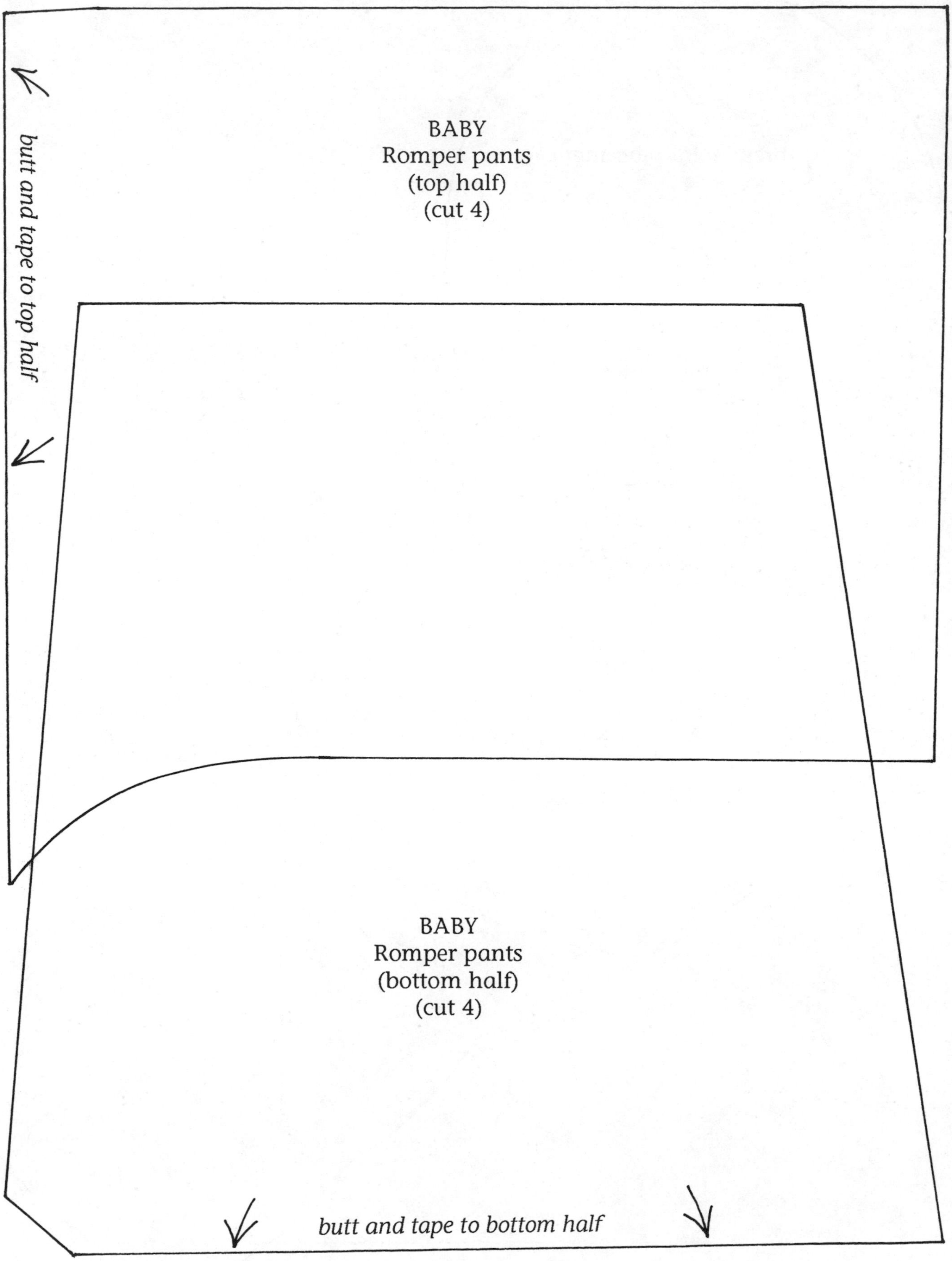

butt and tape to top half

BABY
Romper pants
(top half)
(cut 4)

BABY
Romper pants
(bottom half)
(cut 4)

butt and tape to bottom half

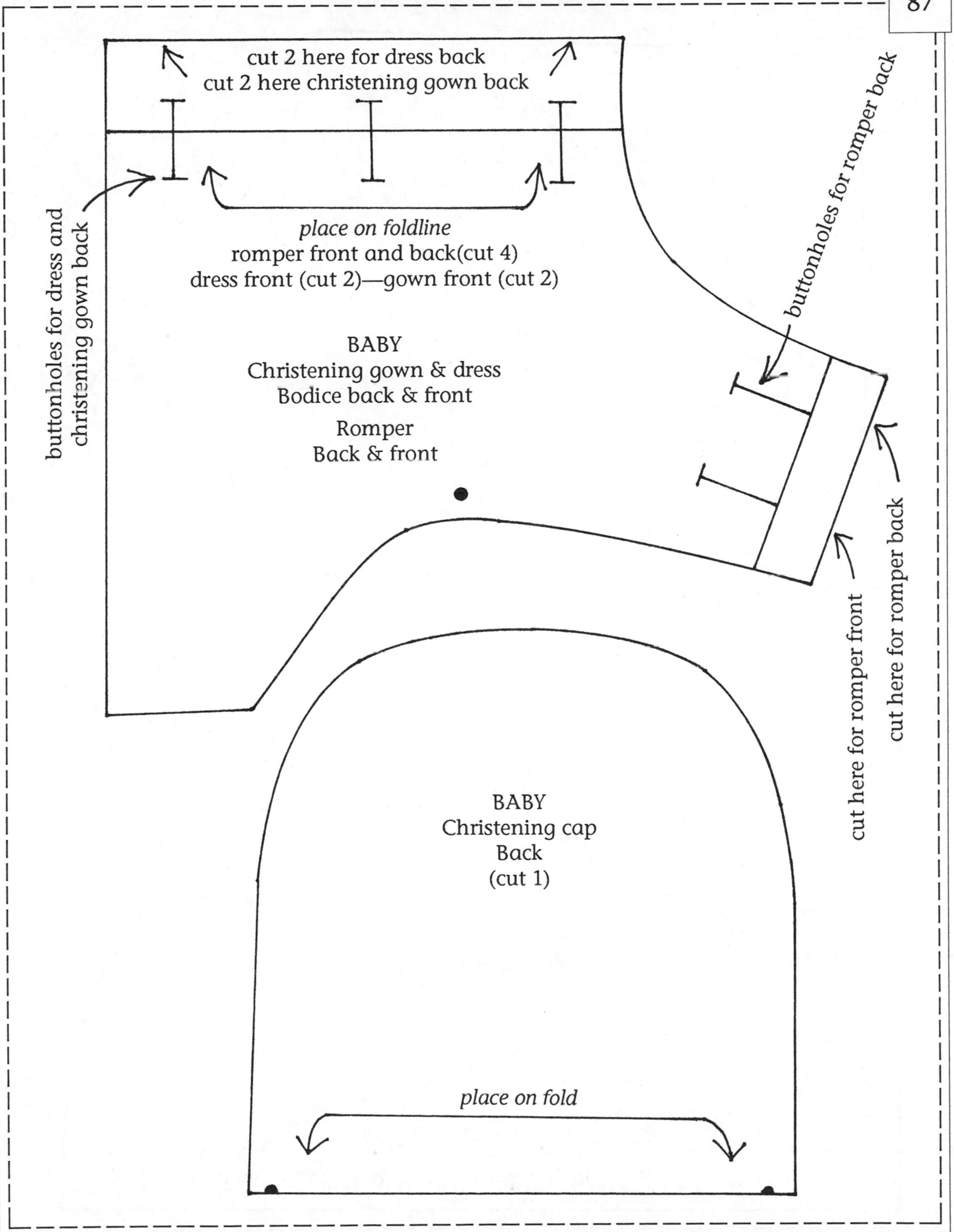

cut 2 here for dress back
cut 2 here christening gown back

buttonholes for dress and
christening gown back

buttonholes for romper back

place on foldline
romper front and back(cut 4)
dress front (cut 2)—gown front (cut 2)

BABY
Christening gown & dress
Bodice back & front

Romper
Back & front

cut here for romper front

cut here for romper back

BABY
Christening cap
Back
(cut 1)

place on fold

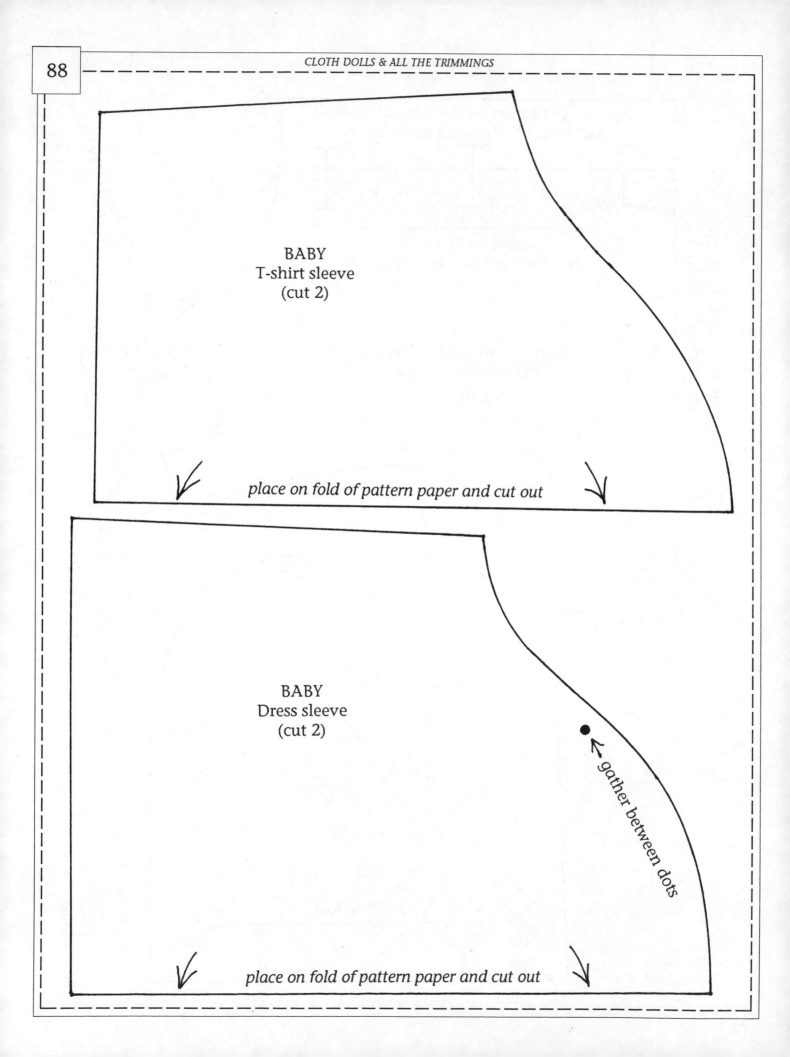

BABY
T-shirt sleeve
(cut 2)

place on fold of pattern paper and cut out

BABY
Dress sleeve
(cut 2)

gather between dots

place on fold of pattern paper and cut out

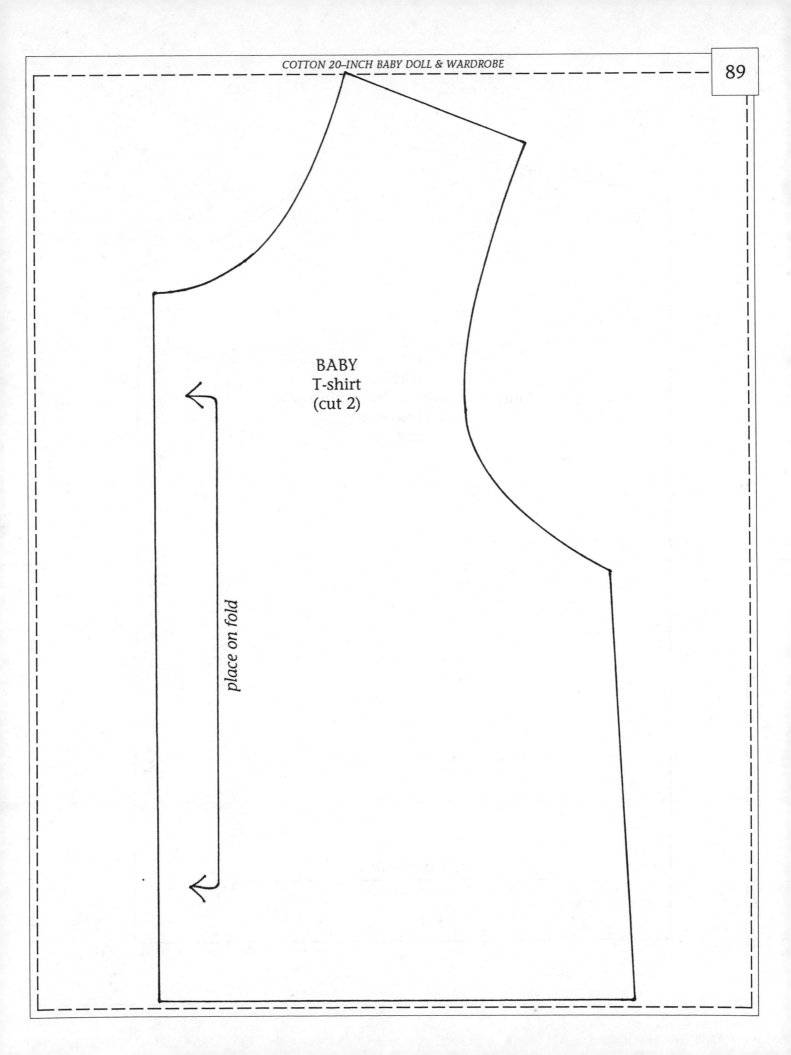

BABY
T-shirt
(cut 2)

place on fold

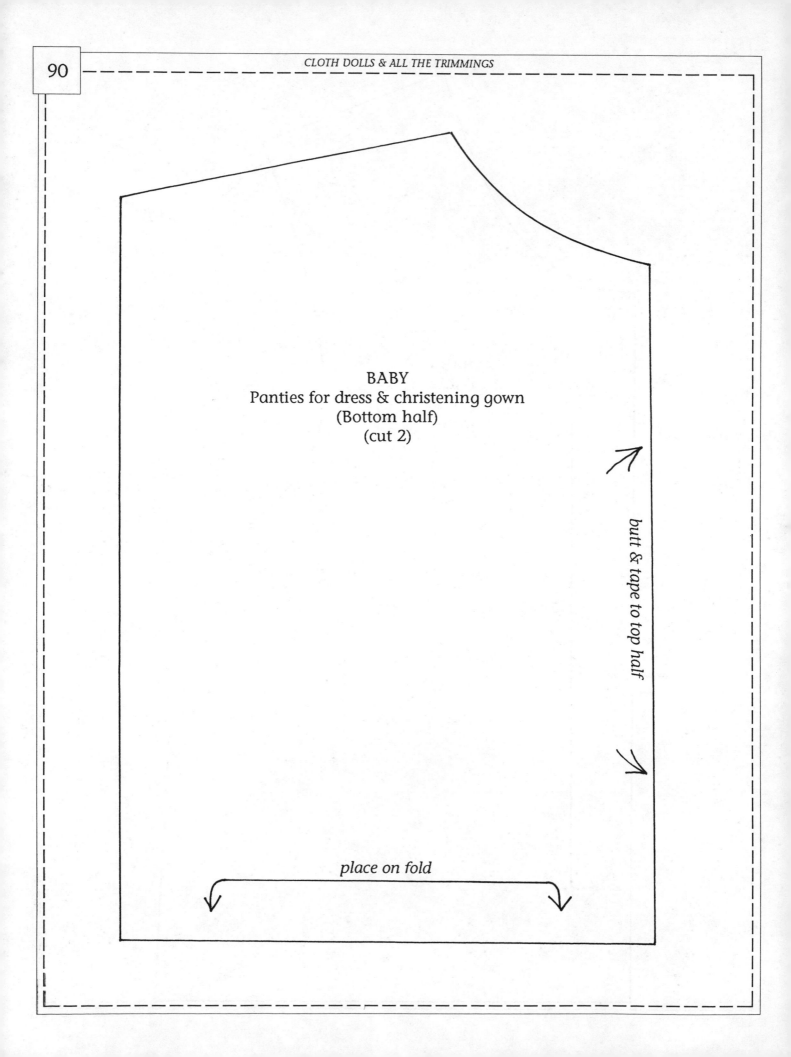

BABY
Panties for dress & christening gown
(Bottom half)
(cut 2)

butt & tape to top half

place on fold

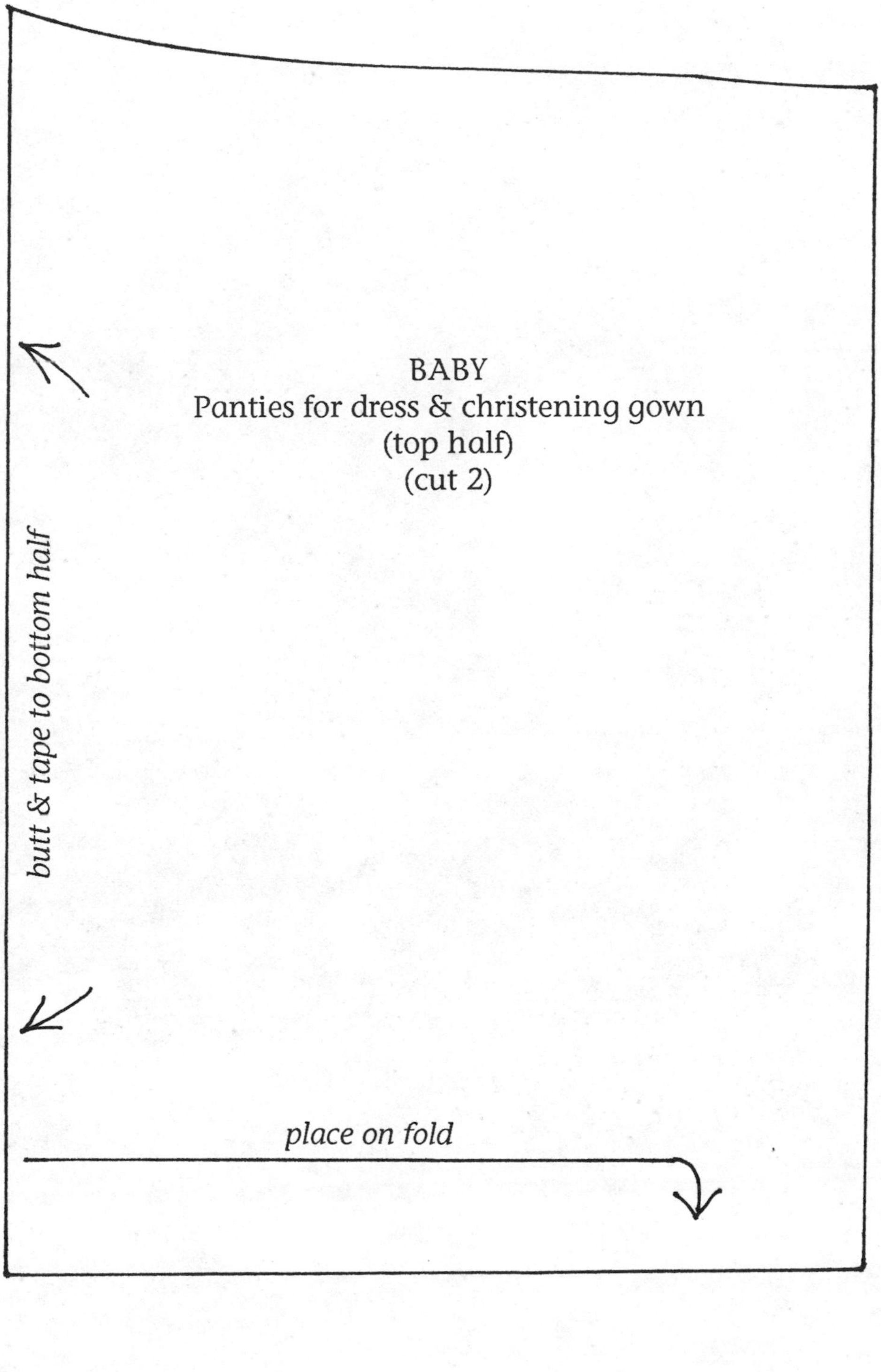

BABY
Panties for dress & christening gown
(top half)
(cut 2)

butt & tape to bottom half

place on fold

CHAPTER ♥ 4

BOY & GIRL 25-INCH DOLLS & WARDROBE

*S*tanding twenty-five inches tall, these friends are ready for any occasion with their easily stitched wardrobe. She wears a puffed sleeve dress with a skirt gathered into a fitted bodice. Her lace-edged bloomers and petticoat peek out from under the hem of her dress. He sports a pair of trousers with suspenders and a button-front shirt. Both wear handmade shoes.

The remainder of their wardrobes contain matching sailor suits, a lacy flannel nightie and bunny slippers for her; a flannel nightshirt and teddy bear slippers for him. To ensure sweet dreams, each carries a favorite toy to bed.

25" BOY & GIRL DOLLS

For each doll:

²/3 yards finely woven muslin or
broadcloth

Matching thread

Embroidery floss: Dark red for mouth,
brown or black for brows, nose, and
pupils, and your choice for eye color

Polyester fiberfill

Two skeins yarn

Matching thread

INSTRUCTIONS

*Note: All seam allowances are ¼" unless instructed
otherwise.*

Following the instructions in chapter 1,
prepare fabrics and patterns, cut out the
fabric, and transfer markings. Do not cut
out the face until you have completed the
embroidery.

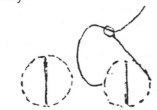

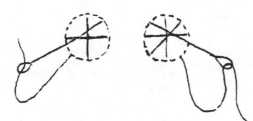

1. Face: Trace the face pattern from the
book. Tape the tracing to a window. Lay the
muslin face over the face pattern. With a soft
lead pencil, trace the face onto the muslin.
Using three strands of embroidery floss form
the eyebrows and nose with backstitches. To
embroider the eyes, make a stitch from the
center top to the center bottom of the pen-
ciled circle. Make another stitch horizontally
from the center side left to the center side
right of the eye. Fill in the stitches.

Fill in the upper and then lower lips of
the mouth with satin stitches. Cut out face.

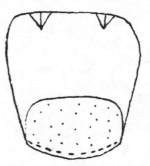

2. Body: Using a long
machine stitch gather
the long curved edge
of the back bottom.
Pin, matching edges
and center dots.

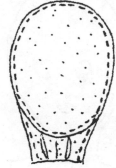

Pin face/front neck to head back/sides. Stitch. Stuff head firmly.

Stitch the darts at the shoulders of the body front and back. Stitch the body front to the body back, leaving an opening between the dots at the neck for turning.

Clip curves. Turn. Stuff body firmly.

3. Head: Stitch darts in neck fronts. Stitch neck fronts together along neck front seam, right sides facing.

Make darts and tucks on face. Pin neck front to lower edge of face, matching center front seam of neck to dot on chin of face. Stitch.

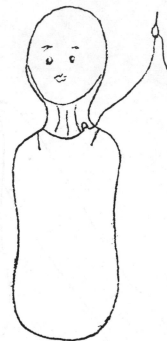

Turn under ¼" on bottom edge of head. Handstitch to top of body, covering the opening at the top of the body. Before completing the last few stitches, push some fiberfill into the neck to make it very firm; otherwise, the doll's head will be wobbly. Finish stitching.

4. Arms: Lay two arms on a flat surface, thumbs facing one another, wrong sides facing up. Make darts from wrong sides so you will have a right and a left arm.

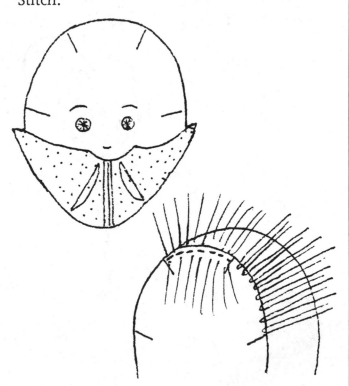

Pin rounded edge of head side backs to head center back, easing to fit. Stitch.

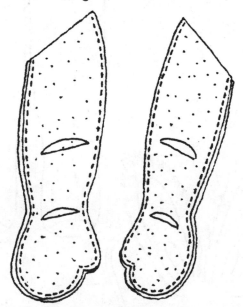

Stitch arms together, right sides facing, pairing one darted arm with one undarted arm, and leaving the tops of the arms open. Trim seam allowances to ⅛" along hand. Clip into seam allowances along curves. Turn arms right side out.

Stuff firmly, starting with tiny pieces in the fingers. Turn under ¼" at tops of arms. Whipstitch closed. Whipstitch to body, making sure the thumbs are pointing up and the darts are toward the front of the doll.

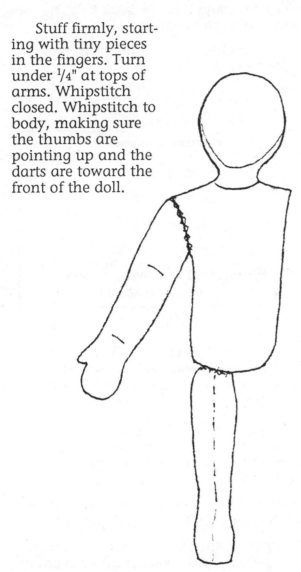

5. Legs: Stitch legs together, leaving the tops open. Pin sole to bottom raw edges of foot, matching large dot to seam at front of foot and small dot to seam at back of leg.

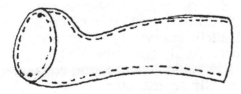

Clip seam allowances at curves. Turn. Stuff firmly. Turn under ¼" at tops of legs. Whipstitch closed. Whipstitch to body bottom, making sure the toes are pointing toward the front.

6. Using a gentle touch and a ball of cotton, apply blush to the doll's cheeks. Soften the color with clean cotton.

GIRL

From one pattern, you can make a dress of calico or corduroy for everyday wear and velvet or satin for dress-up. Add plenty of lace, ribbons, bows, and ribbon flowers to make this dress a little girl's dream. For a snappy sailor's suit, make the dress of navy fabric and top it off with a collar.

When the sun sets, dress your doll in her pretty nightie. Choose a flowery, feminine flannel for warm winter dreams, a light cotton — plain or print — or eyelet for warm summer nights. She'll be cute as a button in her bunny slippers. And don't forget to tuck her in with her favorite doll.

Hair

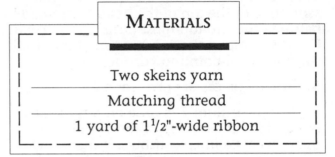

MATERIALS

Two skeins yarn
Matching thread
1 yard of 1½"-wide ribbon

INSTRUCTIONS

Note: All seam allowances are ¼" unless instructed otherwise.

1. Cut 45 pieces of yarn, each 40" long. Draw a 2¼"-long line on a piece of paper. Lay the centers of the yarn evenly along the line. Machine stitch along the line through the yarn centers and paper.

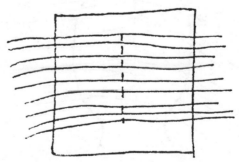

Tear the machine stitching and yarn from the paper.

2. Handstitch the machine stitching on the yarn to just in front of the seam line of the

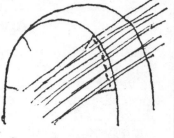

head, starting at the top-most dart on one side of the head and continuing down the side of the head to the next (middle) dart.

Repeat steps one and two for the other side of the head.

3. Cut 60 pieces of yarn each 8" long. Draw a 4"-long line on a piece of paper. Lay the centers of the pieces of yarn evenly along the line. Stitch along the line, through the centers of the yarn. Carefully tear the paper away from the yarn.

4. For bangs, place the stitching along the seam line at the top of the head, easing to fit between the two top-most darts on the head. Hand sew along the machine stitching. Fold the backward-pointing yarn to the front.

5. Cut 200 pieces of yarn, each 40" long.

6. Draw a straight 7½" line on a piece of paper. Find the centers of the yarn and lay them over the line, distributing the yarn to fill the 7½" evenly. Machine stitch through the yarn and paper. Tear the paper away.

7. Place the stitched "part" of the hair piece on a vertical line down the center back of the head, starting at the center top of the doll's head, just overlapping the bangs. Ease the fullness so that the bottom of the stitching ends about 2" above the neck seam at the back of the doll's head. Handstitch to the head along the part.

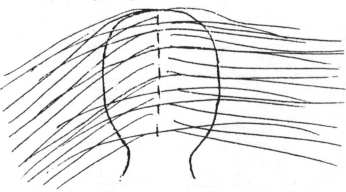

8. Divide each side of the hair from step 7 into two bunches. Braid the hair into two braids. Treat the yarn stitched to the side of the head in step 2 as the third of the three

bunches, bringing it to the back first. Tie the ends with a piece of yarn.

9. Cut ribbon in half. Tie ribbons in bows over the ends of the braids.

DRESS

MATERIALS
⅞ yard dress fabric
Matching thread
Interfacing
Three ½" buttons
1⅓ yards of 1½"-wide ribbon for dress waist tie

INSTRUCTIONS

Note: All seam allowances are ¼" unless instructed otherwise.

Prepare fabric and patterns as instructed in chapter 1. Cut and mark fabric. Cut a skirt for the dress 11" x 45". Cut the neck ruffle 1½" x 24".

1. Stitch front to back bodices at shoulders and sides, for both bodice and bodice lining.

2. Fold neck ruffle in half lengthwise, right sides together. Stitch short ends. Trim seams. Turn. Press. Using a long machine stitch, gather the length of the neck ruffle. Pin to right side of shorter curved edge of one neckband, between the dots. Baste.

Fuse or stitch interfacing to wrong side of second neckband. Lay second neckband, right side down, over first neckband and ruffle, matching raw edges. Pin. Stitch along one short side, shorter curved edge, and second short side, leaving long edge open. Trim and clip seams. Turn. Press.

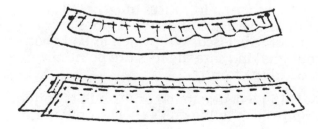

3. Pin both raw edges of neckband to neck edge of bodice, right sides together. Pin second (lining) bodice on top. Stitch from bottom of back edge, around neck edge, and down second back. Trim corners. Clip curves. Turn. Press.

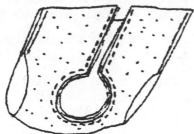

4. Turn under the bottom edges of the sleeves 2". Cut two pieces of elastic, each 6" long. Holding the raw ends of the elastic at the side edges of the sleeve, zigzag stitch the elastic in place, along the raw edge of the turned up bottom edge of the sleeve. Hold the ends of the elastic firmly, stretching the elastic as you sew.

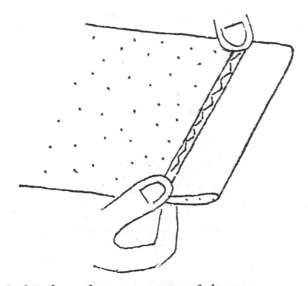

5. Stitch underarm seams of sleeves.

6. Using a long machine stitch, gather the top, curved edge of a sleeve between the dots. Match dots to dots on bodice. Pin, leaving bodice lining free. Pull up on gather stitches. Even out the fullness and pin. Stitch. Turn under ¼" on armhole edge of bodice lining. Pin over seam allowances. Handstitch in place. Repeat for other sleeve.

7. Match short raw edges of dress skirt, right sides facing. Using a ½" seam allowance stitch center back seam of dress skirt. Use a regular machine stitch half way, backstitch

to secure, and continue with a basting stitch to the top. Press the seam open.

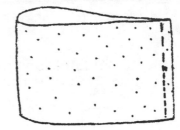

Turn under ¼" on each seam allowance. Topstitch a scant ¼" from either side of the seam. Remove basting stitches.

Turn under ¼" and then another ¼" on the bottom of the skirt. Topstitch.

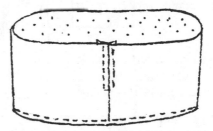

8. Using two rows of gathering stitches, gather the top edge of the skirt. Pin the skirt to the bottom of the bodice with center backs matching, leaving bodice lining free. Adjust gathers. Stitch. Turn ¼" on bottom edge of bodice lining to inside. Pin over seam allowances. Handstitch.

9. Make buttonholes on bodice. Try on doll. Mark positions for buttons. Sew buttons on.

10. Tie ribbon around doll's waist, making a big bow at the back.

PANTALOONS & PETTICOAT

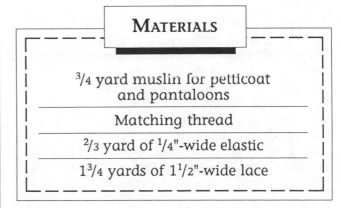

MATERIALS

¾ yard muslin for petticoat and pantaloons
Matching thread
⅔ yard of ¼"-wide elastic
1¾ yards of 1½"-wide lace

INSTRUCTIONS

Note: All seam allowances are 1/4" unless instructed otherwise.

Make patterns, cut out fabric and mark as instructed in chapter 1. Cut the petticoat 12" x 45".

Pantaloons

1. Stitch inside leg seams. Press open.

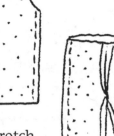

2. Pin long, curved crotch seams, right sides together, matching inside leg seams.

3. Press under 1/4" at bottom of legs for hem. Pin lace on under side of hem, right side facing wrong side of fabric. Topstitch.

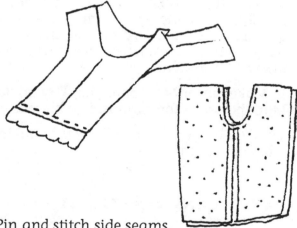

4. Pin and stitch side seams.

5. Press under 1/4" at waist. Press under 5/8" to form casing for elastic. Topstitch close to both folded top edges, leaving a 1/2" gap in the bottom stitching to insert elastic. Cut a piece of elastic 14" long. Insert elastic through casing by attaching a safety pin to one end and running it through the casing. Try on doll. Adjust elastic. Overlap raw edges of elastic and stitch back and forth to secure. Topstitch gap in casing closed.

Petticoat

1. To make hem, press under 1/4" on one long edge. Press under another 1/4". Pin lace to underside of hem, right side of lace facing wrong side of fabric. Topstitch in place.

2. Stitch center back seam, right sides together, including ends of lace in seam.

3. To make casing for elastic, press under 1/4" on the top edge of the petticoat. Press under another 5/8". From the right side topstitch close to both folded edges, leaving a 1/2" opening in the bottom stitching to insert the elastic. Insert a 14"-long piece of elastic into the casing. Overlap ends 1/2" and stitch to secure. Topstitch gap in casing closed.

GIRL'S SAILOR SUIT

MATERIALS
1 yard navy blue medium weight cotton or wool fabric
Matching thread
Three 1/2" buttons
4 yards middy braid
Matching thread
1/4 yard red cotton fabric for tie
One snap

INSTRUCTIONS

Note: All seam allowances are 1/4" unless instructed otherwise.

As instructed in chapter 1, make patterns, cut out fabric and mark. Cut the skirt for the dress 12" x 45".

Sailor Dress

1. Stitch front to back bodices at shoulders and side seams, for both bodice and bodice lining.

2. Pin bodice to bodice lining at neck and back edges, matching shoulder seams. Stitch. Trim corners. Clip curves. Turn right side out. Press.

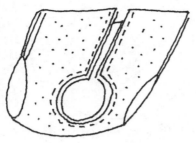

3. Press under the bottom edges of the sleeves ¼". Repeat. Topstitch. Stitch one row of middy braid to sleeve, ¼" from folded edge. Stitch a second row ¼" above the first. Repeat for second sleeve

4. Stitch underarm seams in sleeves.

5. Using a long machine stitch, gather the top, curved edge of the sleeves between dots. Match dots to dots on bodice. Pin, leaving bodice lining free. Pull up on gather stitches. Even out the fullness and pin. Stitch. Turn under ¼" on armhole edge of bodice lining. Pin over seam allowances. Handstitch in place. Repeat for other sleeve.

6. Match short raw edges of dress skirt, right sides facing. Using a ¼" seam allowance stitch center back seam of dress skirt, using a regular machine stitch half way, backstitching to secure, and continuing with a basting stitch to the top. Press the seam open. Turn under ¼" on each seam allowance. Topstitch a scant ¼" from either side of the seam. Remove basting stitches.

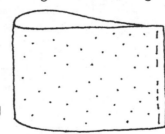

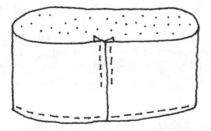

7. Turn under ¼" and then another ¼" on the bottom of the skirt. Topstitch.

8. Using two rows of gathering stitches, gather the top edge of the skirt. Pin the skirt to the bottom of the bodice, having center

backs match, leaving bodice lining free. Adjust gathers. Stitch. Turn ¼" on bottom edge of bodice lining to inside. Pin over seam allowances. Handstitch.

9. Make buttonholes on bodice. Try on doll. Mark positions for buttons. Sew buttons on.

Sailor Collar

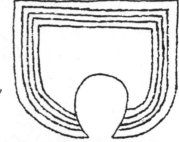

1. Pin and stitch middy braid to right side of three edges of one collar, ½" from the raw edges, as illustrated (excepting neck edge). Stitch both edges of middy braid. Repeat for a second row ¼" from inside of first row.

2. Lay second collar over first, right sides facing. Pin and stitch all but neck edge. Trim corners. Clip curves. Turn right side out. Press.

3. Pin two neckbands together along longest edge. Stitch. Turn right side out. Press.

4. Pin remaining long edge of one neckband to both thicknesses of the collar, right sides facing with short edges of neckband extending ¼" past collar edge. Stitch.

5. Fold collar ties in half along foldline, right sides facing. Stitch along long edge and curve, leaving short straight edge unstitched.

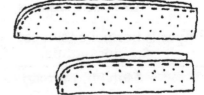

Turn right side out. Press.

6. Turn under ¼" on free, long raw edge of remaining neckband. Pin over seam allowances of other neckband. Turn ¼" at short edges of neckband to inside. Insert raw ends of ties into neckband at these short edges. Fold and pinch the tie to fit inside. Pin. Handstitch short and long edges.

7. Stitch snap in place as shown on collar illustration. To tie, first bring one tie over the top and around the back of the tie.

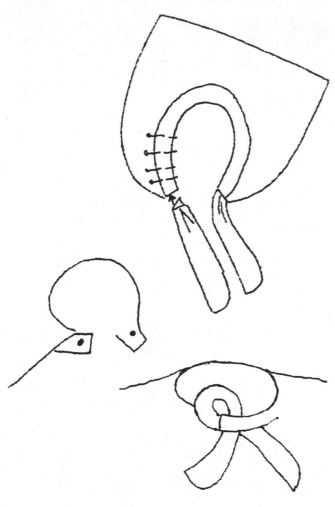

NIGHTIE

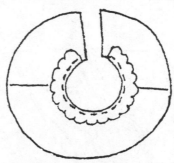

1. Stitch yoke backs to yoke fronts at shoulders, right sides facing. One set will be yoke and the other, yoke lining. Cut a piece of lace 10½" long. Turn under ¼" on each end. Turn under another ¼". Topstitch. Pin lace to yoke. The lace will stop ¼" from each end. Baste.

Right sides facing, pin yokes together along neck edge. Stitch along center back edge, along neck, finishing at lower center back edge of yoke, including the lace in the seam.

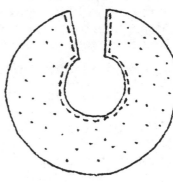

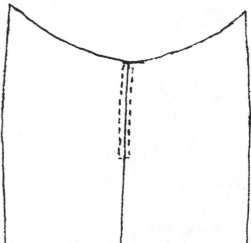

2. Using a ½" seam allowance stitch center back seam. Use a basting stitch from the top to the dot, backstitching at the dot and continuing with a regular stitch to the bottom. Turn ¼" of seam allowance to inside above dot. Topstitch. Remove basting stitches.

3. Press under ¼" on bottom edges of sleeves. Repeat. Pin lace under hem. Topstitch in place. Cut two pieces of elastic, both 5" long. Pin to sleeve 1½" from edge as shown. Zigzag stitch in place stretching the elastic in front of and behind the needle as you sew. Repeat for second sleeve.

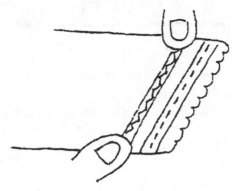

4. Stitch sleeves to nightie body front and back.

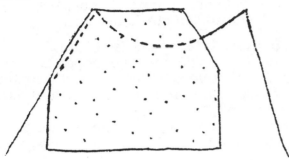

5. Using long machine stitches gather the yoke edge of the nightie body and sleeves between seams.

6. Pin sleeves/nightie front and back to bodice yoke, leaving yoke lining free, matching back edges and sleeve seams to dots on yokes. Adjust gathers. Pin. Stitch. Turn under ¼" on raw edge of yoke lining. Pin over seam allowances. Handstitch.

7. Stitch underarm/side seams as one.

8. Press under ¼" on hem. Repeat. Top-stitch.

9. Make buttonholes at back of yoke. Try on doll. Mark dots for buttons. Sew buttons in place.

10. Tie ribbon into a bow. Tack in place (or safety pin from inside).

BUNNY SLIPPERS

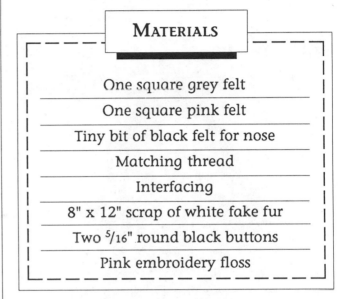

MATERIALS
One square grey felt
One square pink felt
Tiny bit of black felt for nose
Matching thread
Interfacing
8" x 12" scrap of white fake fur
Two ⁵⁄₁₆" round black buttons
Pink embroidery floss

INSTRUCTIONS

Note: All seam allowances are ¼" unless instructed otherwise.

Prepare patterns and cut fabric as instructed in chapter 1.

1. Right sides facing, pin and stitch the two long edges of two slipper straps together. Turn. Press. Repeat for second set.

2. Apply interfacing to one slipper sole. Pin straps between dots on side of sole without interfacing. Lay second slipper sole over first sole and strap. Pin. Stitch, leaving a 1" opening for turning. Turn. Press. Handstitch opening closed.

3. Pin and stitch fur ears to felt ears, leaving bottoms open. Turn.

4. Make a crimp in ears. Baste ears to right side of fur head, pink of ears facing fur head, as shown.

Pin felt bunny head to fur bunny head, right sides facing, stuffing ears inside. Stitch, leaving a 1" opening in the stitching for turning. Turn. Handstitch opening closed. Sew eyes in place. Cut a nose out of felt. Glue in place. Handstitch bunny's head to slipper strap.

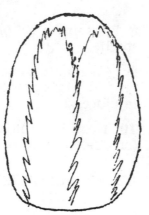

DOLL'S DOLL

INSTRUCTIONS

Note: All seam allowances are 1/4" unless instructed otherwise.

Prepare patterns and cut fabric as instructed in chapter 1.

1. Stitch two muslin doll bodies together, leaving a 1" opening in the stitching at one leg side for turning. Clip into seams at curves. Turn. Stuff. Handstitch opening closed.

2. Embroider face, making French knots for eyes.

3. To form bangs, handstitch loops to the top 2" of the head along the seam line.

4. Cut thirty 12"-long pieces of yarn. Draw a line 1 1/2" long on a piece of paper. Lay the middles of the yarn on the paper, distributing the yarn evenly along the line. Stitch through the yarn and the paper.

Pin stitching to head as shown. Handstitch in place. Braid yarn. Tie with a piece of yarn.

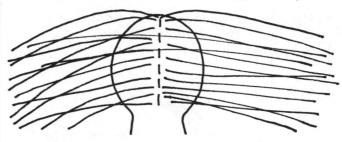

5. Stitch one shoulder seam in dress. Fold 3/8" at neck edge to inside. Pin the ends of a 4 1/2" piece of elastic to the wrong side of the dress, over the turned under raw edge as shown. Holding both ends of the elastic and dress, stretch and zigzag stitch the elastic in place.

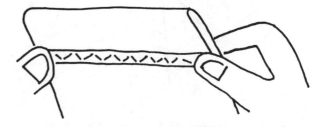

Stitch second shoulder seam.
Turn 3/8" to inside at wrist edge. Zigzag a 3" piece of elastic over raw edge, stretching the elastic as you sew. Repeat for the second sleeve.
Stitch underarm seams.
Press under 1/4" at dress hem. Turn under another 1/4". Topstitch.

BOY

Hair

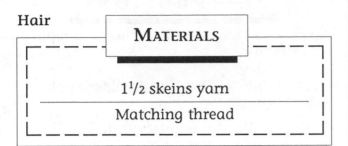

INSTRUCTIONS

1. Draw a 16" line on a piece of paper. Lay yarn in continuous loops with 3"-long loops on either side of the line as shown. Fill the line evenly with about 260 of these loops. Machine stitch along the line through yarn and paper. Tear paper away.
    Make another row of yarn on another piece of paper in the same manner, using the same measurements.
    Make five more rows of yarn in the same way using the following measurements:

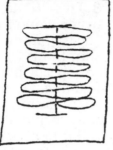

220 loops on a	14" line
180 loops on a	12" line
140 loops on a	10" line
120 loops on a	7" line
60 loops on a	3" line

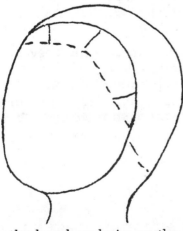

2. With a soft lead pencil, draw a line along the doll's head as illustrated. Pin the middle of the first row of yarn on the line at the center of the doll's forehead. Bring the ends around the respective sides of the head and pin on the line where they meet at the back of the head. Handstitch the first, 16" row of yarn to the doll's head along the pencil line. Ease the fullness of the string of yarn as you stitch, since the stitching will have stretched as it was removed from the paper.

3. Stitch the second 16" row to the head in the same manner, spacing it approximately ½" inside the first row.

4. Repeat for the remaining rows, spacing each approximately ½" behind the preceding row.

5. Stitch the seventh, final string of yarn to the top of the head as if it was a part in the boy's hair.

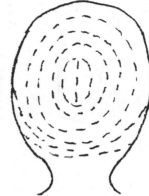

PANTS

INSTRUCTIONS

Note: All seam allowances are ¼" unless instructed otherwise.

As instructed in chapter 1, prepare fabric and patterns, and cut and mark the fabric.

1. Sew the short inner leg seams, right sides together. Press open.

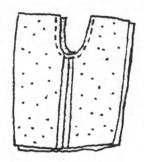

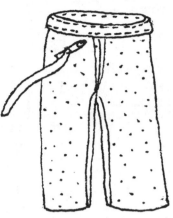

2. Pin and stitch the curved crotch seam, right sides facing.

3. Match the long, outside leg seams. Pin and stitch.

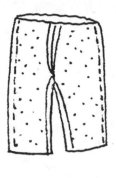

4. Press under ¼" along the waistline opening. Press under an additional ⅝". Topstitch close to both folds, leaving a ½" opening in the stitching on the lower fold for inserting the elastic. Run a 14" piece of elastic through the casing. Try the pants on the doll. Adjust the elastic, if necessary. Overlap and stitch the raw ends of the elastic. Stitch the gap in the casing closed.

5. Press under ¼" on the bottom edges of the pant legs. Press under another ¼". Topstitch.

6. Cut buttonholes in suspenders as marked. Stitch buttons to pants, 1¾" to each side of the center crotch seam, both front and back. Put buttons through holes in suspenders.

SHIRT

MATERIALS

⅔ yard fabric for shirt

Matching thread

Interfacing

Four ½" buttons

INSTRUCTIONS

Note: All seam allowances are ¼" unless instructed otherwise.

1. Stitch fronts to back at shoulders, right sides facing.

2. Cut a collar out of interfacing. Fuse to wrong side of one collar (will be under collar). Pin collars, right sides together, along longer edge and two short ends. Stitch, leaving shorter edge open. Trim corners. Turn. Press.

3. Press ¼" to inside along front edges of front. Fold shirt fronts to wrong side along fold line. Pin top edges to shirt, right sides facing. Pin collar to neck edge, so that far edges of collar touch edge of front facing. Stitch from front edge to front edge, catching collar.

Trim corners. Turn.

Press front along fold line. Topstitch ⅛" from the front edge and again ½" from the first stitching. Repeat for the second side. Make buttonholes as marked on left front.

4. Stitch side seams.

5. Press under ¼" and ¼" again on lower edge of shirt. Topstitch just less than ¼" from the edge.

6. Stitch the underarm seams of the sleeves. Press under ¼" and another ¼" for hem of sleeves sleeve. Topstitch barely ¼" from the edge. Pin sleeve to armhole, matching seam in sleeve with side seam of shirt, easing the sleeve to fit. Stitch. Repeat for other sleeve.

7. Sew buttons in place.

BOY'S SAILOR SUIT

MATERIALS

1¹/₃ yards fabric for pants

Matching thread

¹/₄"-wide elastic

Eight ⁵/₈" buttons

4 yards middy braid

Matching thread

¹/₄ yard red cotton fabric for tie

One snap

INSTRUCTIONS

Note: All seam allowances are ¹/₄" unless instructed otherwise.

As instructed in chapter 1, make patterns, and cut and mark fabric.

Shirt

1. Stitch fronts to back at shoulders, right sides facing.

2. Press ¹/₂" to inside at both shirt front edges. Topstitch. Repeat.

Pink or zigzag stitch the longest curved edge of neck facing. Pin neck facing to neck edge, right sides facing with short facing edges extending ¹/₄" past shirt front edges. Stitch.

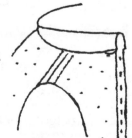

Clip curves. Turn facing to wrong side. Turn ¹/₄" at short front edges of facing to inside. Hand-stitch. Press.

Make buttonholes on left front as marked.

3. Stitch side seams.

4. Stitch underarm seams of sleeves.

5. Press under ¹/₄" and another ¹/₄" along hems of the sleeves. Topstitch barely ¹/₄" from the edges.

6. Pin sleeve to armhole, matching underarm seam in sleeve with side seam of shirt, easing the sleeve to fit. Stitch. Repeat for other sleeve.

7. Press under ¹/₄" and ¹/₄" again on lower edge of shirt. Topstitch just less than ¹/₄" from the edge.

8. Sew buttons in place.

Pants

Make pants for boy doll as shown on page 105, using navy blue fabric (included in Materials list above.)

Sailor Collar

Make sailor collar as instructed for girl doll on page 101.

NIGHTSHIRT

MATERIALS

⁷/₈ yard fabric for nightshirt

Matching thread

Four ¹/₂" buttons

INSTRUCTIONS

Note: All seam allowances are ¹/₄" unless instructed otherwise.

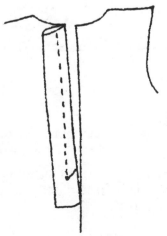

1. Fold front placket in half lengthwise. Pin to front along slash, matching raw edges at top and along slash. Stitch. Repeat for other placket.

2. Clip diagonally from bottom of slit to dot through nightshirt front and both layers of placket.

3. Turn right placket out flat pushing bottom extension to wrong side of nightshirt front. Turn left placket out flat, with bottom extension of placket on outside. Turn under left (now top) extension ¾". Topstitch a box with a V in it through all layers. Clip the excess inside placket extension close to stitching.

Stitch front to back at shoulder seams.

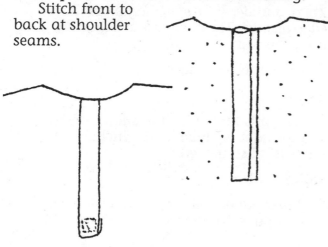

4. With right side of neck facing wrong side of nightshirt neck opening, pin neck facing to neckline, matching center backs and leaving ¼" of neck facing extending past neckline edge in front. Stitch. Trim corners.

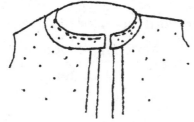

5. Turn facing to right side of neckline. Turn under ¼" on raw edges of facing. Pin in place. Topstitch close to edge.

6. Pin sleeve to nightshirt matching large dot to shoulder seam. Stitch.

7. With right sides together, stitch underarm sleeve and side seams as one continuous seam.

8. Turn under ¼" at sleeve edge. Press under another ¼". Topstitch. Repeat for other sleeve.

9. Turn under ¼" at hem. Press under another ¼". Topstitch.

10. Make buttonholes on left front placket and neck facing as marked.

11. Sew buttons in place.

TEDDY BEAR SLIPPERS

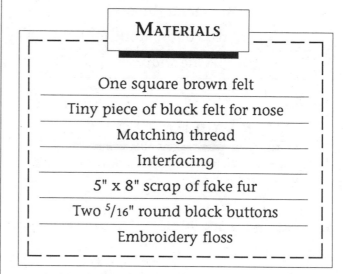

MATERIALS
One square brown felt
Tiny piece of black felt for nose
Matching thread
Interfacing
5" x 8" scrap of fake fur
Two 5/16" round black buttons
Embroidery floss

INSTRUCTIONS

Note: All seam allowances are ¼" unless instructed otherwise.

Prepare patterns and cut fabric as instructed in chapter 1.

1. Right sides facing, pin and stitch the two long edges of two slipper straps together. Turn. Press. Repeat for second set.

2. Apply interfacing to one slipper sole. Pin straps between dots on right side of sole. Lay second slipper sole over first sole and strap. Pin. Stitch, leaving a 1" opening for turning. Turn. Press. Handstitch opening closed.

3. Pin fur teddy bear head to felt teddy bear head, right sides facing. Stitch, leaving a 1" opening in the stitching for turning. Turn. Handstitch opening closed. Sew eyes in place. Cut felt nose. Glue in place. Handstitch bear head to slipper strap.

DOLL'S TEDDY BEAR

MATERIALS

7" x 16" piece of fake fur fabric

Matching thread

Polyester fiberfill

Two $5/16$" round black buttons for eyes

Tiny scrap of black felt for nose

INSTRUCTIONS

Note: All seam allowances are $1/4$" unless instructed otherwise.

Following the instructions in chapter 1, make the patterns and cut and mark the fabric.

1. Pin the bear front to bear back, right sides together. Stitch, leaving a $1^1/2$" opening in one side leg for turning. Stitch. Turn. Stuff. Handstitch opening closed.

2. Sew eyes in place. Cut nose out of black felt. Glue in place.

BOTH DOLLS' SHOES

MATERIALS

$1/4$ yard vinyl

Matching thread

Two $1/4$" buttons

Elastic thread

INSTRUCTIONS

Note: All seam allowances are $1/4$" unless instructed otherwise.

Prepare the patterns and cut out the vinyl as instructed in chapter 1. Transfer dots.

1. Stitch back seam of shoe top, right sides facing.

2. Matching small dot on shoe sole to back seam of shoe top and large dot on sole to large dot on shoe top, pin shoe top to shoe sole. Stitch. Trim seam allowances to $1/8$".

3. Make small holes for elastic with seam ripper. Push one end of elastic through hole in shoe side from inside. Push elastic through strap from wrong side. Put button on elastic. From right side push end of elastic back through hole on strap. Push elastic back through the hole on the shoe side. Make a large knot in elastic on inside of shoe. If you have to enlarge the holes to get the elastic through, put a clip like the ones that hold buttons on a card through the knot.

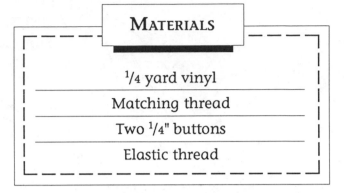

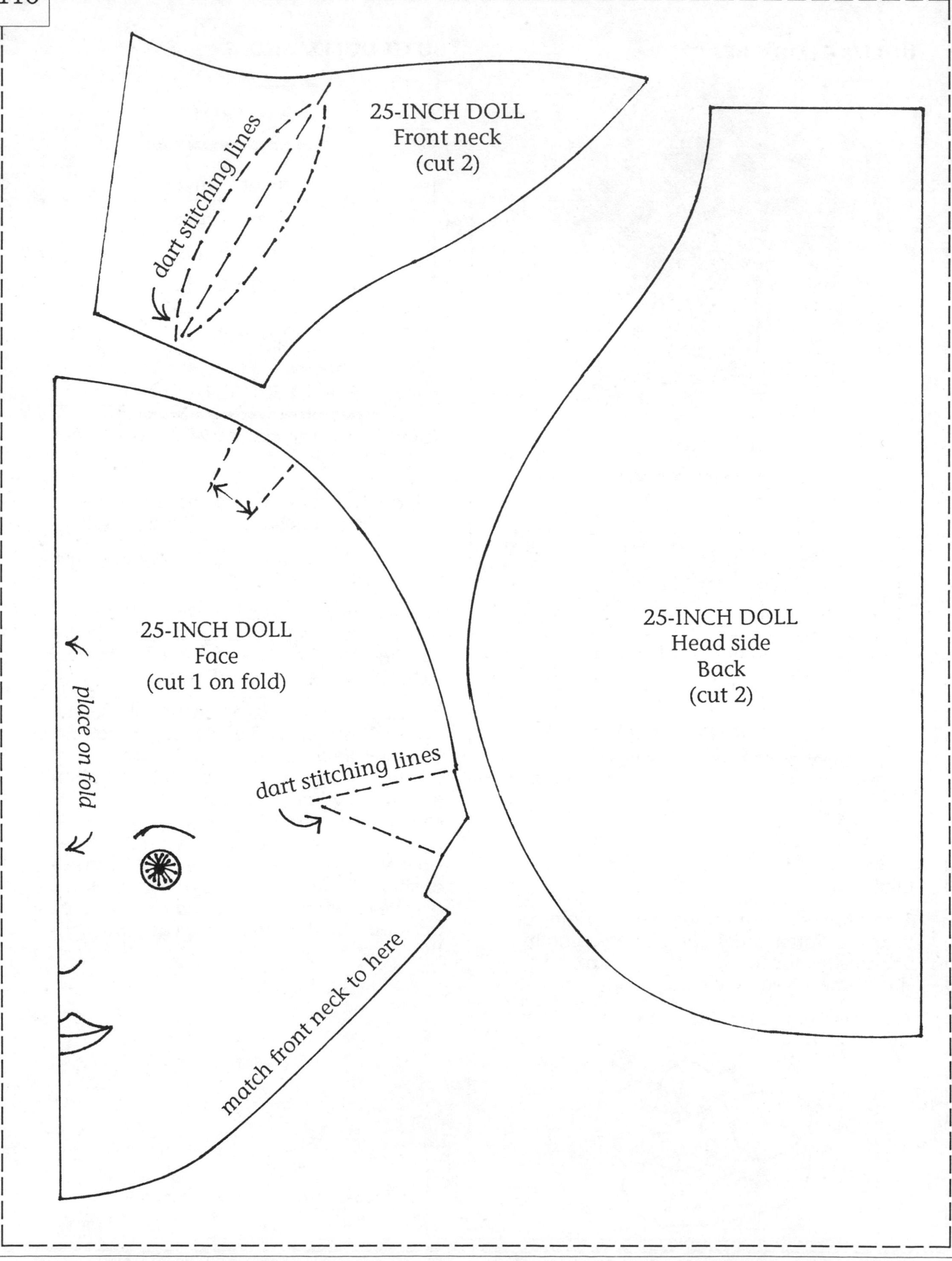

dart stitching lines

25-INCH DOLL
Front neck
(cut 2)

place on fold

25-INCH DOLL
Face
(cut 1 on fold)

25-INCH DOLL
Head side
Back
(cut 2)

dart stitching lines

match front neck to here

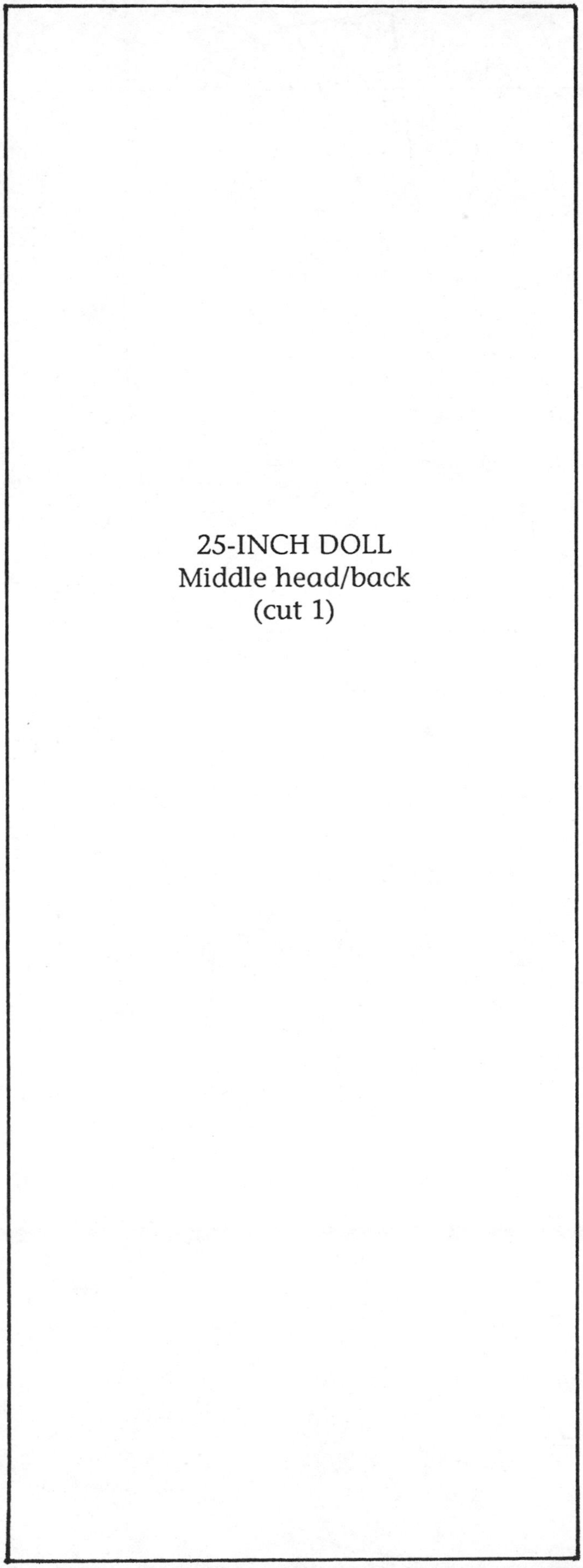

25-INCH DOLL
Middle head/back
(cut 1)

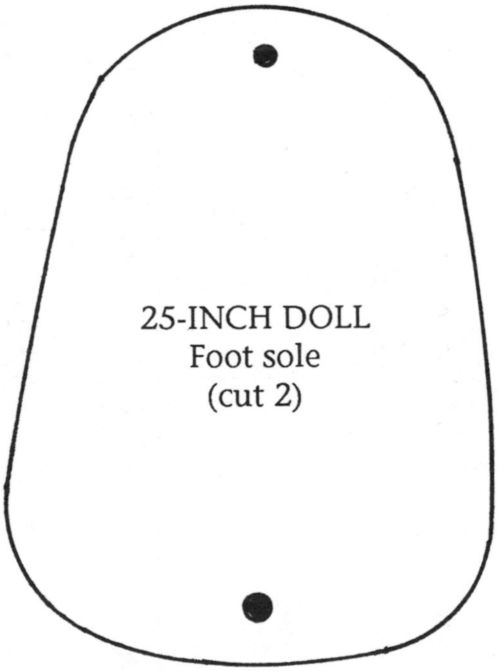

25-INCH DOLL
Foot sole
(cut 2)

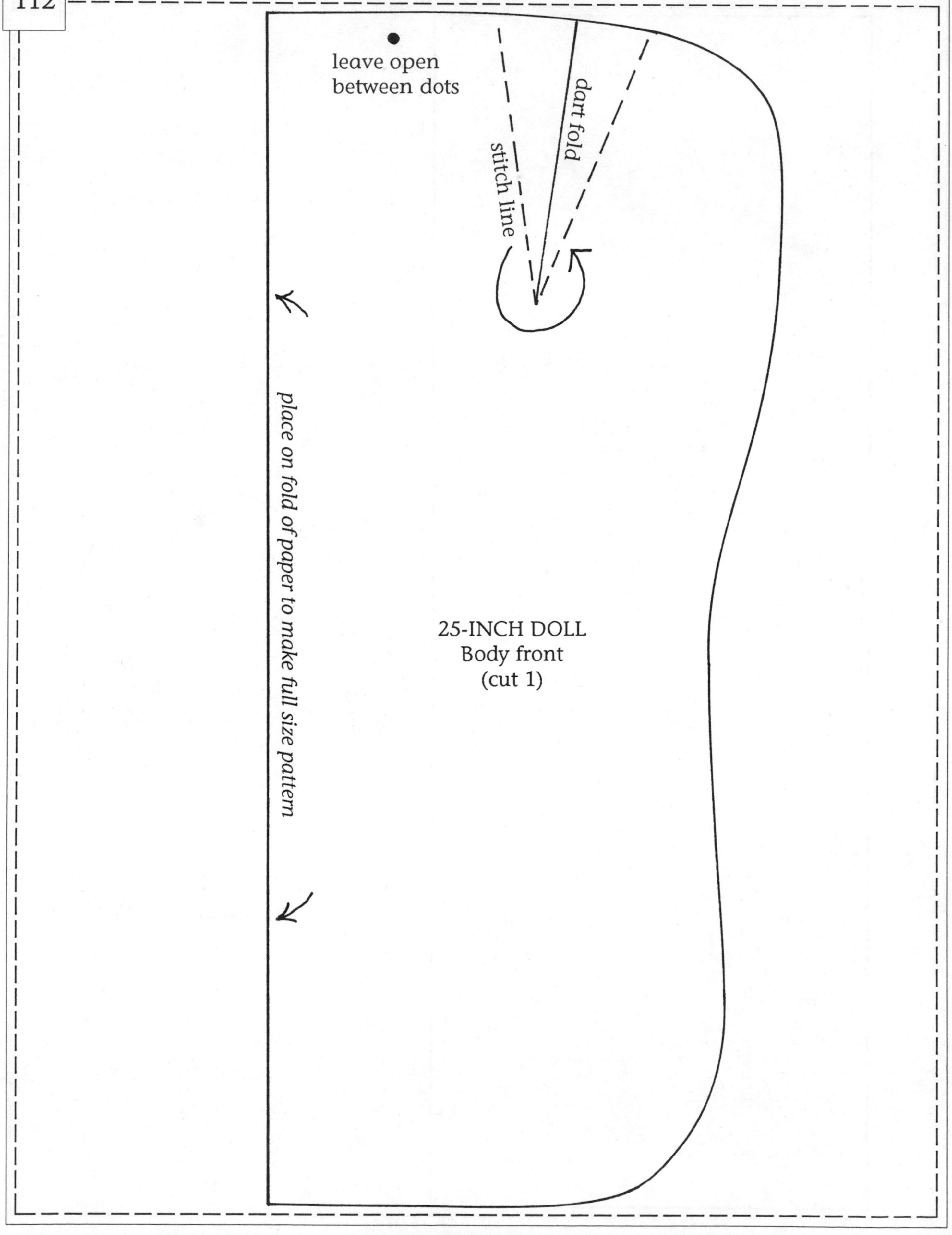

leave open
between dots

stitch line

dart fold

place on fold of paper to make full size pattern

25-INCH DOLL
Body front
(cut 1)

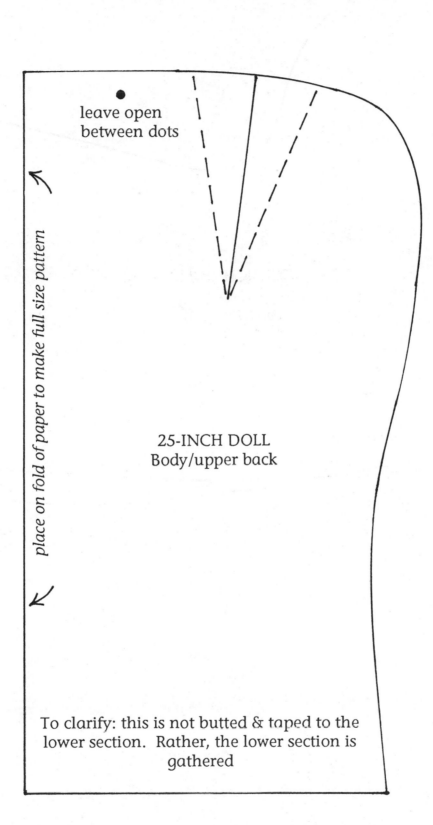

leave open
between dots

place on fold of paper to make full size pattern

25-INCH DOLL
Body/upper back

To clarify: this is not butted & taped to the
lower section. Rather, the lower section is
gathered

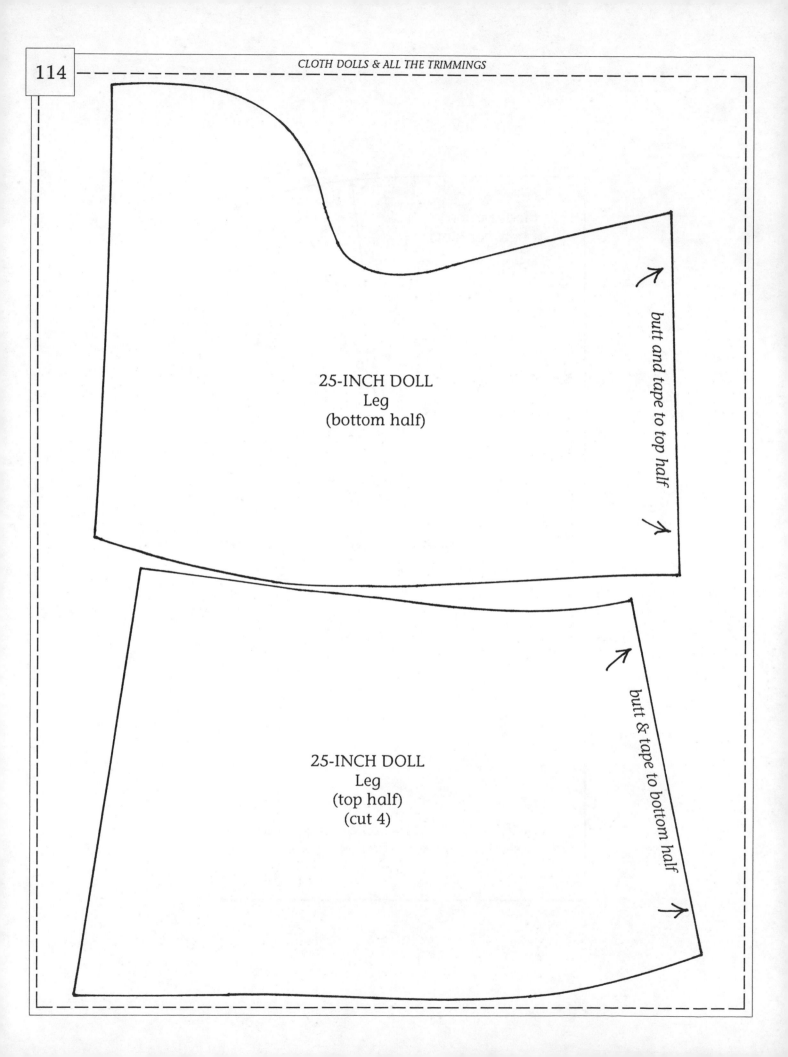

25-INCH DOLL
Leg
(bottom half)

butt and tape to top half

25-INCH DOLL
Leg
(top half)
(cut 4)

butt & tape to bottom half

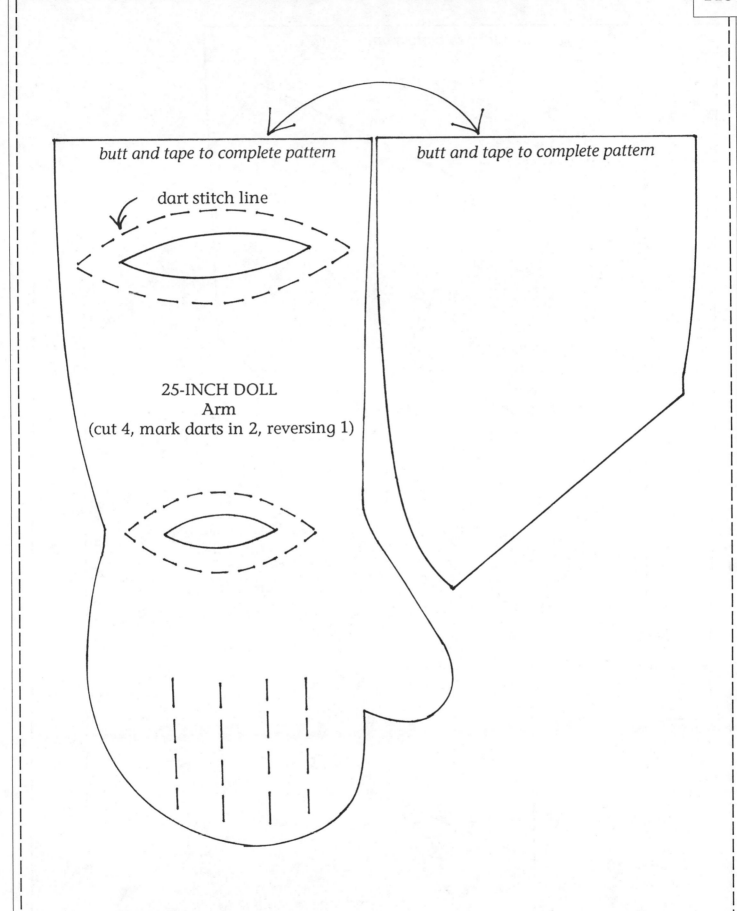

butt and tape to complete pattern

butt and tape to complete pattern

dart stitch line

25-INCH DOLL
Arm
(cut 4, mark darts in 2, reversing 1)

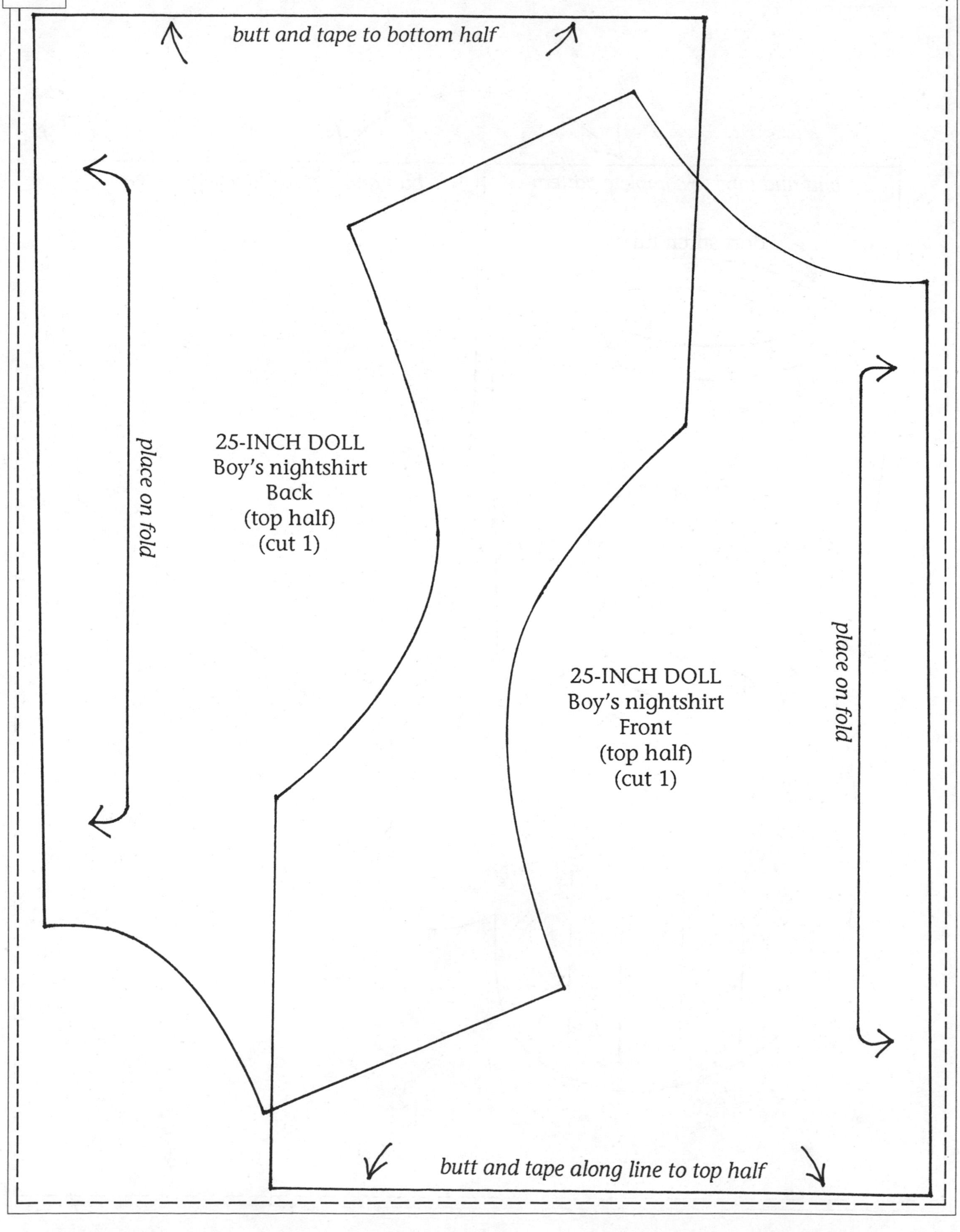

butt and tape to bottom half

place on fold

25-INCH DOLL
Boy's nightshirt
Back
(top half)
(cut 1)

25-INCH DOLL
Boy's nightshirt
Front
(top half)
(cut 1)

place on fold

butt and tape along line to top half

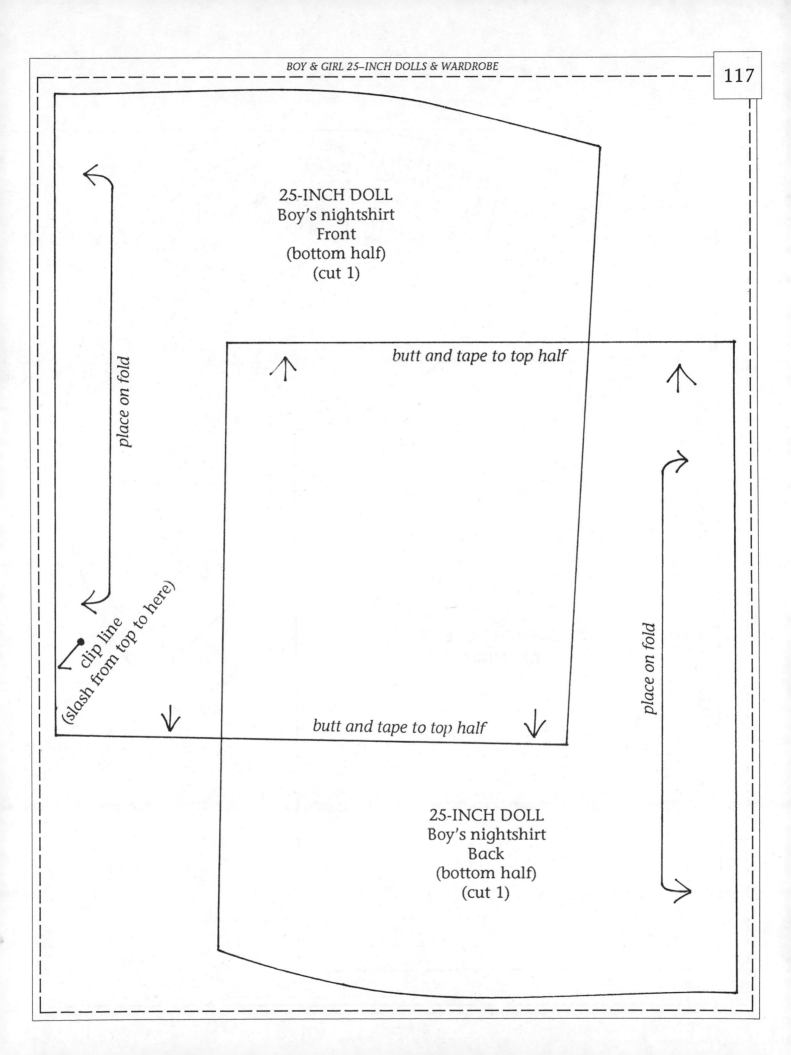

25-INCH DOLL
Boy's nightshirt
Front
(bottom half)
(cut 1)

place on fold

butt and tape to top half

clip line
(slash from top to here)

butt and tape to top half

place on fold

25-INCH DOLL
Boy's nightshirt
Back
(bottom half)
(cut 1)

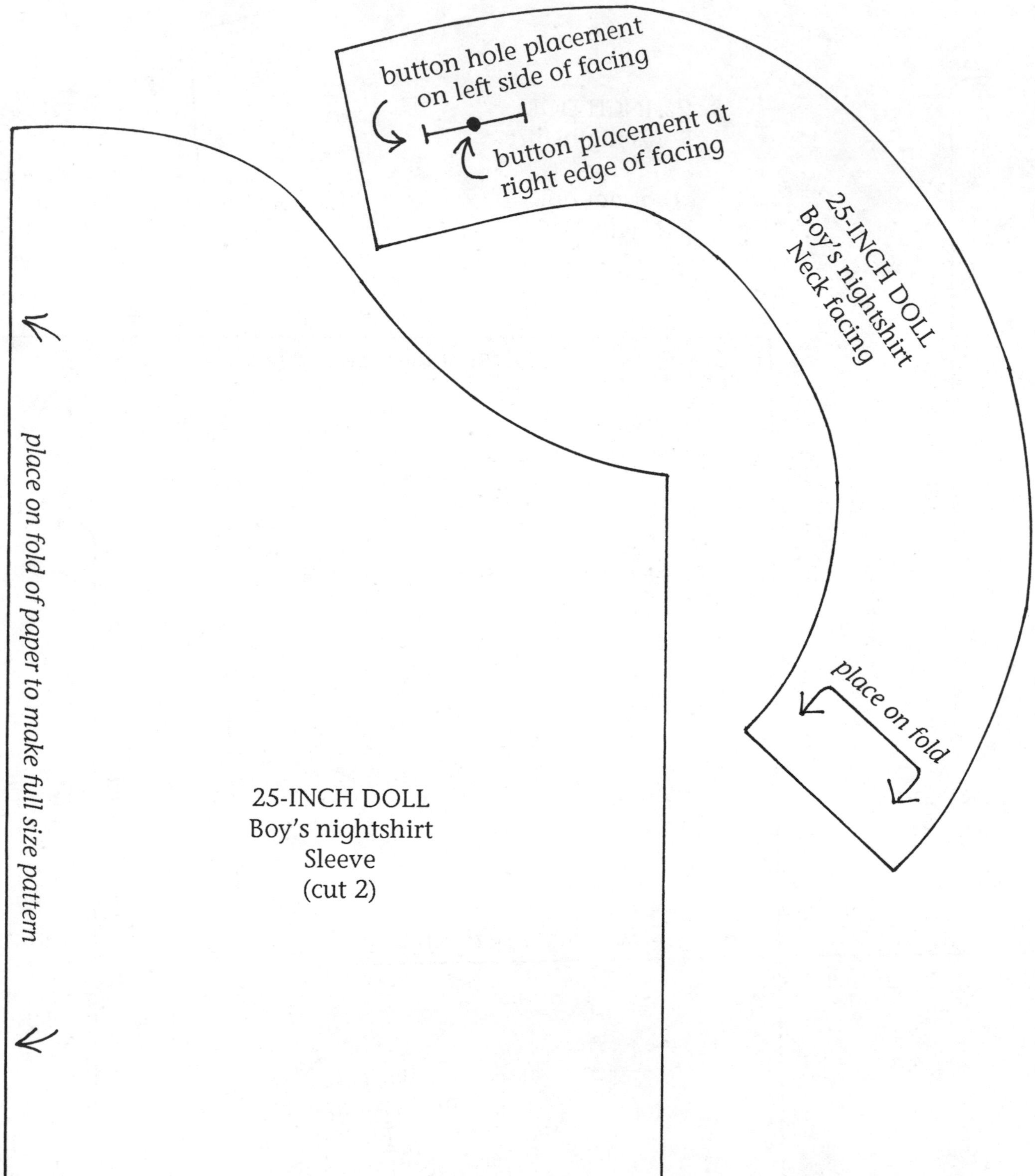

button hole placement
on left side of facing

button placement at
right edge of facing

25-INCH DOLL
Boy's nightshirt
Neck facing

place on fold

place on fold of paper to make full size pattern

25-INCH DOLL
Boy's nightshirt
Sleeve
(cut 2)

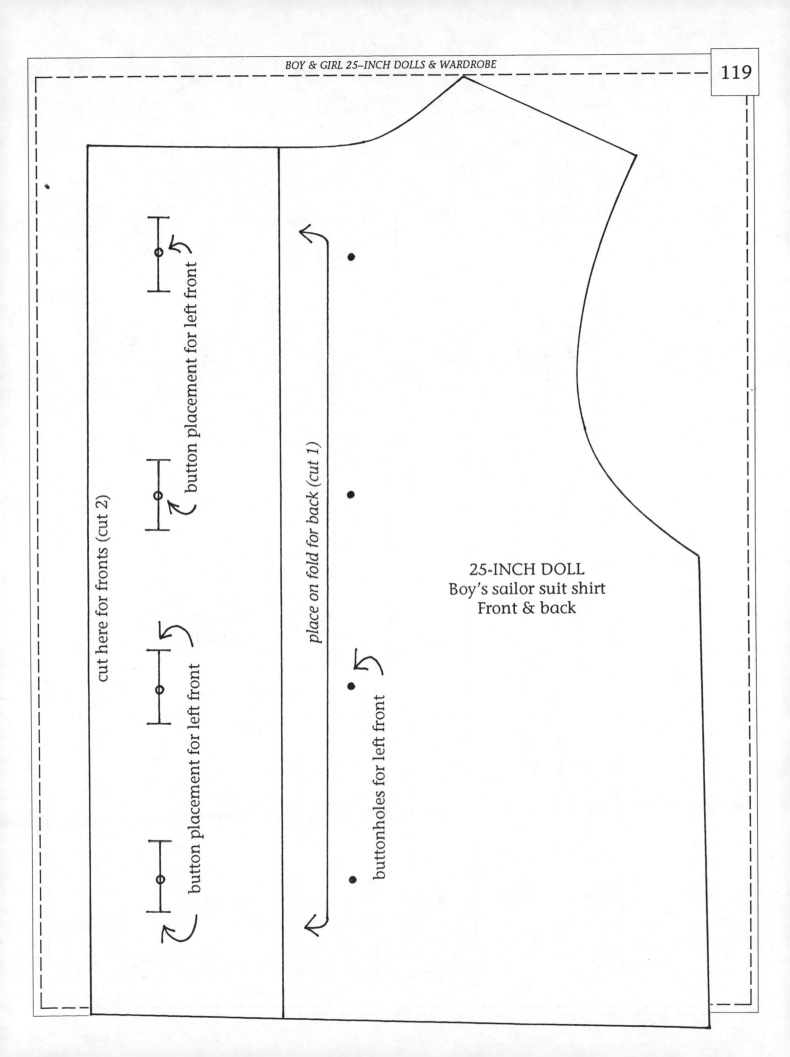

cut here for fronts (cut 2)

button placement for left front

button placement for left front

place on fold for back (cut 1)

buttonholes for left front

25-INCH DOLL
Boy's sailor suit shirt
Front & back

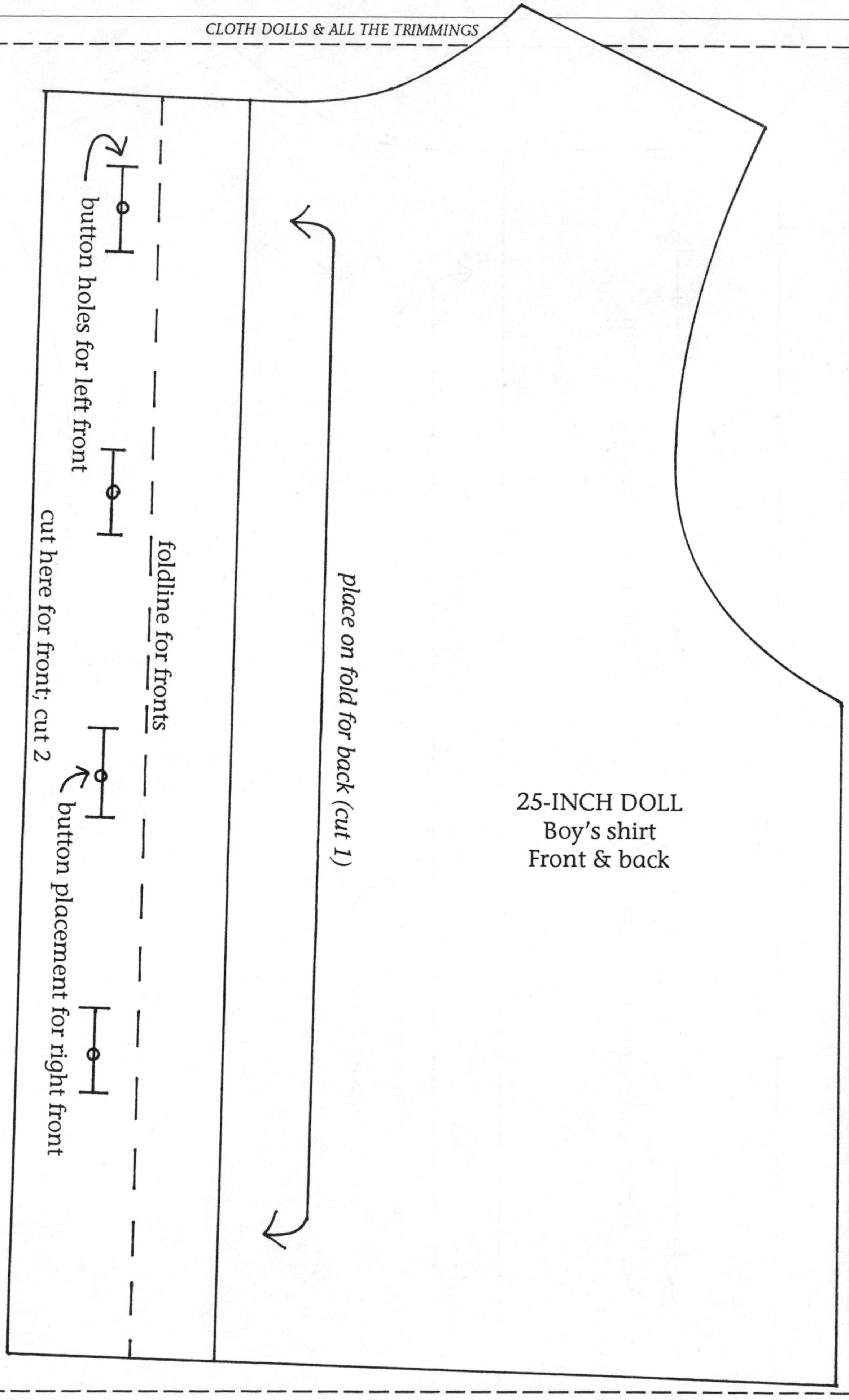

button holes for left front

cut here for front; cut 2

foldline for fronts

button placement for right front

place on fold for back (cut 1)

25-INCH DOLL
Boy's shirt
Front & back

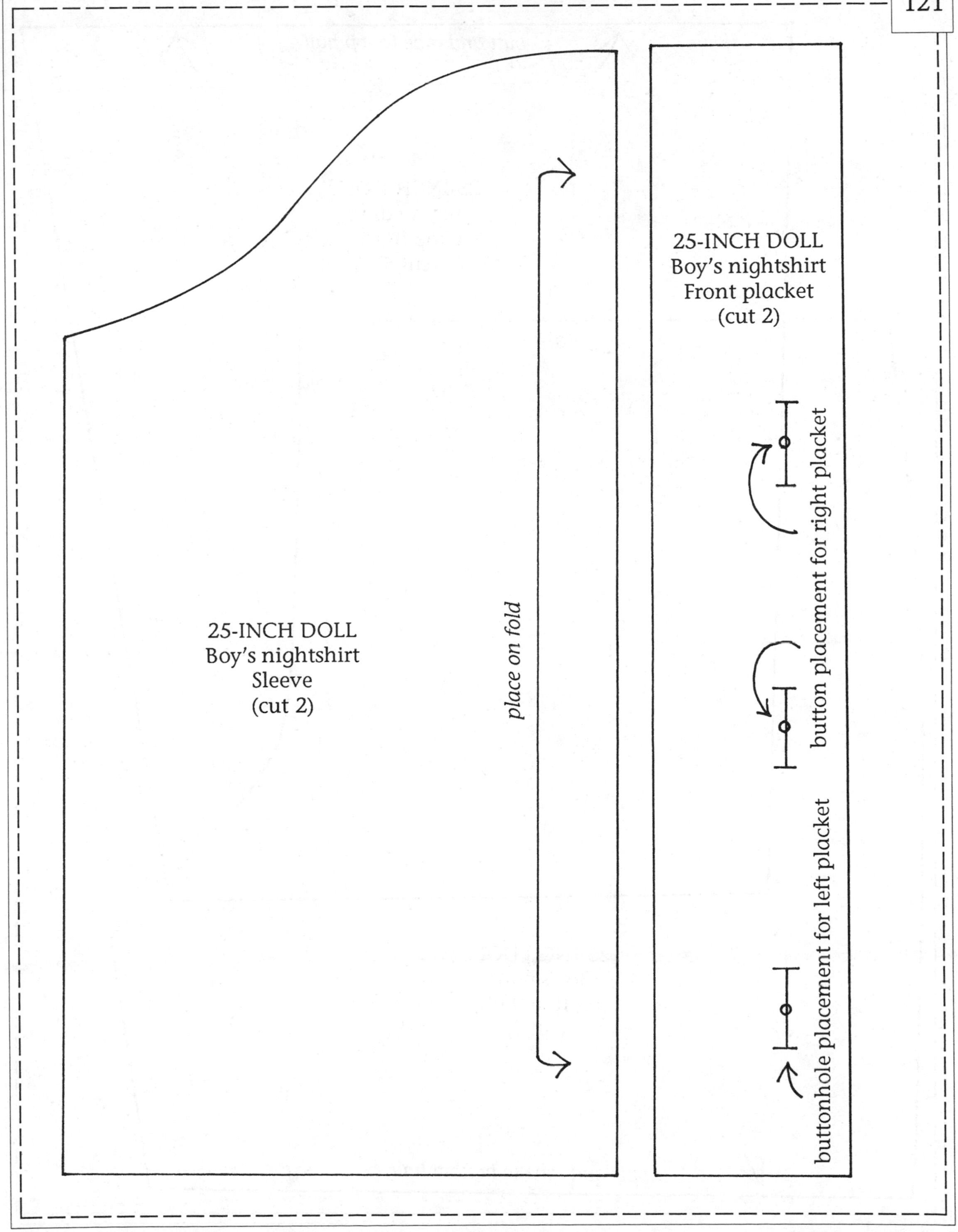

25-INCH DOLL
Boy's nightshirt
Front placket
(cut 2)

button placement for right placket

25-INCH DOLL
Boy's nightshirt
Sleeve
(cut 2)

place on fold

buttonhole placement for left placket

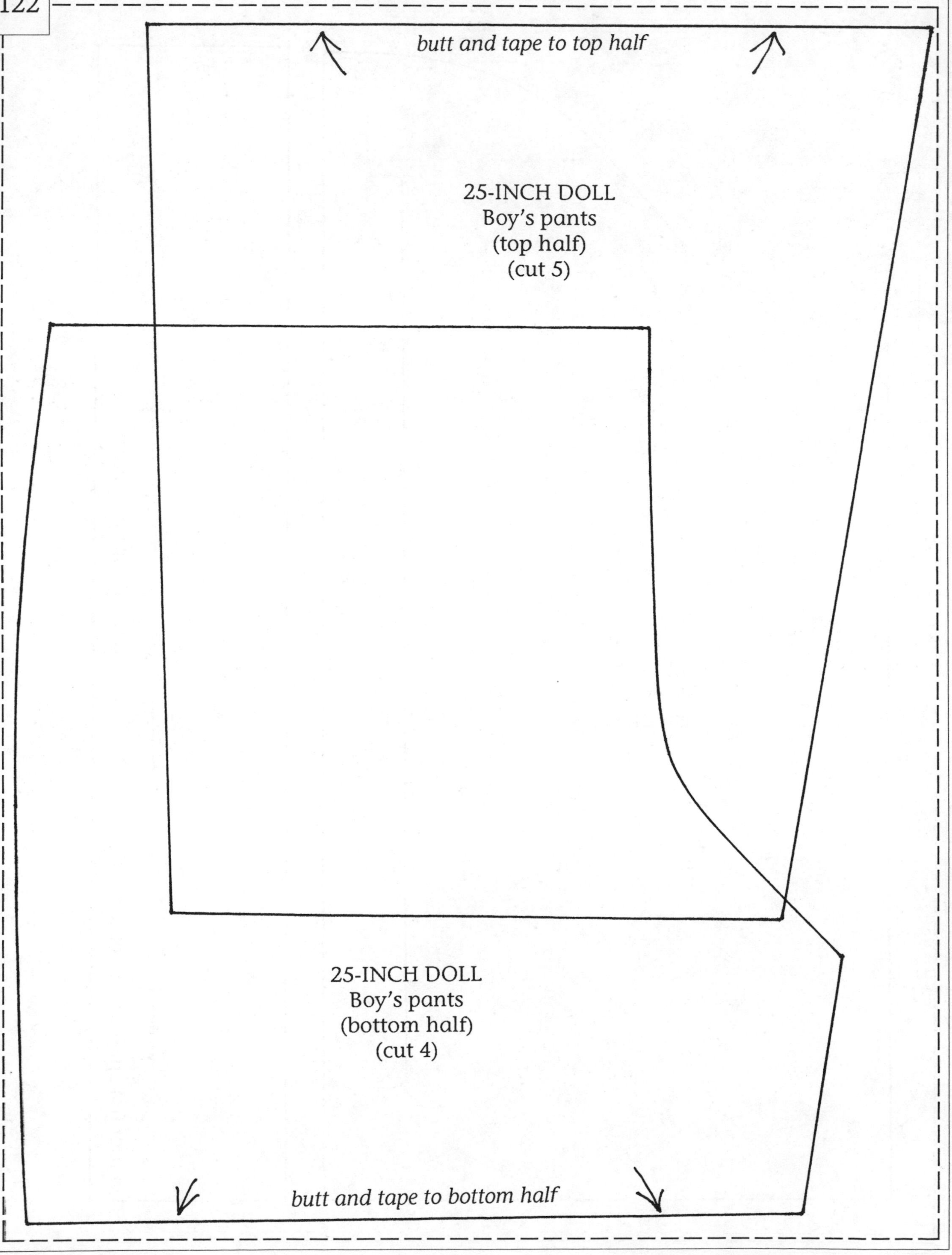

butt and tape to top half

25-INCH DOLL
Boy's pants
(top half)
(cut 5)

25-INCH DOLL
Boy's pants
(bottom half)
(cut 4)

butt and tape to bottom half

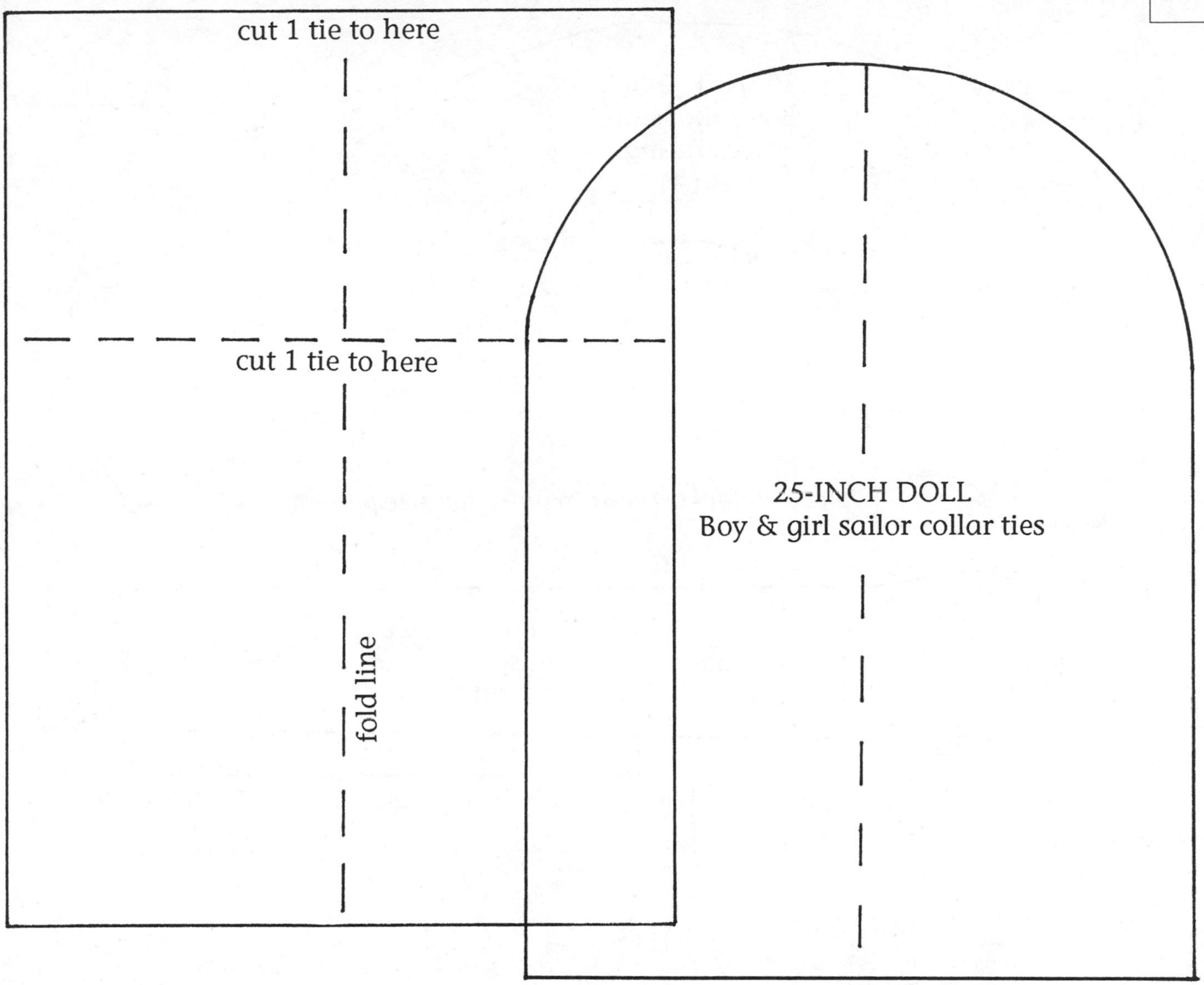

cut 1 tie to here

cut 1 tie to here

fold line

25-INCH DOLL
Boy & girl sailor collar ties

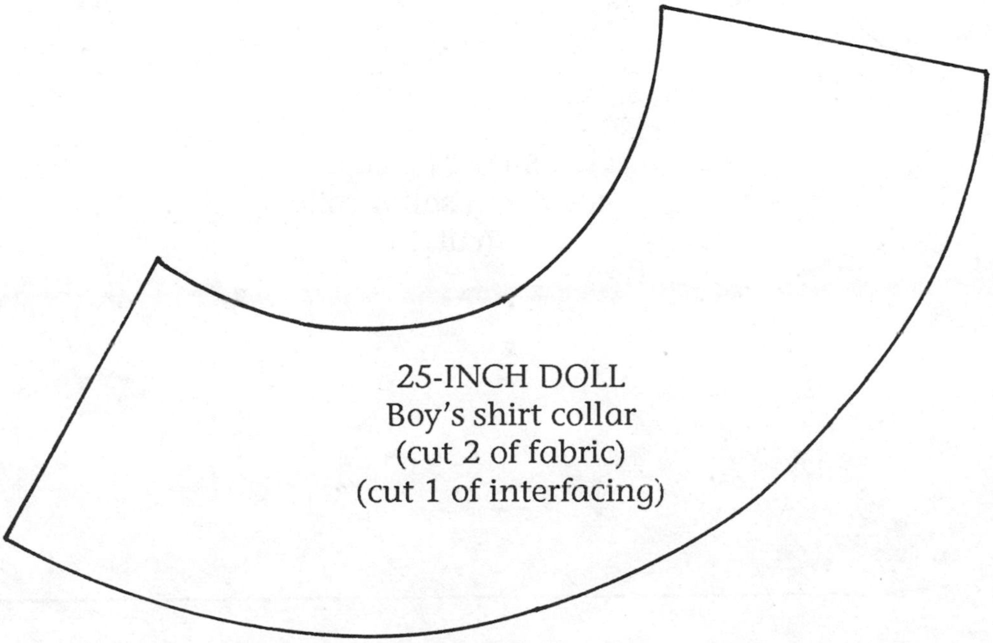

25-INCH DOLL
Boy's shirt collar
(cut 2 of fabric)
(cut 1 of interfacing)

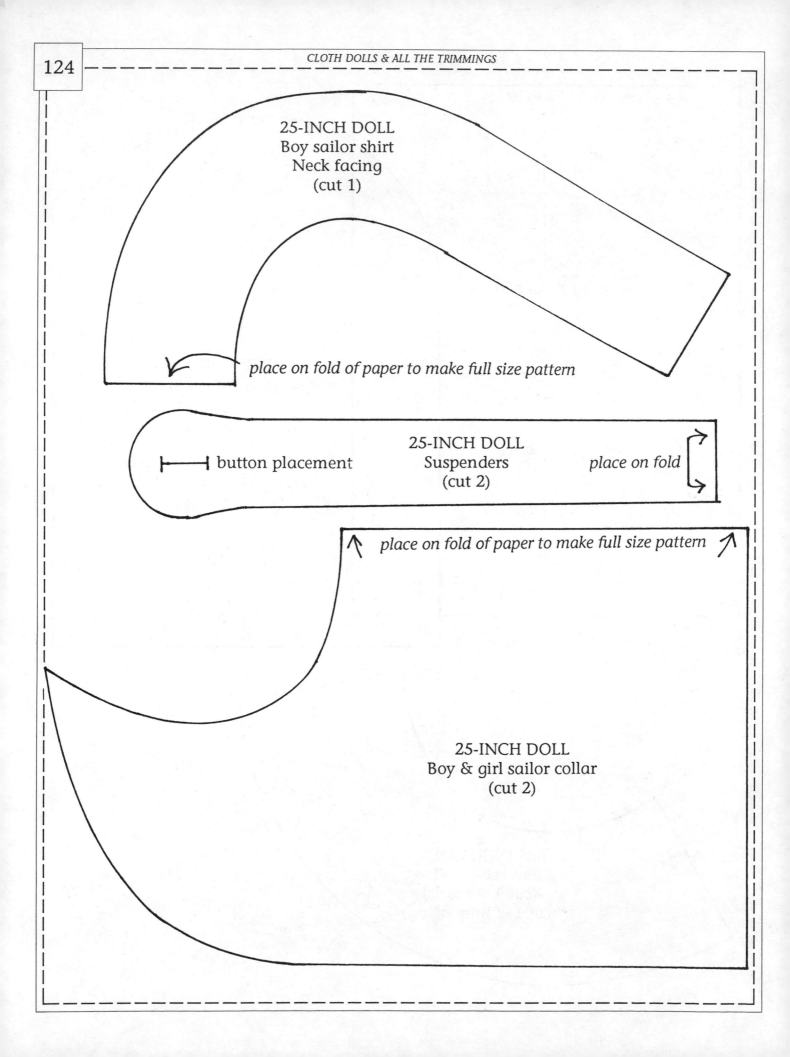

25-INCH DOLL
Boy sailor shirt
Neck facing
(cut 1)

place on fold of paper to make full size pattern

⊢——⊣ button placement

25-INCH DOLL
Suspenders
(cut 2)

place on fold

place on fold of paper to make full size pattern

25-INCH DOLL
Boy & girl sailor collar
(cut 2)

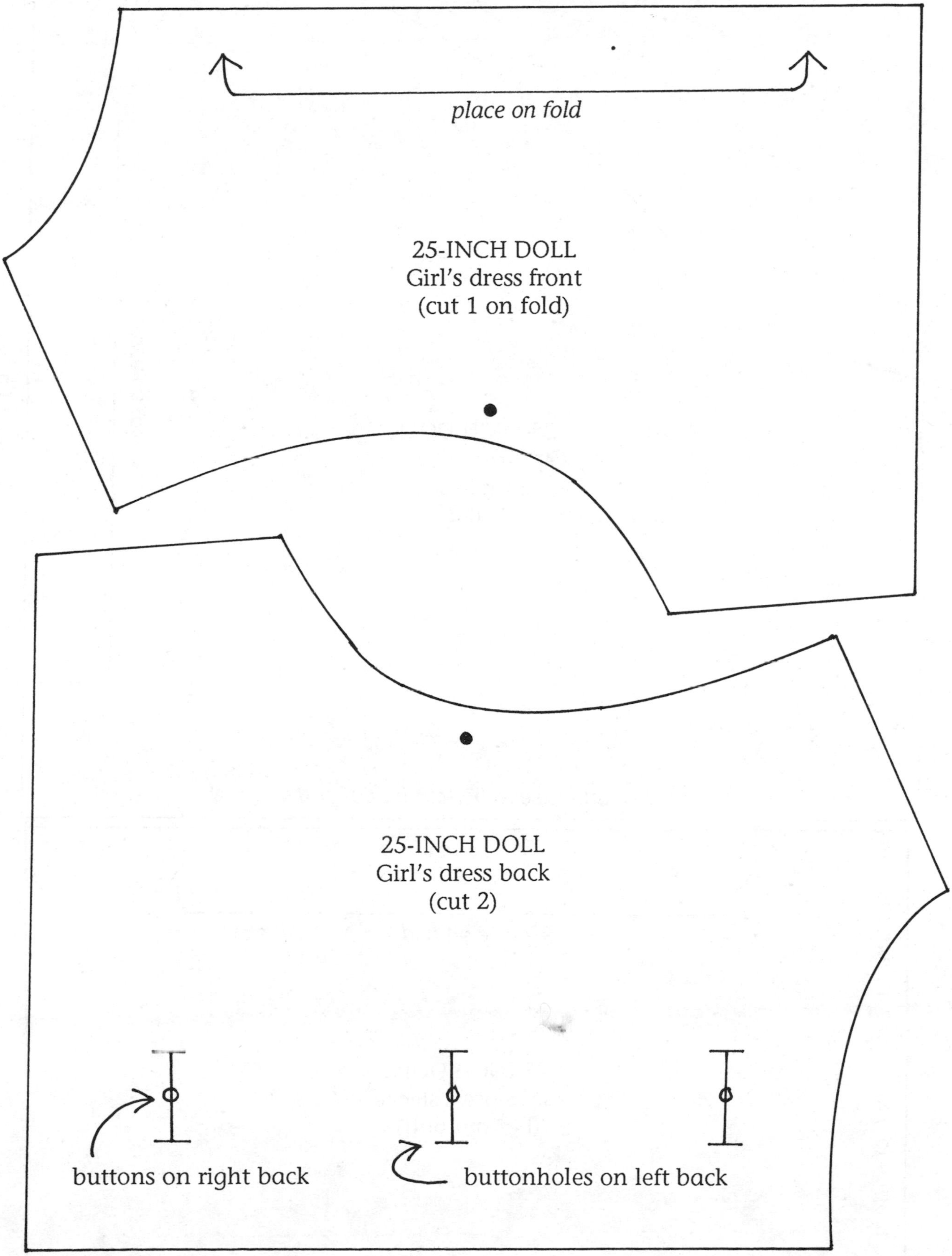

place on fold

25-INCH DOLL
Girl's dress front
(cut 1 on fold)

25-INCH DOLL
Girl's dress back
(cut 2)

buttons on right back   buttonholes on left back

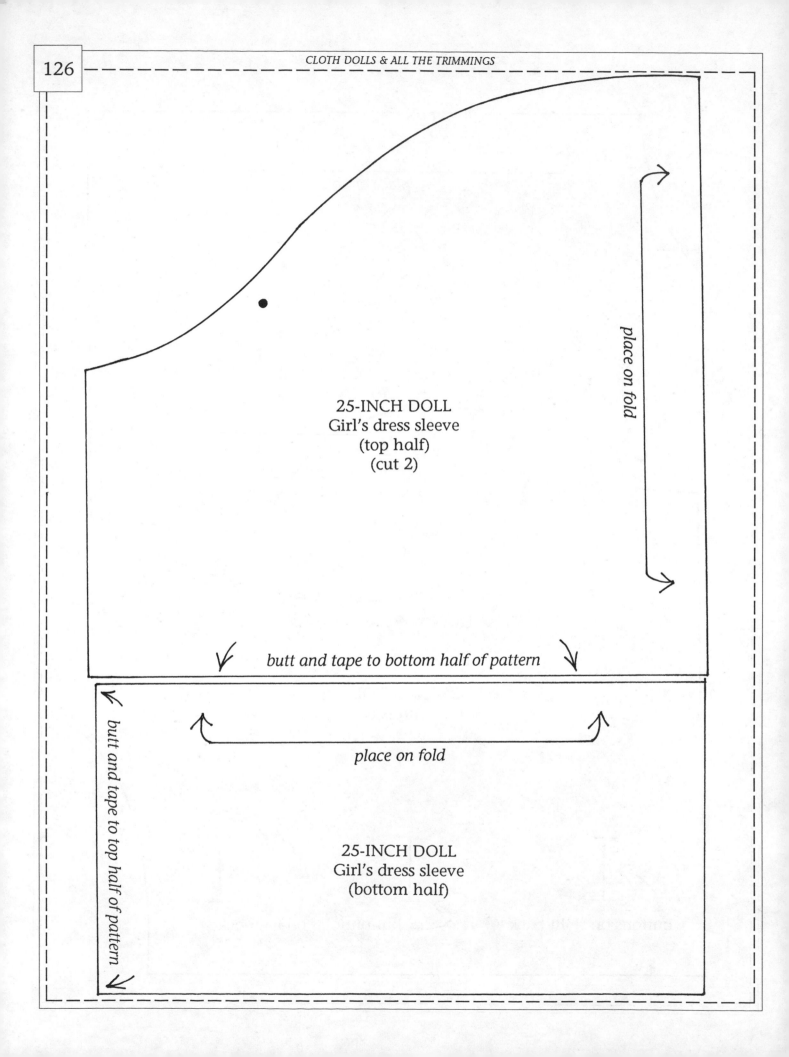

25-INCH DOLL
Girl's dress sleeve
(top half)
(cut 2)

place on fold

butt and tape to bottom half of pattern

place on fold

butt and tape to top half of pattern

25-INCH DOLL
Girl's dress sleeve
(bottom half)

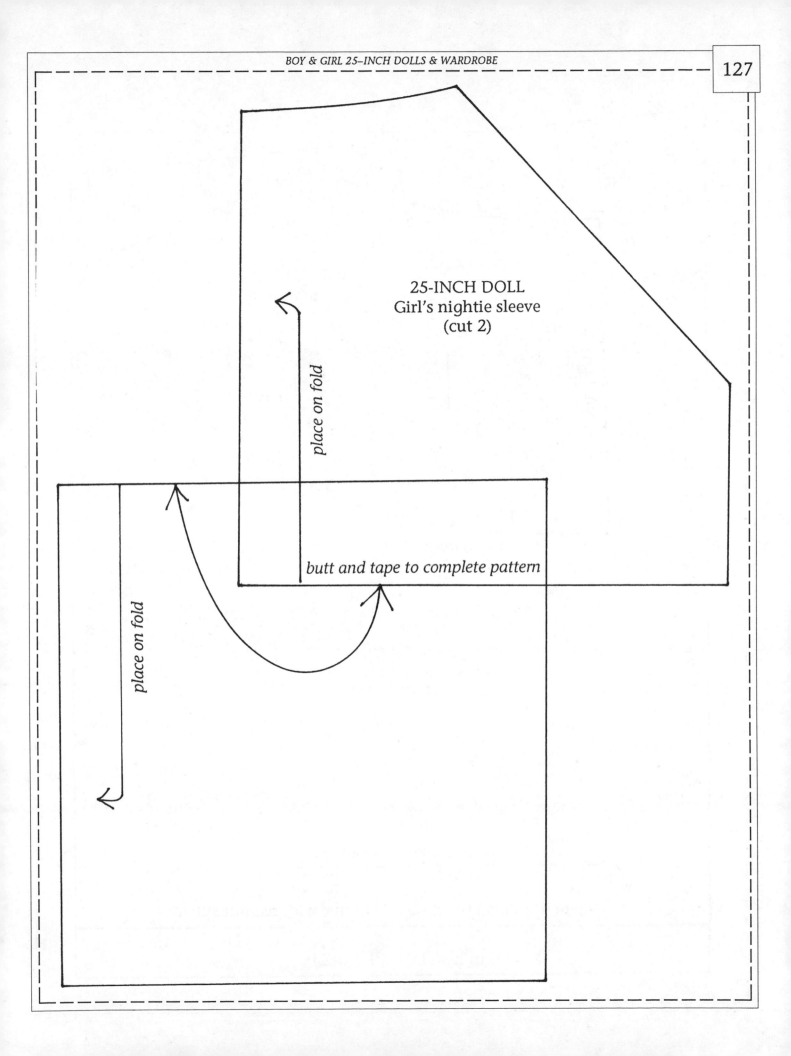

25-INCH DOLL
Girl's nightie sleeve
(cut 2)

place on fold

butt and tape to complete pattern

place on fold

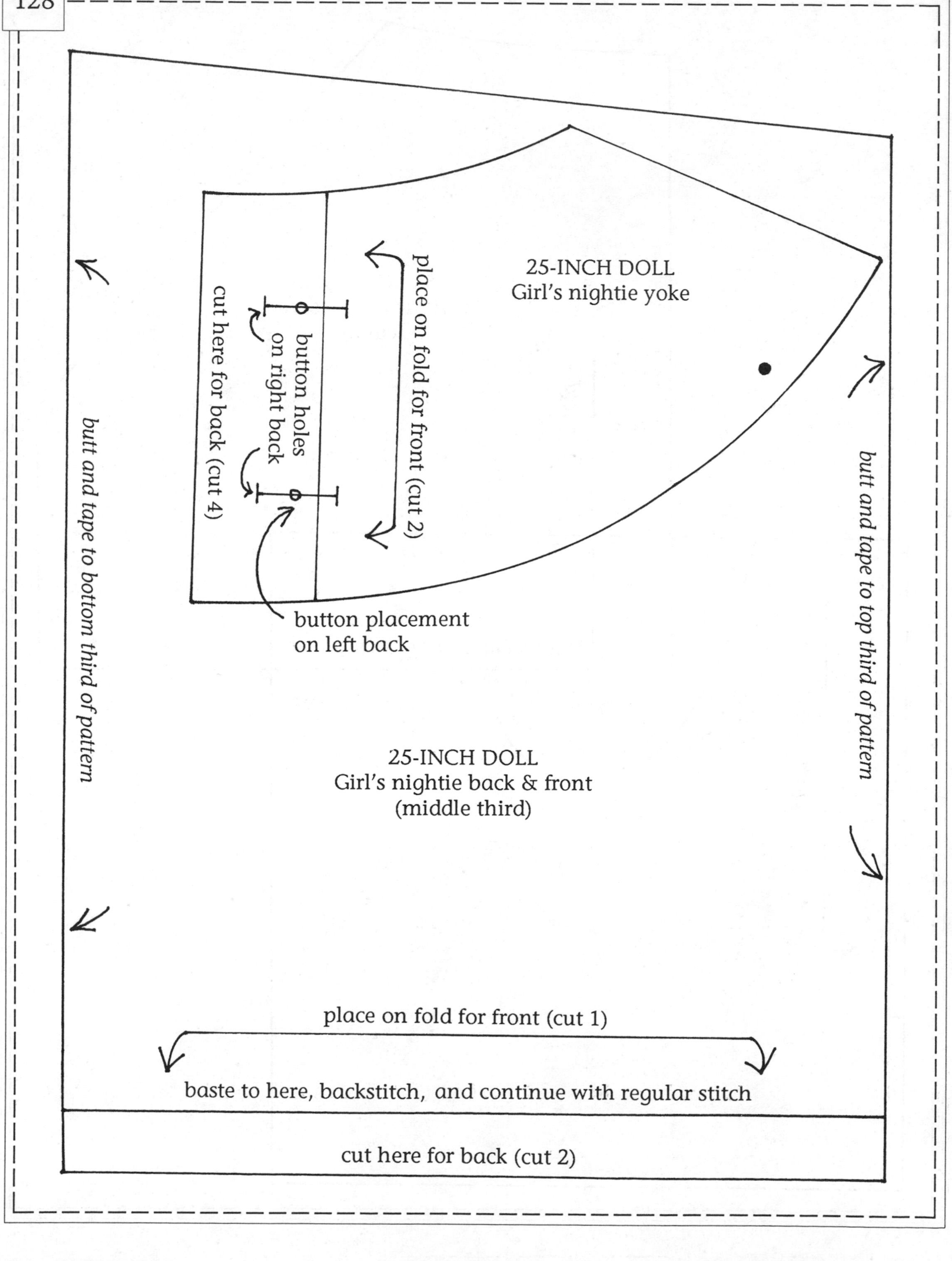

25-INCH DOLL
Girl's nightie yoke

place on fold for front (cut 2)

cut here for back (cut 4)

button holes
on right back

button placement
on left back

butt and tape to bottom third of pattern

butt and tape to top third of pattern

25-INCH DOLL
Girl's nightie back & front
(middle third)

place on fold for front (cut 1)

baste to here, backstitch, and continue with regular stitch

cut here for back (cut 2)

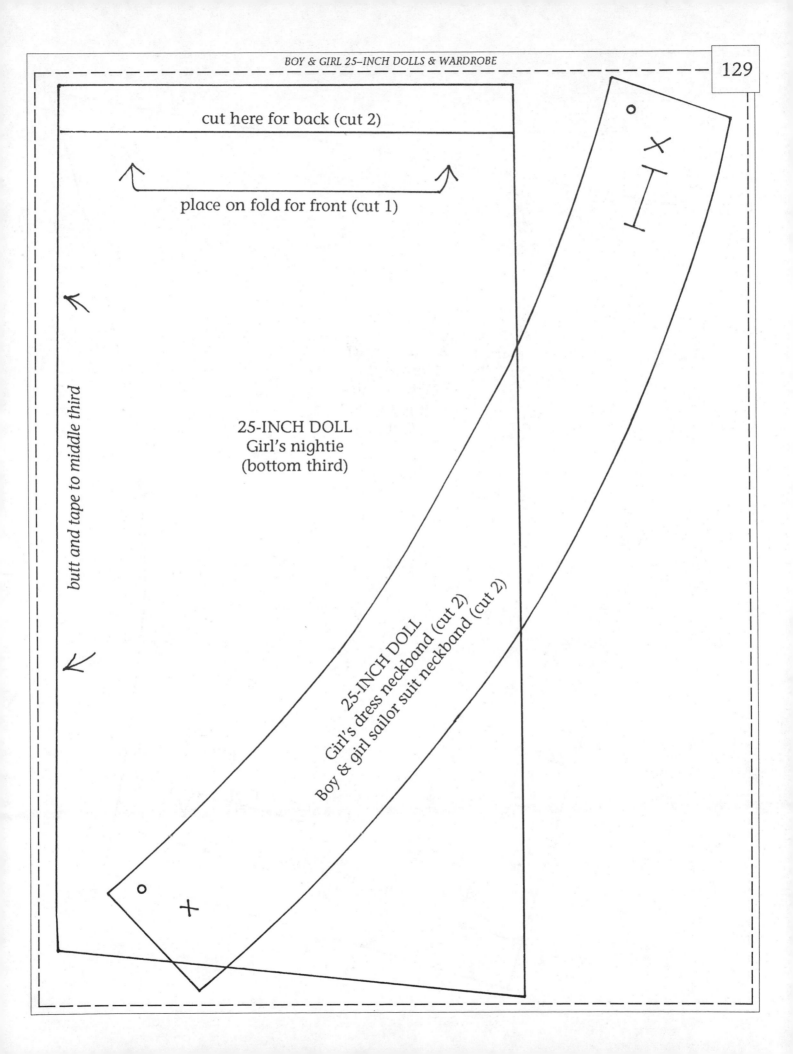

cut here for back (cut 2)

place on fold for front (cut 1)

butt and tape to middle third

25-INCH DOLL
Girl's nightie
(bottom third)

25-INCH DOLL
Girl's dress neckband (cut 2)
Boy & girl sailor suit neckband (cut 2)

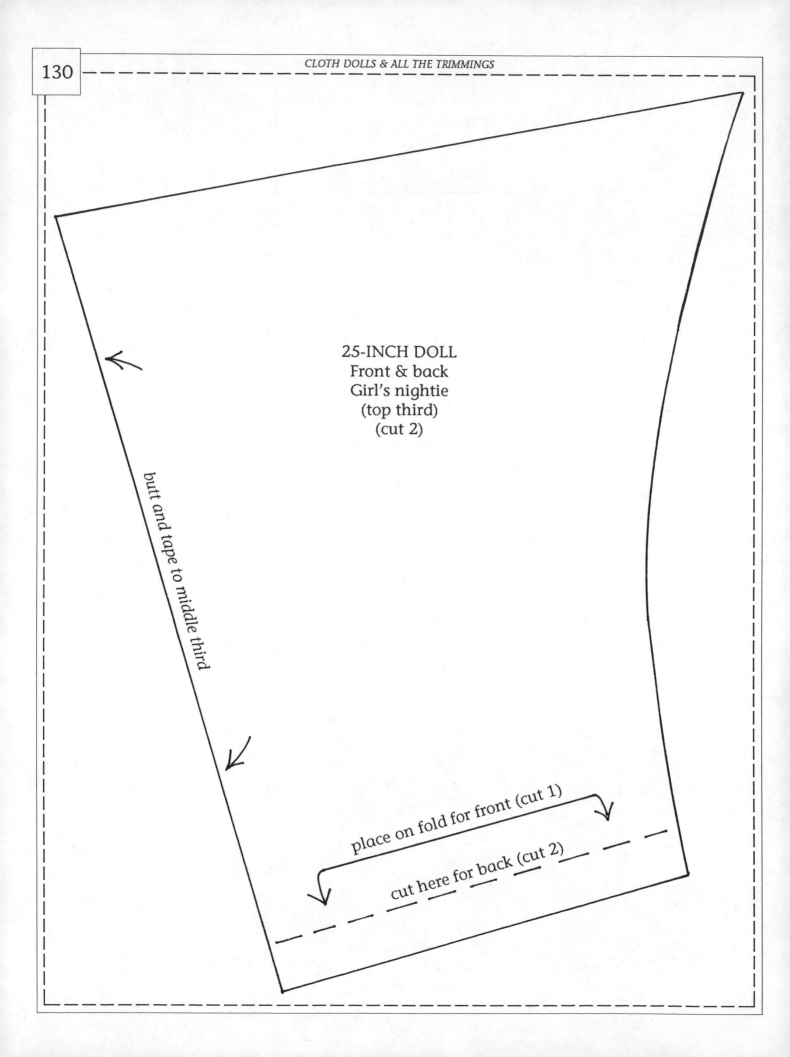

25-INCH DOLL
Front & back
Girl's nightie
(top third)
(cut 2)

butt and tape to middle third

place on fold for front (cut 1)

cut here for back (cut 2)

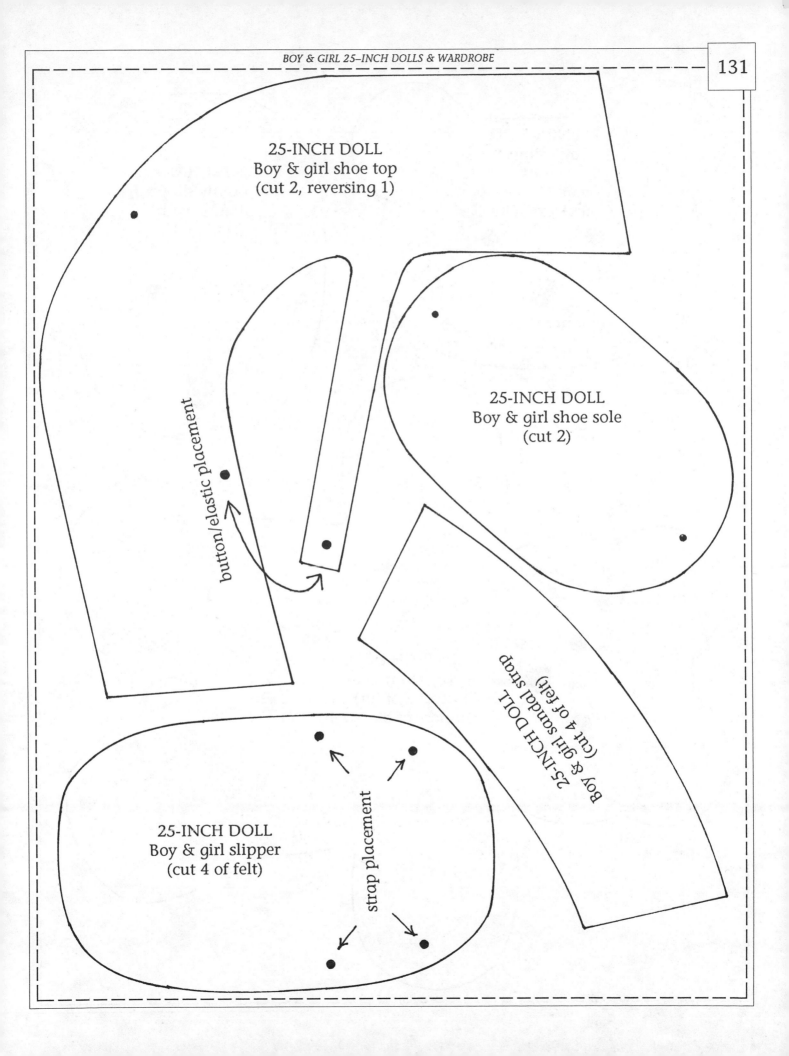

25-INCH DOLL
Boy & girl shoe top
(cut 2, reversing 1)

25-INCH DOLL
Boy & girl shoe sole
(cut 2)

button/elastic placement

25-INCH DOLL
Boy & girl sandal strap
(cut 4 of felt)

25-INCH DOLL
Boy & girl slipper
(cut 4 of felt)

strap placement

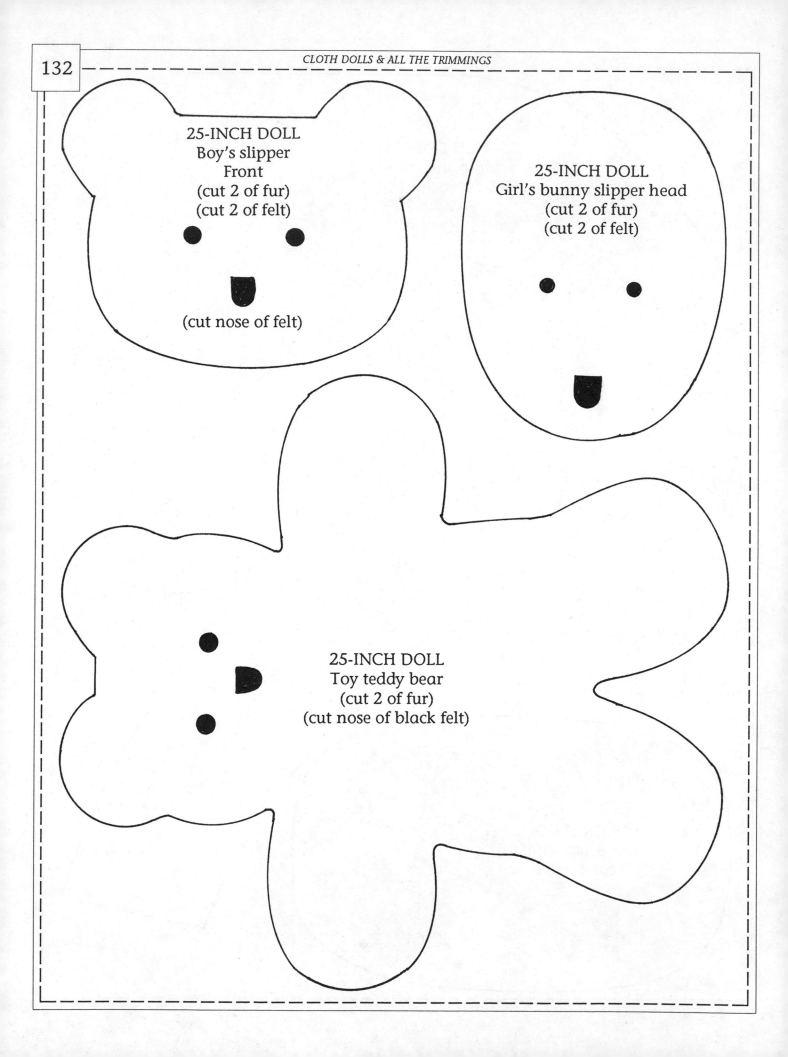

25-INCH DOLL
Boy's slipper
Front
(cut 2 of fur)
(cut 2 of felt)

(cut nose of felt)

25-INCH DOLL
Girl's bunny slipper head
(cut 2 of fur)
(cut 2 of felt)

25-INCH DOLL
Toy teddy bear
(cut 2 of fur)
(cut nose of black felt)

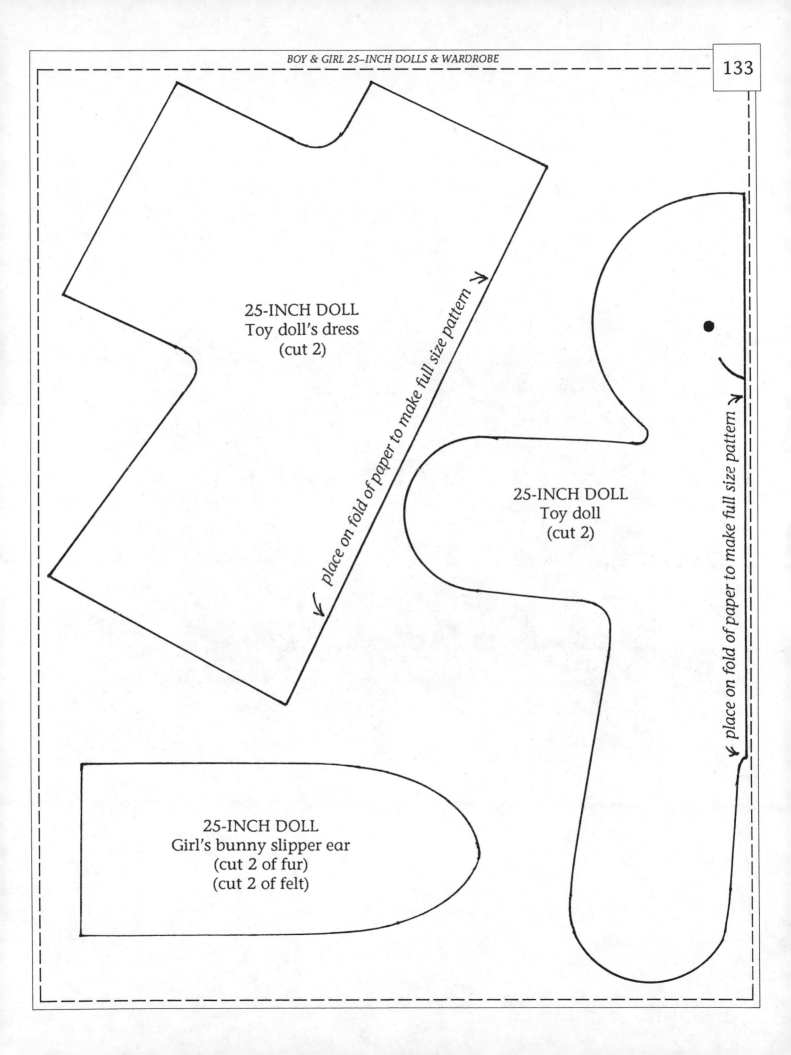

25-INCH DOLL
Toy doll's dress
(cut 2)

place on fold of paper to make full size pattern

25-INCH DOLL
Toy doll
(cut 2)

place on fold of paper to make full size pattern

25-INCH DOLL
Girl's bunny slipper ear
(cut 2 of fur)
(cut 2 of felt)

CHAPTER ♥ 5

DOLLS AROUND THE WORLD

*U*sing one pattern, simply vary body fabric, face embroidery and clothing to create a world of dolls: a homespun country boy and girl, a Japanese kimono doll; a Chinese doll; a traditional African doll; a traditional Amish boy and girl; a fancy Victorian doll; a Pilgrim couple; and a Native American Indian squaw and brave. These 18" dolls have jointed arms, giving them flexibility in handling and in posing.

To make the dolls:

MATERIALS

²/₃ yard finely woven muslin
or broadcloth

Matching thread

One pair of 30 mm plastic doll joints
(see Sources)

Embroidery floss: red for mouth, your
choice for the eyes, brown or black for
the eyebrows, nose, and eye outline.

Polyester fiberfill

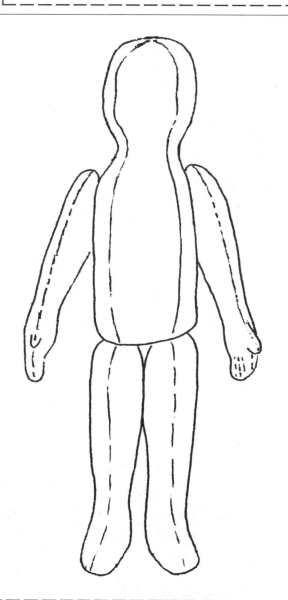

INSTRUCTIONS

Note: All seam allowances are ¼" unless instructed otherwise.

As instructed in chapter 1, transfer the patterns to heavy paper, cut out the pattern pieces, and pin to the fabric. Trace pattern on fabric. Transfer all markings. For arms, trace pattern and transfer markings for one arm, flip the pattern for a second arm. Cut all pattern pieces out of fabric. Trace the face pattern, including outline of head sides, from the book. Set aside.

1. Body and head: Lay body/head front over one body side having the front edge (curved face, round tummy) facing to the right. Pin the side front (facing right) seam. Stitch.

Lay the body back over the remaining body side, having the front of the side facing to the left. Pin and stitch the side back (facing right) seam.

Pin the two halves of the body/head assemblies together, right sides facing, matching seams at top of head, curves, bottom edges.

Clip curves. Turn.

2. Arms: Right sides facing, stitch two arms together, leaving an opening between the dots for turning. Trim to ⅛" from stitching around hand and fingers. Clip curves. Turn. Repeat for other arm.

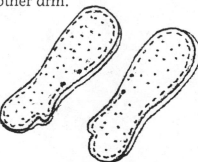

3. Jointing: For joint holes, fold the fabric at the dot and fold again, so that the dot is at the tip of the point. Cut across the folded point. You may wish to practice on a piece of scrap fabric since it is easy to mistakenly cut too large a hole. Apply Fray Chek® to the hole to strength it. Allow to dry. Repeat for both inside arm holes, both leg holes, and for dots on the body/head sides.

Assemble the joint as illustrated. The stationary disk (the one with the threaded screw-like protrusion) always goes in the limb with the screw part sticking out of the hole in the fabric. Push the screw into the hole in the body side of the doll. Check to be sure the limb is pointing in the correct direction (thumbs and toes up and to front of doll). From the inside of the doll's body, place the washer (large flat disk) on the screw with the rounded edge facing the stationary disk. Push the flat side of the locking disk onto the screw. Use an empty thread spool to press and lock the disk firmly in place, perhaps placing the assembly on a table and using your weight to get a tight fit.

Stuff the body to within 1¹/₂" of bottom. Fold the bottom of the body as you would wrap a package and slipstitch in place.

Stuff the arms firmly. Handstitch the opening closed.

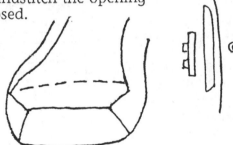

4. Legs: Stitch front and back leg seams, leaving the tops open.

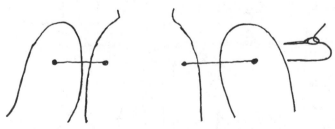

To form toes, match front and back seams at center of toes. Pin. Stitch along marked, curved line.

Trim seam allowances along toes to ¹/₈". Turn.

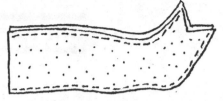

Stuff firmly to within 1¹/₂" of top of leg. Turn ¹/₄" at tops of legs to inside. Whipstitch closed. Whipstitch legs to body bottom, ¹/₂" from the front edge of the bottom of the doll, making sure the toes are pointing toward the front.

5. Face: Go over traced face pattern several times with regular lead pencil or white pencil, depending on color of doll fabric. From the back of the face pattern put a pin through the paper at the large dot. Push the pin into the top of the doll's head where the four seams meet. Center the face pattern over the face. Hold the paper flat against the fabric and rub the pencil lines onto the fabric with your thumb nail. Remove paper.

Using three strands of embroidery floss, form the eyebrows and nose with backstitches. Embroider the eyes with satin stitches.

Fill in the mouth with satin stitches. Using a cotton ball and a light touch, dab a bit of blush on the doll's cheeks. Soften it by dabbing off some of the color with a fresh cotton ball.

6. Making fingers: Thread a needle with heavy thread. Tie a double knot in one end. Push the needle into an arbitrary point on the back of the hand. Emerge from the fabric at the palm end of a marked line. Pull the thread until the knot pops into the fabric and seats itself in the fiberfill. Using a backstitch and leaving ¹/₈" between the stitches, handstitch along the traced lines on the hands, forming indentations suggesting fingers.

To finish, follow instructions for individual dolls.

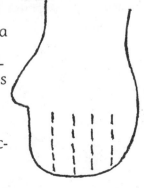

COUNTRY BOY & GIRL

Stepping out of our country's past, this friendly duo reminds us of the simple pleasures of rural life.

The girl wears a calico print dress and homespun apron and bonnet. She carries a basket of flowers she just picked from the meadow. Wearing his rugged denim overalls, the boy is returning from the family orchard where he harvested a bucket of shiny apples to be baked into a luscious pie.

COUNTRY GIRL

MATERIALS

1 skein yarn
Matching thread
1/2 yard ribbon to match dress for hair ties
1/2 yard calico fabric for dress
Matching thread
1/4"-wide elastic for dress sleeves
Three 3/8" buttons for dress
1/3 yard osnaburg or other homespun-looking fabric
Matching thread
Scrap of Thermolan™ or batting
Small basket
Dried flowers
Glue
Clay or floral styrofoam

INSTRUCTIONS

Note: All seam allowances are 1/4" unless instructed otherwise.

As instructed in chapter 1, prewash and press fabrics, transfer patterns from book, cut and mark fabric. Cut a piece of calico 9" x 25" for dress skirt. For apron cut a rectangle 7" x 20" and cut a tie measuring 4" x 35", both from osnaburg. Also from osnaburg, cut two bonnet ties, each 1 1/2" x 10".

Hair

1. Cut 150 pieces of yarn, each 28" long.

2. Draw a straight line on a piece of paper 4 1/2" in length. Find the centers of the yarn and lay them over the line, distributing the yarn to fill the 4 1/2" evenly. Machine stitch through the yarn and paper.

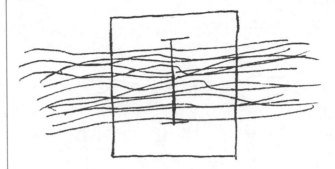

Carefully tear the paper away.

3. Place the stitched "part" of the hair piece on the center top of the doll's head, starting at the forehead (as in the picture of the doll) about 1 1/4" to the front of the junction of the seams at the top of the head with the bottom of the stitching 4 1/2" straight down the back of the neck. In the process of tearing the paper from the yarn the stitching will have stretched, so ease the fullness between these two points. Handstitch along the part, catching the stitching.

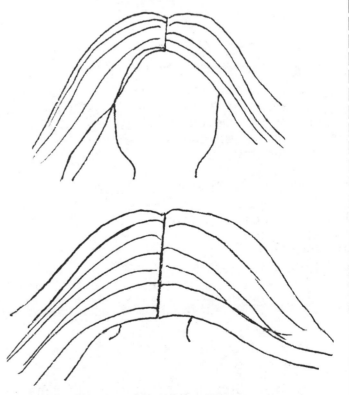

4. Cut folds in ends of hair. Braid the hair. Tie the ends with a piece of yarn.

5. Cut hair ribbon in half. Tie ribbons in bows over the ends of the braids.

Dress

1. Stitch front to back bodices at shoulders. Repeat for second set: one will be the bodice, one the lining.

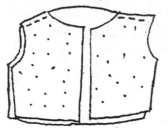
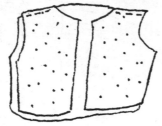

2. Pin bodice to lining along neck edge and center backs, matching shoulder seams. Stitch. Clip curves. Trim corners. Turn.

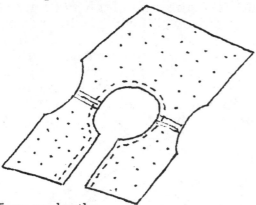

3. Turn under the bottom edges of the sleeves 2". Cut two pieces of elastic, each 5" long. Lay the elastic over the raw, turned-under edge on the wrong side of the sleeve. Pin one end of the elastic over the raw edge, placing the end of the elastic even with the side edge of the sleeve. Repeat for the other end of the elastic. Zigzag stitch the elastic in place, along the raw edge of the turned-up bottom edge of the sleeve. Hold the ends of the elastic firmly and stretch the elastic as you sew. Repeat for second sleeve.

4. Using a long machine stitch, gather the top edge of the sleeve between dots. Match dots to dots on bodice. Pin, treating bodice and bodice lining as one. Pull up on gather stitches. Even out the fullness and pin. Stitch through sleeve, bodice, and bodice lining. Repeat for other sleeve.

5. Right sides together, sew the underarm and side seams as one, matching sleeve/bodice seams.

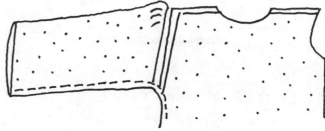

6. Using a ¹/₂" seam allowance, stitch center back seam of dress skirt. Start with a basting stitch for top half, backstitch half way down the seam, and continue with a regular stitch.

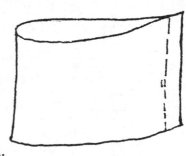

Press the seam open. Turn under ¹/₄" on each seam allowance. Topstitch a scant ¹/₄" from either side of the seam. Remove basting stitches.

7. To form hem, turn under ¹/₄" and then another ¹/₄" on the bottom edge of the skirt. Topstitch.

8. Using two rows of gathering stitches, gather the top edge of the skirt. Pin the skirt to the bottom edge of the bodice, right sides facing, matching center backs. Leave bodice lining free. Adjust gathers. Pin. Stitch.

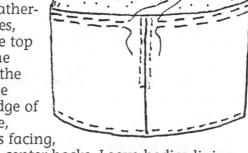

Turn under ¹/₄" on raw edge of bodice lining. Handstitch over seam allowances.

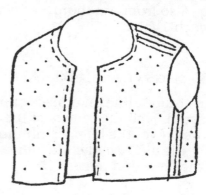

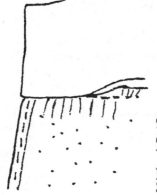

9. Make buttonholes on bodice as marked. Try on doll. Mark positions for buttons. Sew buttons on.

Apron

1. Press waist tie in half. Fold long raw edges in to meet at center. Press.

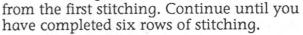

2. Press one long edge of apron under ¼" and ¼" again. Topstitch a scant ¼" from folded edge. Press under ¼" twice on short sides. Topstitch.

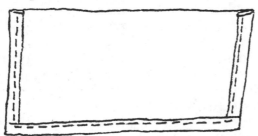

3. Using a long machine stitch, gather the long, unstitched (top) edge of the apron. Unfold the waist tie. Fold the waist tie in half. Mark the center with a pin. Unfold. Measure 2" on either side of the center pin and place a pin in both places. Match the center and the side edges of the gathered top edge of the apron to the pins on the tie, right sides facing. Pin. Pull up on and adjust the gathering stitches on the apron between the pins. Pin and stitch.

4. Fold tie along pressed lines. Pin folded edge to apron. Pin fold evenly along remaining lengths of tie, matching top and bottom folds. Topstitch close to double-folded edge.

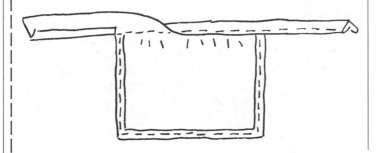

5. Make knots in ends of ties.

Bonnet

1. Fold bonnet flap in half along fold line. Stitch short ends.
 Turn right side out. Press.

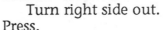

2. Press bonnet brim in half along fold line. Sandwich Thermolan™ or batting inside. Pin. Topstitch ¼" from folded edge through all thicknesses, again ¼" from the first stitching. Continue until you have completed six rows of stitching.

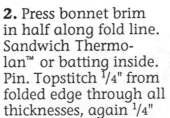

3. Using a long machine stitch, make two rows of gathering stitches along the rounded edge of the bonnet back, the first just inside the ¼" seam line and the second between the first stitching and the raw edge. Pin to bonnet brim, matching raw edges. Pull up on gathering threads. Adjust gathers. Pin. Stitch.

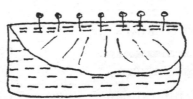

4. Using a long machine stitch, make two rows of stitching on the bottom of the bonnet back. Pin bonnet flap to bottom of bonnet back and bonnet brim assembly. Pull up on gathering threads. Adjust gathers. Pin. Stitch.

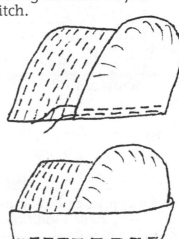

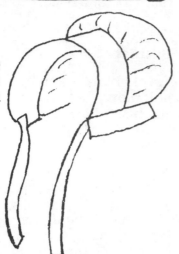

5. Press ties in half lengthwise. Press under both long edges to meet at the center. Turn ends to the inside. Topstitch close to edge.

Pin to seam allowances at intersection of bonnet brim and bonnet flap. Stitch.

Basket of Flowers

1. Form clay or cut styrofoam to fit inside basket, coming to about ½" from the brim. Glue clay or styrofoam to bottom inside of basket.

2. Poke dried flower stems into clay or styrofoam, cutting the stems to desired lengths.

COUNTRY BOY

Materials
1 skein yarn
Matching thread
Lightweight cardboard
⅓ yard denim fabric
Matching thread
Two ½" metal buttons
⅓ yard chambray or calico fabric
Matching thread
Scrap of fusible interfacing
Three ⅜" buttons
10" x 10" square of handkerchief fabric
7"-diameter straw hat
Rope, jute, or baling twine to tie around hat

INSTRUCTIONS

Note: All seam allowances are ¼" unless instructed otherwise.

Prepare fabrics and patterns. Cut and mark fabrics.

Hair

1. Cut a thin piece of cardboard into four strips:

one 12" x 2"
one 11" x 4"
one 7" x 4"
one 3" x 4"

Draw a crosswise line across the top and bottom of the length of each cardboard piece, ½" from the top and bottom edges. Draw a line lengthwise down the center of each piece of cardboard. Cut along this second line. Tape the two halves of the cardboard together, leaving a small gap between them.

Starting at the top crosswise line of the first cardboard piece, wind yarn around the cardboard, continuing until you reach the bottom crosswise line.

Machine stitch along the lengthwise gap through the yarn.

Sliding the blade of your scissors between the edge of the cardboard and the loops of the yarn, cut the yarn.

Pull the cardboard away.

Repeat for the three remaining pieces of cardboard and batches of yarn.

2. Lay the middle of the first stitched string of yarn on the doll's forehead about 1¼" from the point where the four seams meet at the top of the head. Pin. Bring the ends around the head to the back of the neck where the nape of the doll's hair will be, about 5" from this starting point, over the head and straight down the back of the head. Pin. Stitch the string of yarn around the head, easing the fullness as you go, checking that the stitching line is symmetrical on each side of the head.

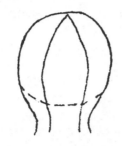

3. Stitch the second row to the head in the same manner, spacing it approximately 1/2" from the first row.

4. Repeat for the third row.

5. Stitch the fourth and final string of yarn to the top of the head as a part in the boy's hair.

Overalls

1. Stitch inside leg seams. Press seams open.

2. Pin long, curved crotch seams, right sides together, matching inside leg seams. Stitch.

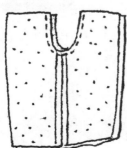

3. Pin and stitch side seams.

4. Press under 1/4" at waist. Press under 5/8".

5. Stitch three sides of two bibs together, right sides facing. Turn. Press. Turn under 1/4" at bottom of unstitched edge of bib to inside. Press. Press under 1/4" on one edge of bib pocket. Topstitch a scant 1/4" from folded edge. Press under 1/4" on three remaining edges of bib pocket. Pin in place on bib with topstitched edge toward top of bib, away from opening in bib. Topstitch through pocket and bib on three remaining sides of pocket.

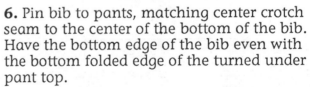

6. Pin bib to pants, matching center crotch seam to the center of the bottom of the bib. Have the bottom edge of the bib even with the bottom folded edge of the turned under pant top.

7. Topstitch a scant inch from folded, top edge of pants, sewing through all layers of pants and bib at front. Topstitch close to top folded edge of pants.

8. Turn under ¹/₄" on pant leg for hem. Press under another ¹/₄". Topstitch a scant ¹/₄" from bottom edge. Repeat for second leg.

9. Press suspender in half lengthwise. Press long edges to meet in center. Turn raw edges to inside on one end of suspender. Topstitch close to folded edge.

Pin and stitch unfinished ends of suspenders to inside back of pants 1¹/₂" to either side of the center seam.

Bring suspenders over shoulders, pin them to top corners of bib. Sew a button over them, through the bib.

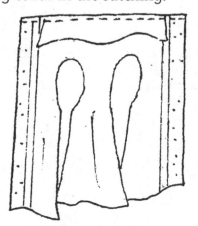

Shirt

1. Stitch fronts to back at shoulders, right sides facing.

2. Fuse to wrong side of one collar (will be under collar). Pin collars, right sides together, along longer curved edge and two short ends. Stitch, leaving shorter, inside curve open. Trim corners. Clip curve. Turn. Press.

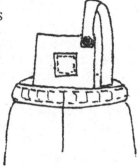

3. Press under ¹/₄" along front edges of front. Press shirt fronts along fold line to outside. Pin top edges to shirt. Pin collar to neck edge so that far edges of collar touch edge of front facing. Stitch from front edge to front edge, catching collar in the stitching.

Trim corners. Turn.

Press front along fold line. Topstitch ¹/₈" from the front edge and again ¹/₂" from the first stitching. Repeat for the second side. Make buttonholes on left front as marked.

4. Stitch side seams of shirt.

5. Press under ¹/₄" and ¹/₄" again on lower edge of shirt. Topstitch just less than ¹/₄" from the edge.

6. Match the two short sides of a sleeve. Stitch.

Press under ¹/₄" and another ¹/₄" along one raw edge of the sleeve. Topstitch barely ¹/₄" from the edge.

Pin sleeve to armhole, matching seam in sleeve with side seam of shirt, easing the sleeve to fit. Stitch. Repeat for other sleeve.

Handkerchief

1. Press ¹/₄" to wrong side all around handkerchief. Press under another ¹/₄". Topstitch.

2. Roll as shown and tie around neck over shirt but under collar.

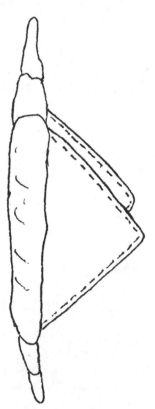

Strawhat

1. Tie rope around hat brim. Tack in place.

TRADITIONAL AFRICAN DOLL

Bursting with pride in her heritage, this doll wears her colorful ethnic tunic proudly. Choose two paisley or batik prints for the tunic and headwrap. Visit the bead section of your favorite craft store to find interesting wooden, glass, and ceramic beads to adorn the doll's neck and wrists. Layer them on, making the strands of various lengths.

MATERIALS

½ yard fabric for tunic body
½ yard contrasting fabric for tunic facings and headwrap
Matching thread
One hook and eye
1"-diameter wire hoops for earrings
Assorted colored and gold beads
Gold soutache or other braid for bracelet
Glue
¼ yard brown or beige felt, Ultra-suede™ or double-sided suede for sandals (see Sources)
Craft glue

INSTRUCTIONS

Note: All seam allowances are ¼" unless instructed otherwise.

Prepare fabrics and patterns following instructions in chapter

1. For headwrap cut a 16" x 16" square from contrasting fabric.

Tunic

1. Clip seam allowance at center front to dot as indicated on pattern.

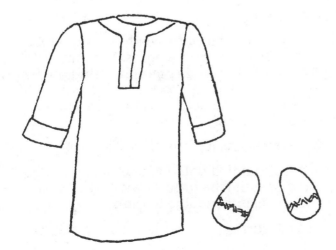

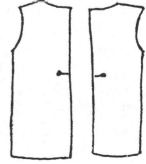

2. Stitch front to back tunics at shoulders.

3. Press under ¼" on bottom of front facings as indicated on pattern.

4. With right side of facing to wrong side of tunic, pin facing to neckline and front opening of tunic, matching center backs and front edges. Stitch.

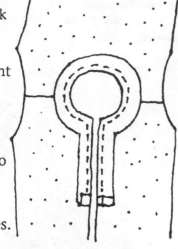

Trim corners, clip curved seam allowances. Turn facing to right side. Press.

Pin facing to right side of tunic. From right side use a zigzag stitch to sew over raw edges of facing, through tunic, all the way around outer edge of facing.

5. With right side of the sleeve facing, facing to the wrong side of sleeve, pin facing to one long edge of sleeve. Stitch. Turn facing to right side. Press. Pin in place. From 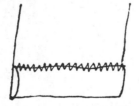 right side, use a zigzag stitch to sew raw edge of facing in place. Repeat for second sleeve.

6. Pin other long raw edge of sleeve to armhole of tunic, right sides together. Stitch.

7. Right sides facing, stitch center front seam from dot down to bottom edge of tunic.

8. Pin and stitch underarm/side seam as one.

9. Press under ¼" on bottom edge of tunic. Press under another ¼". Topstitch in place, a scant ¼" from bottom, folded edge.

10. Sew the hook and eye to the inside top of the front opening of the tunic.

Headwrap

1. Press under ¼" on two opposing raw edges. Press under another ¼". Topstitch a scant ¼" from folded edge.

2. Repeat for the two remaining edges.

3. Fold headwrap in half diagonally to form a triangle. Place center of folded edge on doll's forehead, the middle point facing upward. Wrap the left side of the triangle around the doll's head to the back. Roll the point of the headwrap from the top of the head toward the back. Wrap right side of triangle to the back. Adjust. Handstitch edges in place to secure.

Sandals

1. Glue the two sandal soles together, wrong sides facing. Repeat for second sandal.

2. Immediately insert the uncut end of the sandal strap between the two soles at one dot. Press the soles together to sandwich the strap end, adding more glue if needed.

3. Braid the free ends of the sandal strap all the way to the end. Tuck the end in between the soles on the opposite side. Add more glue if needed. Press to secure. Repeat steps 1, 2, and 3 for second sandal.

4. Place sandal on doll's foot. Attach sandal to foot by taking a few stitches on both sides of the top of the foot through the sandal strap.

Finishing

1. String beads if not already strung. Make necklaces of varying lengths. Put around doll's neck. For choker length, string the beads to the desired length, place around the doll's neck and tie. To keep necklaces in place tack to back of neck.

2. String beads for bracelets. Tie around wrist.

3. For simulated gold bracelet, wrap flat gold braid or soutache around wrist five times. Tuck ends under. Glue in place.

4. Tack earrings to head under the headwrap.

AMISH BOY & GIRL DOLLS

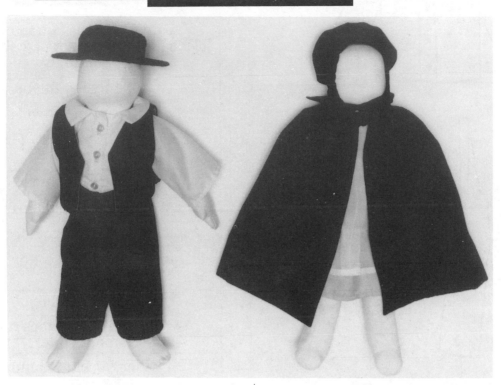

The unique dress style of the Amish is a distinctive symbol of their identity, a reminder of the cultural separation they seek. Amish dress enhances group solidarity and signifies Gelassenheit — submission to the collective order. Amish dress gives the wearer a sense of belonging, of equality, and is a symbol of faith and loyalty to the supremacy of the group.

Since the Amish disapprove of the making of any likenesses (for it fosters vanity), portraits are not made. Likewise, children's dolls are faceless, as are these dolls.

These dolls represent a young Amish girl and boy. Their clothes are examples of what they might wear.

Until age twelve, when the opening shifts to the front and the fastenings become pins, little girls dresses button in back. Though Amish women are restricted to solid colors when choosing fabric for their dresses, with black and gray comprising most of their wardrobes, Amish dresses are far from lacking in color. Deep purple, forest green, lavender, magenta, peacock blue, turquoise, red-violet, blue green, purple, and wine stand out as jewels against a backdrop of stark black.

The sleeve apron, worn by children under the age of twelve, is usually made of white (sometimes black) organdy. The back and front of the sleeve apron is made from one piece, the center front is pleated, and cap sleeves are added.

Traditionally, capes fought off winter's chill, though today many Amish women wear coats. This cape is made of black or charcoal wool and is lined with grey cotton fabric.

Amish women keep their heads covered at all times, a symbol of their subjection to God. As early as age four, Amish girls begin wearing the adult-style cap of Swiss organdy for everyday wear. For daytime wear, both young girls and married women wear white organdy bonnets. This doll wears her black bonnet whenever she goes out in public. Ribbons tie the bonnet under the chin. A large bow is fastened to the back.

The Amish boy wears a durable wool vest and broadfall trousers with suspenders. His shirt is purple, blue, pink or white and buttons up the front. His traditional black hat is an Amish signature.

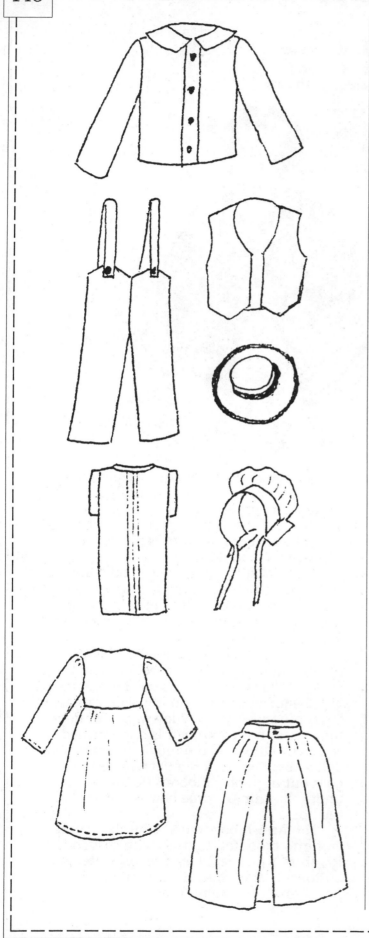

MATERIALS

1/2 yard solid color cotton or cotton blend fabric in a color described above for dress

Matching thread

Two 5" pieces of 1/4"-wide elastic

1/3 yard white organdy for sleeve apron

Matching thread

White double-fold bias tape

3/8 yard black wool for cape

3/8 yard gray or black cotton fabric for lining

Matching thread

5/8 yard of 3/8"-wide black ribbon for bonnet ties

One 1/2" black button

1/3 yard black cotton or lightweight wool fabric for bonnet

Matching thread

Scrap of Thermolan™ or batting

INSTRUCTIONS

Note: All seam allowances are 1/4" unless instructed otherwise.

As instructed in chapter 1, prepare fabrics and patterns. Cut fabric. Transfer all markings. For dress skirt, cut out a rectangle, 9" x 25". Cut one 12" x 30" piece of black wool fabric for cape and one 12" x 30" piece of gray or black cotton for lining.

Dress

1. Stitch front to back bodices at shoulders and sides. Repeat for second set: one will be the bodice, one the lining.

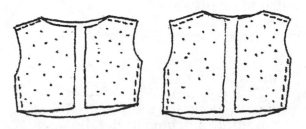

2. Pin bodice to lining along neck edge and center backs, matching shoulder seams. Stitch. Clip curves. Trim corners. Turn.

3. Pin one long side of sleeve to armhole, treating bodice and lining as one, easing the sleeve to fit. Stitch. Repeat for other sleeve.

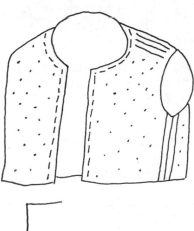

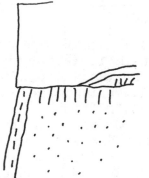

4. Stitch sleeve and underarm seam as one. Repeat for other side.

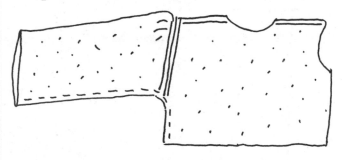

5. Press under 1/4" and another 1/4" along remaining long raw edge of the sleeve. Topstitch barely 1/4" from the edge. Repeat for second sleeve.

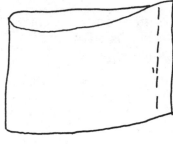

6. Using a 1/2" seam allowance, stitch center back seam of dress skirt, starting at the top of the skirt with a basting stitch, backstitching half way down the seam, and finishing with a regular machine stitch to the bottom.

Press the seam open. Turn under 1/4" on each seam allowance. Topstitch a scant 1/4" from either side of the seam. Remove basting stitches.

7. To form hem, turn under 1/4" and then another 1/4" on the bottom (regular stitched end) edge of the skirt. Topstitch.

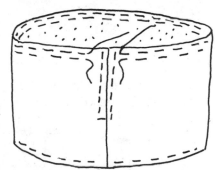

8. Using two rows of gathering stitches, gather the top edge (basting stitch end) of the skirt. Pin the skirt to the bottom edge of the bodice, right sides facing, matching center backs. Leave the bodice lining free. Adjust gathers. Pin. Stitch. Turn under 1/4" on bottom edge of bodice lining. Handstitch over seam allowances.

9. Make buttonholes on bodice as marked. Try on doll. Mark positions for buttons. Sew buttons on.

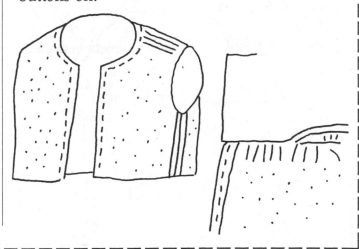

Sleeve Apron

Note: For strong, neat seams, use zigzag stitches for the organdy and trim seam allowances close to stitching.

1. Press under ¼" on center back edges of apron. Press under another ¼". Topstitch a scant ¼" from the folded edge.

2. Right sides together, fold the front of the sleeve apron along the center front. To form center front pleat, stitch along line indicated on pattern. Press pleat open.

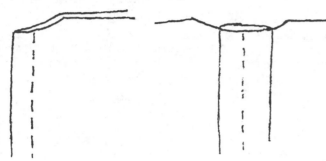

3. Fold front of sleeve apron to back along foldline. Using a zigzag stitch, stitch shoulder seam.

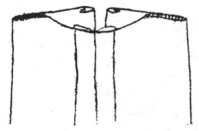

4. To finish neck edge and form ties, cut a piece of bias tape 20" long. Pin bias tape to neck edge, centering it over the neck opening. Topstitch close to the open edge of the bias tape, starting at the far end of one tie, continuing along the neck edge, stitching along the second tie, turning under the raw ends of the ties ¼".

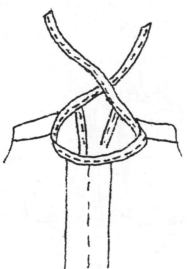

5. Stitch the short ends of the sleeve together. Fold as shown, right sides facing.

6. To make armholes, carefully cut a 4"-long slit in the apron along the marked (fold) line from the zigzag stitching at the shoulder down. Pin the sleeve to the armhole opening, right sides together. This is easier if the sleeve is on the inside of the sleeve apron. Stitch. Turn sleeve to outside.

Cape

1. Pin cape to cape lining, right sides facing. Stitch down one short side, along one long side, and up the next short side. Trim corners. Turn. Press.

2. Using a long machine stitch gather the top (unstitched) edge of the cape through both layers.

3. Fold the neckband in half lengthwise, buttonhole marking to inside. Stitch along the short edges.

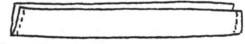

Turn. Press.

4. Pin the top edge of the cape to the buttonhole-marked neckband, right sides together, leaving the other long edge of the neckband free. Pull up on the threads and adjust gathers. Pin. Stitch.

    Fold the neckband over the top raw edge of the cape, encasing it. Turn under ¼" on the free edge of the neckband and pin to inside of cape. Handstitch in place.

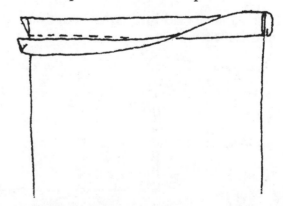

5. Make buttonhole as indicated on pattern. Try on doll. Mark position for button. Stitch button in place.

Bonnet

1. Fold bonnet flap in half along fold line. Stitch short ends.

Turn right side out. Press.

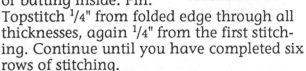

2. Press bonnet brim in half along fold line. Sandwich Thermolan™ or batting inside. Pin. Topstitch 1/4" from folded edge through all thicknesses, again 1/4" from the first stitching. Continue until you have completed six rows of stitching.

3. Using a long machine stitch, make two rows of gathering stitches along the rounded edge of the bonnet back, the first just inside the 1/4" seam line and the second between the first stitching and the raw edge. Pin to bonnet brim, matching raw edges. Pull up on gathering threads. Adjust gathers. Pin. Stitch.

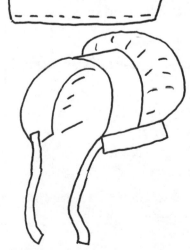

4. Using a long machine stitch, make two rows of stitching on the bottom of the bonnet back. Pin bonnet flap to bottom of bonnet back and bonnet brim assembly. Pull up on gathering threads. Adjust gathers. Pin. Stitch.

5. Cut tie ribbon in half. Pin one end to each side of bonnet at seam allowances at intersection of bonnet brim and bonnet flap as shown. Stitch.

BOY DOLL

MATERIALS

2/3 yard black wool fabric for pants and vest

Matching thread

Two 1/2" black buttons

1/3 yard fabric for shirt

Matching thread

Scrap of fusible interfacing

Three 3/8" buttons

1/4 yard black or gray cotton for vest lining

1/4 yard black felt

Scrap of black cotton or lining fabric

Heavyweight fusible interfacing

Lightweight cardboard

Craft glue

Black double-fold bias tape

3/8 yard of 5/8" grosgrain ribbon

INSTRUCTIONS

Note: All seam allowances are 1/4" unless instructed otherwise.

Following the instructions in chapter 1, prepare the fabrics and the patterns, cut out the fabric, and transfer markings.

Broadfall Pants

1. Stitch inside leg seams.

Press seam open.

2. Pin long, curved crotch seams, right sides together, matching inside leg seams. Stitch.

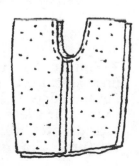

3. Pin and stitch side seams.

4. Stitch sides of facings together, right sides facing.

Finish the bottom, straight, raw edges of facing with a zigzag stitch.

5. Pin facing to top of pants, right sides together, matching side seams and curves and points of front. Stitch.
Turn. Press.

6. Press suspender in half lengthwise. Press long edges to meet in center.

7. Pin and stitch one end of each suspender to inside back of pants 1 1/2" to either side of the center front and back seams. Handstitch in place.

8. Bring suspenders over shoulders, pin them to underside of points at pants top. Place a button over the pant points and sew it to the pants, through the suspender.

9. Turn under 1/4" on pants leg for hem. Press under another 1/4". Topstitch a scant 1/4" from bottom edge. Repeat for second leg.

Amish Boy's Shirt

1. Stitch fronts to back at shoulders, right sides facing.

2. Fuse to wrong side of one collar (will be under collar). Pin collars, right sides together, along longer curved edge and two short ends. Stitch, leaving shorter, inside curve open. Trim corners. Clip curve. Turn. Press.

3. Press under 1/4" along front edges of front. Press shirt fronts along fold line to outside. Pin top edges to shirt. Pin collar to neck edge so that far edges of collar touch edge of front facing. Stitch from front edge to front edge, catching collar in the stitching.

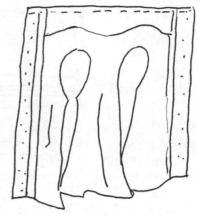

Trim corners. Turn.
Press front along fold line. Topstitch 1/8" from the front edge and again 1/2" from the first stitching. Repeat for the second side. Make buttonholes on left front as marked.

4. Stitch side seams of shirt.

5. Press under 1/4" and 1/4" again on lower edge of shirt. Topstitch just less than 1/4" from the edge.

6. Match the two short sides of a sleeve. Stitch.
Press under 1/4" and another 1/4" along one long raw edge of the sleeve. Topstitch barely 1/4" from the edge.
Pin remaining raw edge of sleeve to armhole, matching seam in sleeve with side seam of shirt, easing the sleeve to fit. Stitch. Repeat for other sleeve.

Amish Boy's Vest

1. Stitch fronts to back at shoulders, right sides facing.

2. Pin vest to vest lining, right sides facing, matching shoulder seams, corners, and points. Stitch both armholes and all around outside edges, leaving sides and between dots on back open.
Trim corners. Turn. Press.

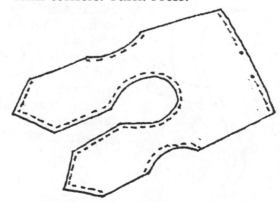

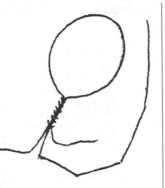

4. Turn raw edges on sides to inside along seam line. Butt turned edges of side. Hand-stitch.

5. Handstitch opening at bottom back closed. Press vest.

Amish Boy's Hat

1. Following manufacturer's directions, apply interfacing to felt hat top and side.

2. Stitch short straight edges of hat side together. Repeat for hat side lining.

3. Pin and stitch felt hat top to felt hat side. Repeat for linings.

4. Clip a scant 1/4" into seam allowance along inside of both felt hat brims.

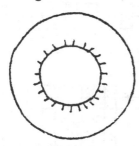

5. Pin and stitch one felt hat brim to felt hat side/felt hat top, right sides facing.

6. Pin and stitch hat side lining/hat top lining to second felt brim, as illustrated above.

7. Place bottom of hat, the felt brim attached to the lining side and top, flat on a table, wrong sides of lining facing up, brim flat on table. Lay cardboard brim over felt brim (1/4" of outside edge of felt brim will show past the cardboard). Glue cardboard to brim. Put felt hat on top, right side up. Match brim raw edges. Glue top felt brim to cardboard and to bit of felt bottom brim sticking out past cardboard.

8. Glue bias tape to edge of hat brim, encasing edges of both layers of felt. Let dry.

9. Push lining into hat top. Shape hat to stand squarely.

10. Cut the 5/8"-wide black ribbon into three pieces; one 6", one 5", one 2". Glue the 6" piece to the bottom of the hat side, overlapping the raw ends. Overlap the raw ends of the 5" piece 1/2". Fold the 2" piece into thirds and glue over the folded 5" piece, as shown. Glue over visible raw end of ribbon glued to hat. Allow to dry. Rub away any traces of glue with a paper towel dampened with warm water.

SUNSHINE AND SHADOW DOLL QUILT

In Amish society, art for art's sake was considered unacceptable. It was perceived as worldly and a waste of time. Therefore, the creative spirit found expression in utilitarian subjects, such as flower gardens, hooked rugs, samplers, and quilts. Limited to plain, solid color fabrics, Amish women became masters of color, often abruptly juxtaposing the purples, yellows, and greens with dark, striking black. The patchwork was then embellished with elaborate quilting. Intricate feathers and wreaths, all requiring long, tedious hours of work, are trademark Amish patterns. And each tiny stitch is perfect.

Our doll quilt is borrowed from this Amish tradition. A popular pattern, this Sunshine and Shadow quilt is quickly stitched on the sewing machine and completed with a minimum of (optional) hand or machine quilting.

Finished size is 13 1/2" square.

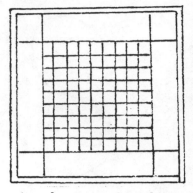

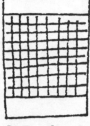

MATERIALS

¼ yard each or scraps of solid color cotton fabrics in nine colors
¼ yard black cotton fabric
17" x 17" piece of backing fabric; black or to match one of the front fabrics
17" x 17" piece of polyester fiberfill
Natural color thread
Black thread
Quilting thread

INSTRUCTIONS

Note: All seam allowances are ¼" unless instructed otherwise.

1. Cutting: Following the line drawing of the quilt decide which colors will fit where in the quilt. Count how many squares of each fabric will be needed and cut colored fabrics into 1½" squares. For the border, cut four corner squares, each 2½" square; four border strips 2½" x 9½" each, and four black binding strips, each 2½" x 16".

2. Piecing: On a flat surface, lay out the 1½" squares as they will appear in the finished quilt. Starting at the top left, sew the top left corner square to the one below it. Without pulling the piece from under the pressure foot, feed the top two pieces in the second row from the left together.

Continue until the first two pieces in each row are sewn together. Now sew the third piece in each row to the second piece, which you have just sewn to the first.

Do the same for each succeeding row until the nine strips are complete. Press all seams of each strip in one direction.

Lay out the strips in the order they will appear in the finished quilt top. Sew the first strip to the second, carefully matching seams, pinning if you need to. Sew the third to the second. Continue until all the strips are sewn together.

Press the seams in one direction, gently stretching the fabric to make a 9½" square.

3. Border: Sew one of the 9½" x 2½" border strips to one side of the pieced square. Sew the second 9½" x 2½" border strip to the opposite side. Press seams toward the border strip.

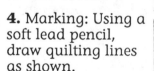

Stitch one 2½" square to each end of the two remaining 9½" x 2½" border strips.

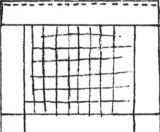

Press seams toward long border strips. Pin these strips to the two remaining opposite sides of the quilt. Stitch. Press seams toward border.

4. Marking: Using a soft lead pencil, draw quilting lines as shown.

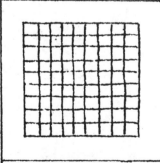

5. Assembly: Lay backing on flat surface. Lay batting on top. Lay pieced top, right side up, over both. Pin.

6. Quilting: With a small running stitch and the quilting thread, quilt along the marked lines.

7. Trim edges of batting. Pin one strip of binding to one edge of front of quilt, right sides facing. Machine stitch in place. Repeat for opposite side of quilt. Turn binding to back of quilt. Turn under ¼". Pin. Handstitch in place. Trim ends of binding even with edge of quilt.

Pin two remaining binding strips to two remaining raw front edges of the quilt. Stitch. Turn and handstitch to back as for first two strips, turning ends to inside to hide them.

JAPANESE KIMONO DOLL

MATERIALS

One skein black yarn

Matching thread

Heavy paper

Silk flowers

Glue or glue gun

$7/8$ yard fabric for kimono

$7/8$ yard matching lining fabric

Matching thread

$1/4$ yard collar fabric for undercollar and obi

$1/8$ yard collar fabric for outercollar

Safety pin

$1/4$ yard brown or beige felt or vinyl for sandals

$1/3$ yard gold braid

Dressed in her traditional kimono, this lovely doll smiles with elegance. Find an oriental-style print or choose a black and gold fabric for the kimono. The collar and obi are made of two matching or contrasting fabrics. Her hair is pulled into a bun and decorated with silk flowers.

INSTRUCTIONS

Note: All seam allowances are $1/4$" unless instructed otherwise.

Prewash all fabrics, make patterns, cut fabric and transfer markings as instructed in chapter 1. Cut one kimono out of lining and one from fabric, each 9" x 15". Cut obi 3" x 15".

Hair

1. Cut 200 lengths of yarn, each 18" long.

2. Draw a straight line on a piece of paper 10" in length. Find the centers of the yarn and lay them over the line, distributing the yarn to fill the 10" evenly. Machine stitch through the yarn and paper. Carefully tear the paper away.

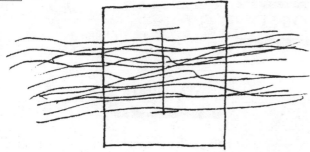

3. Place the middle of the stitching of the hair piece on the center top of the doll's head, starting at the forehead about 1¼" in front of the junction of the four seams at the top of the head. Bring the ends around the sides of the head, having them meet at the back about 4½" below and behind your starting point. In the process of tearing the paper from the yarn the stitching will have stretched, so ease the fullness around the side of the head between these two points. Handstitch along the machine stitching.

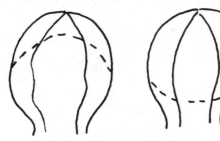

4. Cut folds in ends of hair. Pull the hair to the back of top of the head in a high pony tail, combing it with your fingers to straighten and smooth it out. Tie a piece of yarn around it close to the head.

5. Roll the ends of the yarn away from the center, under themselves to form bun, working around the circle of the bun. Trim away as much of the ends of the yarn as needed to form the bun.

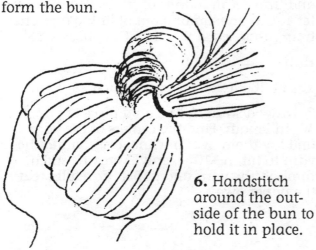

6. Handstitch around the outside of the bun to hold it in place.

7. Glue one big silk flower to the circle at the inside back of the bun and more flowers to the front of the hair.

Kimono

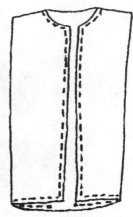

1. Pin kimono fronts to kimono back at shoulders. Pin sides from dots down. Stitch. Clip seam allowance to stitching at dot.

Repeat for kimono linings. Press seams open.

2. Pin lining to kimono at neck, front, and bottom edges, leaving armholes open. Stitch, leaving a 2" gap in the stitching at bottom back for turning.

Turn right side out. Press. Handstitch the opening at the bottom back closed.

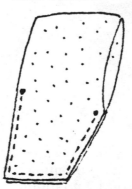

3. Fold sleeve in half along foldline. Pin and stitch from dot to dot around side bottom and bottom edges, as shown. Clip seam allowances into dot.

Repeat for sleeve lining.

Turn sleeve right side out. Put sleeve inside sleeve lining, matching wrist opening (opening on long edge that doesn't go off on a diagonal) to the bottom. Pin. Stitch from dot to dot.

Turn right side out so sleeve is on outside. Repeat for other sleeve.

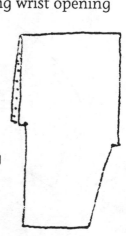

4. Pin raw edges of sleeve to armhole of kimono, treating sleeve lining and sleeve as one, leaving kimono lining free. Stitch from dot to dot. Turn kimono lining under ¼". Pin over sleeve seam. Handstitch.

5. Fold collars in half across their lengths. Stitch along raw edges, leaving a 1"-long gap in the stitching for turning.

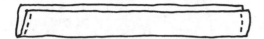

Trim corners. Turn. Press.

6. Pin long, unseamed edges of collars together. Pin them to neck edge as shown. Handstitch in place.

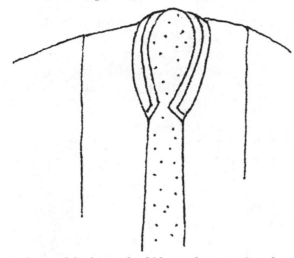

7. Obi: Fold obi in half lengthwise. Stitch along all raw edges, leaving an opening 1"-wide for turning. Trim corners. Turn. Press. Handstitch opening closed.

Find a point about one third from one end of the obi. Place this at the center front of the waist of the doll, just under her arms. Bring the ends of the obi around to the back of the doll. Tie a single knot at the back. Safety pin the short end of the obi to the knot. Run the end of the remaining length of obi under the obi from top. Keep doing this until you have used up the remaining length of obi. Hide end under the obi.

Sandals

1. Cut two sandal straps from the gold braid, each 5½" long.

2. Glue the two sandal soles together, wrong sides facing. Repeat for second sandal.

3. Immediately insert ¾" of one end of the sandal strap between the two soles at the dot on one side. Press the soles together to sandwich the strap end, adding more glue if needed. Repeat for the other side of the strap.
Repeat for second sandal.

4. Place sandal on doll's foot. Attach sandal to foot by taking a few stitches through the sandal strap on each side of the foot.

TRADITIONAL CHINESE DOLL

This charming doll wears her traditional jacket and pants. The jacket closes with snaps and is tied with a sash at the waist. She wears her hair straight and has sandals on her feet.

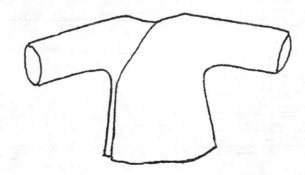
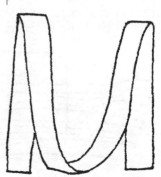

INSTRUCTIONS

Note: All seam allowances are 1/4" unless instructed otherwise.

Follow instructions in chapter 1 to prepare fabrics and patterns and to cut out and mark fabric. Cut sash 4 1/2" x 40".

Hair

1. Cut 45 pieces of yarn, each 4" long.

2. Draw a straight line on a piece of paper 1 1/2" long. Lay the centers of the pieces of yarn over the line, distributing them evenly over the length of the line. Machine stitch through the yarn and the paper.
   Tear the paper from the yarn.

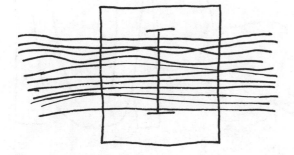

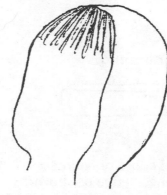

3. Place the stitching across the front of the doll's head over the junction of the seams. Handstitch the yarn bangs to the head.

4. Cut 120 lengths of yarn, each 12" long.

5. Draw a straight line on a piece of paper 3" in length. Find the centers of the yarn and lay them over the line, distributing the yarn to fill the 3" evenly. Machine stitch through the yarn and paper. Carefully tear the paper away.

6. Place one end of the chain of stitching over the back edge of the bangs. Extend the other end of the stitching straight down the back of the head. Stitch in place. Trim ends of yarn.

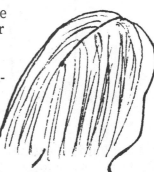

Jacket

1. Stitch jacket fronts to back at shoulders and underarms/sides. Repeat for lining.

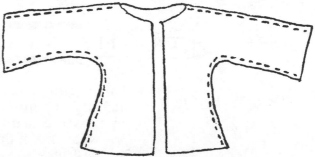

2. Pin jacket to jacket lining, right sides facing. Stitch, leaving a 2"-wide opening at the bottom back for turning.

Turn. Press. Handstitch gap in stitching closed.

3. Turn ¹/₄" to inside of wrist openings of jacket and jacket lining. Handstitch together.

4. Sash: Fold sash in half lengthwise. Stitch along all raw edges, leaving a 1"-wide opening in the middle of long edge for turning. Trim corners. Turn. Press. Handstitch opening closed. Put center of sash at front of doll's waist. Bring free ends to back, twist them once, and bring them to the front again. Tie them in a knot.

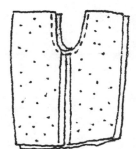

Pants

1. Sew the short inner leg seams, right sides together. Press open.

2. Pin and stitch the crotch seam, right sides facing.

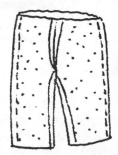

3. Match the long, outside leg seams. Pin and stitch.

4. Press under ¹/₄" along the waistline opening. Press under an additional ⁵/₈". Topstitch close to both folds, leaving a ¹/₂" opening in the stitching on the lower fold for inserting the elastic. Run a 7¹/₂" piece of elastic through the casing. Try the pants on the doll. Adjust the elastic, if necessary. Overlap

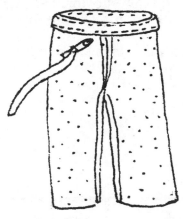

and stitch the raw ends of the elastic. Stitch the gap in the casing closed.

5. Press under ¹/₄" on bottom edges of legs. Press under another ¹/₄". Topstitch.

Sandals

1. Cut two sandal straps from the gold braid, each 5¹/₂" long.

2. Glue the two sandal soles together, wrong sides facing. Repeat for second sandal.

3. Immediately insert ³/₄" of one end of the sandal strap between the two soles at one dot. Press the soles together to sandwich the strap end, adding more glue if needed. Repeat for the other side of the strap.
    Repeat for second sandal.

4. Place sandal on doll's foot. Attach sandal to foot by taking a few stitches on either side of the foot through the sandal strap.

SCANDINAVIAN DOLL

Depending upon the country (and region within that particular country), this little lady could hark from Norway, Sweden, or Denmark. She also bears a striking resemblance to our fictional friend from Switzerland, Heidi.

A wide variety of fabric choices are available when making this doll. Black velvet is appropriate for the bodice as are any number of bright or pastel colors. Even a gaily colored striped fabric would be nice. From there choose skirt and apron colors. Or start with a lovely floral ribbon and choose the fabrics to match.

Visit a specialty yarn shop to find an interestingly variegated yarn for the doll's hair.

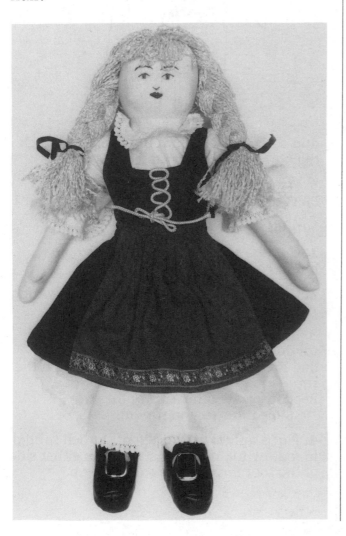

MATERIALS

One skein yarn
Matching thread
$\frac{1}{2}$ yard of $\frac{1}{4}$"-wide ribbon for hair ties
$\frac{1}{4}$ yard fabric for bodice (fronts and back may be two different colors)
Matching thread
Three snaps
$\frac{2}{3}$ yard lacing
$\frac{5}{8}$ yard fine white cotton fabric for blouse and petticoat
Matching thread
2 yards of $\frac{5}{8}$"-wide lace trim
$\frac{1}{4}$ yard fabric for skirt
Matching thread
$\frac{1}{4}$"-wide elastic
$\frac{1}{4}$ yard fabric for apron
Matching thread
$\frac{1}{3}$ yard ribbon for bottom edge of apron
One pair doll tights (see Sources)
$\frac{1}{8}$ yard Ultraleather™, double-sided suede, or vinyl for shoes (see Sources)
Matching thread
Two 1" buckles
$\frac{1}{4}$ yard of 1"-wide grosgrain ribbon for shoes

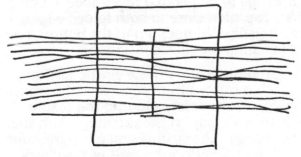

INSTRUCTIONS

Note: All seam allowances are ¼" unless instructed otherwise.

Turn to chapter 1 for instructions on making patterns and cutting and marking fabric. Cut skirt 7½" x 32". Cut petticoat 7½" x 32". Cut apron 7" x 10" and tie 1½" x 26".

Hair

1. Cut 30 pieces of yarn, each 3" long.

2. Draw a straight line on a piece of paper 1½" long. Lay the centers of the pieces of yarn over the line, distributing them evenly over the length of the line. Machine stitch through the yarn and the paper.

Carefully tear the paper away.

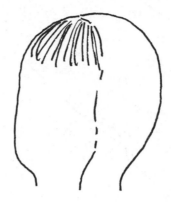

3. Place the stitching across the front of the doll's head, over the junction of the seams. Handstitch the yarn bangs to the head.

4. Cut 120 pieces of yarn, each 28" long.

5. Draw a straight line on a piece of paper 4½" in length. Find the centers of the yarn and lay them over the line, distributing the yarn to fill the 4½" evenly. Machine stitch through the yarn and paper. Carefully tear the paper away.

6. Place one end of the stitched "part" of the hair piece on the center top of the doll's head, starting at the forehead just over the bangs with the bottom of the part 4½" straight down the center back of the head. In the process of tearing the paper from the yarn the stitching will have stretched, so ease the fullness between these two points. Handstitch along the part, catching the thread.

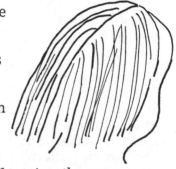

7. Cut folds in ends of hair. Braid the hair. Tie the ends with a piece of yarn.

8. Cut ribbon in half. Tie ribbons in bows over the ends of the braids.

Bodice

1. Stitch fronts to back at shoulders, right sides facing, for both bodice and bodice lining.

2. Pin bodice to bodice lining, right sides facing, matching shoulder seams, corners and points. Stitch both armholes and all around outside edges, leaving open the sides and space between dots on back.

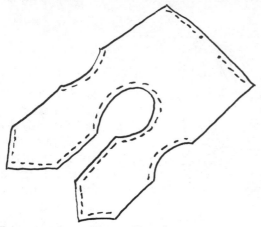

Trim corners. Turn. Press.

4. Turn raw edges on sides to inside along seam line. Butt turned edges of side. Handstitch together.

5. Handstitch opening at bottom back closed. Press bodice.

6. Stitch snaps to bodice front, as marked.

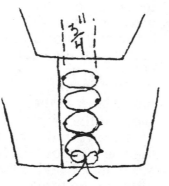

7. To find center of lacing, fold in half. Starting with center at top, tack lacing to front of bodice at dots marked on pattern. Tie bow at bottom.

Blouse

1. Place two blouse bodies together, right sides facing. Stitch one shoulder seam. Press under ³/₈" along neck edge. Press under another ³/₈". Pin lace to wrong side of turned under neck edge, decorative edge of lace showing. Topstitch.

2. Cut a piece of ¹/₄"-wide elastic 8" long. On wrong side of blouse, pin either end of elastic to neck edge where marked placement line meets raw edge. Using a small zig-zag stitch, sew the elastic to the blouse on the marked placement line, stretching the elastic as you go. Hold ends of the elastic along with the edge of the blouse between your fingers.

3. Stitch second shoulder seam, catching ends of elastic in the seam.

4. Press under ³/₈" on one long edge of sleeve. Repeat. Pin lace to wrong side of turned under edge. Topstitch. Repeat for other sleeve.

5. Cut two pieces of baby elastic, each 4¹/₂" long. Lay one on wrong side of sleeve 1" from finished edge. Pin raw ends even with raw edge of short ends of sleeve. Using a small zigzag stitch, stitch the elastic to the

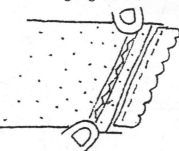

fabric, stretching the elastic to fit as you go. Repeat for second sleeve.

6. Using a long machine stitch, sew two rows of gathering stitches inside the ¹/₄" seam allowance on the second long edge of sleeve. Find the center of the long edge of the sleeve. Pin it to the shoulder seam of the blouse, right sides together. Pin ends to ends of armhole. Pull up on gathering stitches to fit. Stitch. Repeat for other sleeve.

7. Stitch undersleeve/side seams as one.

8. Press under ¹/₄" on bottom edge of blouse. Press under another ¹/₄". Topstitch.

Petticoat

1. Stitch two short ends of petticoat together. Press seam open.

2. Press under ¹/₄" along one long edge. Press under another ¹/₄". Pin lace to wrong side of turned under hem edge, decorative edge of lace showing. Topstitch.

3. Press under ¹/₄" along remaining long, raw edge of petticoat. Press under another ⁵/₈". Topstitch close to both folded edges, leaving one ¹/₂" opening in the bottom row of stitching for elastic insertion.

4. Cut a piece of ¹/₄"-wide elastic 12" long. Attach a safety pin to each end of the elastic. Insert one safety pin into the casing through the gap in the stitching. Push the pin through the casing, emerging from the other end. Overlap the ends of the elastic ¹/₂". Stitch to secure. Stretch the elastic so it pops back into the casing. Topstitch over the gap in the stitching.

Skirt

1. Stitch two short ends of skirt together. Press seam open.

2. Press under $1/4$" along one long edge. Press under another $1/4$". Topstitch.

3. Press under $1/4$" along remaining long, raw edge of skirt. Press under another $5/8$". Topstitch close to both folded edges, leaving one $1/2$" opening in the bottom row of stitching for elastic insertion.

4. Cut a piece of $1/4$"-wide elastic 12" long. Attach a safety pin to each end of the elastic. Insert the safety pin into the casing through the gap in the stitching. Push the pin through the casing, from the other end. Overlap the ends of the elastic $1/2$". Stitch to secure. Stretch the elastic so it pops back into the casing. Topstitch over the gap in the stitching.

Apron

1. Press waist tie in half. Fold long raw edges in to meet at center. Press.

2. Press one long edge of apron under $1/4$" and $1/4$" again. Topstitch a scant $1/4$" from folded edge. Stitch ribbon $1/4$" from folded edge on right side of apron bottom. Press under $1/4$" twice on short sides. Topstitch.

3. Using a long machine stitch, gather the long, unstitched (top) edge of the apron. Unfold the waist tie. Fold the waist tie in half to find the center. Mark the center with a pin. Unfold. Measure $2^{1}/2$" on either side of the center pin and place a pin in both places. Match and pin the center and the side edges of the gathered top edge of the apron to the pins on the tie, right sides facing. Pull up on and adjust the gathering stitches on the apron between the pins. Pin and stitch.

4. Fold tie along pressed lines. Pin folded edge to apron. Pin fold evenly along remaining lengths of tie, matching top and bottom folds, turning ends to inside. Topstitch close to double-folded edge.

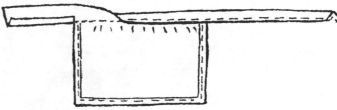

Shoes

1. Stitch front seams in shoe sides, right sides facing.

2. Pin one shoe side to one sole, right sides together, matching large dots at back of shoe side to those on the shoe sole and the small dot on the shoe sole to the seam on shoe side. Stitch. Repeat for second side and sole.

3. Turn one set right side out. Put inside-out set inside this one. Match top back edges. Pin. Topstitch $1/8$" from edge between dots as shown.

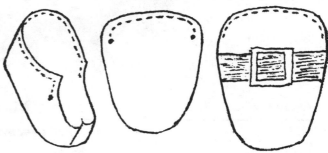

4. Match two shoe tops, wrong sides facing. Topstitch $1/8$" from edge between dots as shown. Repeat for second shoe.

5. Cut a piece of 1"-wide ribbon $2^{1}/4$" long. Put a buckle on it. Pin edges of ribbon to right side of shoe top, having top of ribbon $3/4$" from the top (topstitched) edge of the shoe top. Baste in place. Repeat for second shoe.

6. Pin shoe top to shoe side, right sides facing, between dots as illustrated, matching dot at front of shoe top to seam on shoe side. Stitch between dots, catching both layers of the shoe tops, shoe sides, and the ribbon. Repeat for second shoe.

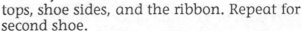

7. Turn right side out. Shape from inside with fingers. Repeat for other shoe.

PILGRIM MAN & WOMAN

MATERIALS

One skein yarn

Matching thread

$1/2$ yard broadcloth or linen-like fabric for doublet and britches

Matching thread

$1/4$ yard crisp, white cotton fabric for collar and cuffs

Matching thread

Hooks and eyes

Lightweight interfacing

Eighteen $1/2$" silver buttons

Three 1" silver buckles

$1/3$ yard of $1/4$"-wide black or matching grosgrain ribbon

$1/4$"-wide elastic

$1/4$ yard black felt for hat

Scrap of black cotton or lining fabric

$3/4$ yard of 1"-wide grosgrain ribbon for hat and shoes

Black thread

Heavy-weight fusible interfacing

Lightweight cardboard

Craft glue

Black double-fold bias tape

$1/8$ yard moss or medium dark green knit fabric for stockings

Matching thread

$1/8$ yard Ultraleather™ double-sided suede, or vinyl (see Sources)

Matching thread

With a bountiful harvest stored as insurance against the suffering of the last winter, this Pilgrim couple takes a respite from their hard work to feast in thankful celebration of their good fortune.

PILGRIM MAN

In his belted doublet with white collar and cuffs, knit stockings, silver buckled shoes, high top hat, and knee britches, this Pilgrim is ready for turkey and pumpkin pie.

Choose a medium-weight cotton for the doublet and breeches in black or dark, rich colors such as French green and warm brown. For instructions on making his shoes and stockings, see page 170.

INSTRUCTIONS

Note: All seam allowances are ¼" unless instructed otherwise.

Prepare patterns and fabric as instructed in chapter 1. Cut and mark fabric.

Hair

1. Cut 100 pieces of yarn, each 14" long.

2. Draw a straight line on a piece of paper 2½" in length. Find the centers of the yarn and lay them over the line, distributing the yarn to fill the 2½" evenly. Machine stitch through the yarn and paper.

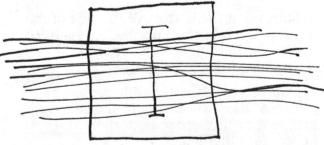

Carefully tear the paper away.

3. Place one end of the stitched "part" of the hair piece on the center top of the doll's head, starting at the forehead 1¼" in front of the junction of the seams at the top of the head. Lay the stitching on the head straight to the back. Handstitch along the part, catching the thread.

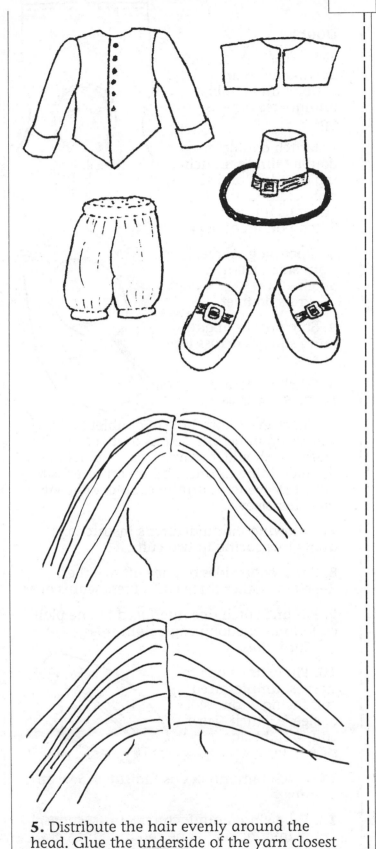

5. Distribute the hair evenly around the head. Glue the underside of the yarn closest to the head in place.

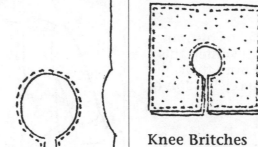

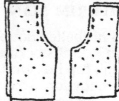

Doublet

1. Stitch fronts to backs at shoulder seams in doublet and doublet lining. Press seams open.

2. Match doublet to doublet lining, matching all edges and seams, right sides facing. Pin. Stitch as illustrated. Stitch bottom of backs.

3. Open side seams. Pin right side together. Stitch.
     Press doublet.

4. Stitch a row of gathering stitches across tops of sleeves.

5. Stitch underarm seams of sleeves.

6. Pin sleeve to armhole of doublet body, matching underarm seams and dot on sleeve to shoulder seam. Treat doublet and doublet lining as one. Pull up on threads to adjust sleeve to fit armhole. Stitch. Repeat for other sleeve.

7. Following manufacturer's instructions, apply interfacing to two cuffs.

8. Stitch short sides of one cuff together. Repeat for other three cuffs. Press seams open.

9. Pin and stitch one interfaced to one plain cuff along one long edge, right sides together. Turn. Press.

10. Pin cuffs as one to sleeves, uninterfaced cuff facing wrong side of sleeve. Stitch. Turn cuff to right side of sleeve. Press.

11. Stitch buttonholes as indicated. Sew on buttons.

12. Following manufacturer's instructions, apply interfacing to one collar. Right sides together, pin and stitch all around raw edges of collar, leaving a 1"-wide opening in the stitching at center back for turning.

Clip corners. Turn. Press. Handstitch opening in stitching closed.

13. Sew hooks and eyes to collar, one close to top and one half way down.

Knee Britches

1. Stitch crotch seams, right sides together.

2. Open pants and match side seams, right sides facing. Stitch.

3. Stitch underleg seam, starting at bottom of one leg and ending at the other.

4. Press under $1/4$" at the waist. Press under an additional $5/8$". Topstitch close to folded edges, leaving a $1/2$" opening in the bottom stitching for inserting elastic. Cut a piece of elastic 11" long. Insert into casing. Overlap raw ends of elastic 1/2". Stitch together to secure. Stitch gap in topstitching closed.

5. Press $1/4$" at bottom of leg. Press under $5/8$" more. Topstitch close to both folded edges, leaving a $1/2$" opening in the top folded edge for inserting elastic. Cut a piece of elastic 6" long. Insert into casing. Overlap raw ends of elastic $1/2$". Stitch together to secure. Stitch gap in topstitching closed. Repeat for second leg.

6. Starting at the bottom of the side of the leg, sew seven buttons up the leg, each $3/4$" apart. The buttons will not reach to the waist. Repeat for second leg.

7. Cut a piece of the $1/4$"-wide grosgrain ribbon 5" long. Tie a knot in the center and tack to leg side close to bottom button. Repeat for other leg.

Hat

1. Following manufacturer's directions apply interfacing to felt hat top and felt hat side.

2. Stitch short seam in hat side.

3. Pin and stitch felt hat top to felt hat side.

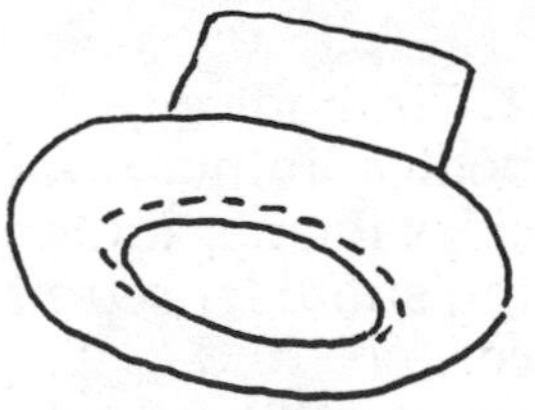

4. Clip a scant ¼" into seam allowance along inside of both felt hat brims.

5. Pin and stitch one felt hat brim to felt hat side, right sides facing.

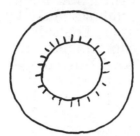

6. Stitch short side seam in hat side lining.

7. Pin and stitch hat top lining to hat side lining, right sides together.

8. Pin and stitch hat side lining to second felt brim, right sides facing.

9. Place bottom of hat, the felt brim attached to the lining side and top, flat on a table, wrong sides of lining facing up, brim flat on table. Lay cardboard brim over felt brim (¼" of outside edge of felt brim will show past the cardboard). Glue cardboard to brim. Put felt hat on top, right side up. Match brim raw edges. Glue top felt brim to cardboard and to bit of felt bottom brim sticking out past cardboard.

10. Glue bias tape to edge of hat brim, encasing edges of both layers of felt. Let dry.

11. Push lining into hat top. Shape hat to stand squarely.

12. Cut a piece of the 1"-wide ribbon 13" long. Put the buckle on the ribbon. Glue the ribbon to the hat as shown, turning the raw end of the ribbon that extends past the buckle to the inside.

Allow to dry. Rub away any traces of glue with a paper towel dampened with warm water.

Pilgrim Woman

The Pilgrim woman wears a pointed collar over her cuffed bodice. Her apron covers a full skirt. A second skirt is split at the front and the ends are tucked into her waistband at the back, forming billows at her sides. Her hair is pulled into a bun and covered with a simple cap.

Choose crisp cotton for the cuffs and collar, and grey, warm russet, French green, or a grayish-blue for the dress.

MATERIALS

One skein yarn
Matching thread
¾ yard fabric for bodice and skirts
Matching thread
3 snaps
¼ yard crisp, white cotton fabric such as batiste
Matching thread
¼"-wide elastic
Light- to medium-weight interfacing
1½ yards of ¼"-wide black grosgrain ribbon
⅜ yard of ⅞"-wide ribbon for collar ties
½ yard of ¼" wide white ribbon for cap ties
⅛ yard Ultraleather™, double-sided suede, or vinyl (see Sources)
Matching thread
Two 1" silver buckle
¼ yard of 1"-wide grosgrain ribbon for shoes

INSTRUCTIONS

Note: All seam allowances are ¼" unless instructed otherwise.

Following the instructions in chapter 1 prepare the fabric and patterns, cut and mark the fabric. Cut two skirts 12" x 30" for underskirt and overskirt. Cut apron 7" x 12" and apron tie 1¼" x 30".

Hair

1. Cut 120 pieces of yarn, each 24" long.

2. Draw a straight line on a piece of paper 2½" in length. Find the centers of the yarn and lay them over the line, distributing the yarn to fill the 2½" evenly. Machine stitch through the yarn and paper.

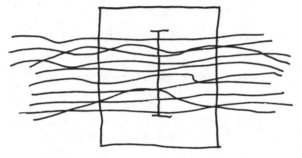

Carefully tear the paper away.

3. Place the stitched "part" of the hair piece on the center top of the doll's head, starting at the forehead about an inch in front of the junction of the seams at the top of the head and running straight back for 2½". Handstitch along the machine stitching.

4. Pull the hair to back of the head, tying it with yarn into a low pony tail at top of the neck. Cut the pony tail to measure 4" long. Turn the yarn to the outside and under itself all the way around to form a bun. Handstitch in place.

Bodice

1. Stitch fronts to back at shoulders, right sides facing, for both bodice and bodice lining.

2. Pin bodice to bodice lining, right sides facing, matching shoulder seams, corners, and points. Stitch both armholes and all around outside edges and across back, leaving open the sides and between dots on back. Trim corners. Turn. Press. Handstitch opening at back closed.

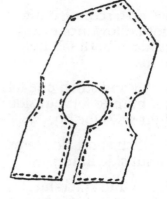

3. Turn raw edges at side of bodice to inside ¼". Butt turned edges. Handstitch. Press bodice.

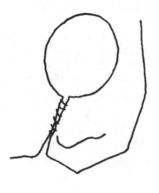

4. Apply interfacing to two cuffs according to manufacturer's instructions. Match and stitch short ends of cuffs, right sides facing.

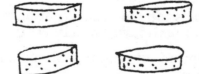

Match two uninterfaced sides of cuffs to two interfaced cuffs. Pin and stitch along one long edge as shown. Turn right side out. Press. Pin cuff to inside of sleeve, right side of cuff facing wrong side of sleeve. Stitch. Turn cuff to right side of sleeve. Press.

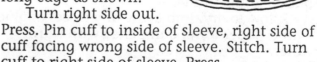

5. Sew snaps to bodice back as marked.

6. Following manufacturer's instructions, apply interfacing to one collar. Right sides together, pin and stitch all around raw edges of collar, leaving a 1"-wide opening in the stitching at center back for turning. Clip corners. Turn. Press. Handstitch opening in stitching closed.

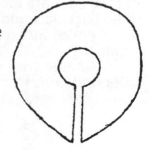

Cut four pieces of ribbon, each 6¹/₂" long. Turn under the ends ¹/₄" and hand sew the ends to the underside of the collar as shown.

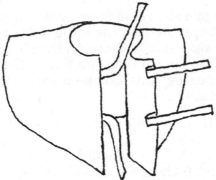

Tie in bows.

Underskirt

1. Stitch ¹/₄" wide black ribbon to one long edge of skirt, 1¹/₂" from the raw edge. Stitch a second row of ribbon ¹/₄" above the first, and a third ¹/₄" above the second.

2. Stitch two short ends of skirt together. Press seam open.

3. Press under ¹/₄" along the ribboned edge. Press under another ¹/₄". Topstitch.

4. Press under ¹/₄" along remaining long, raw edge of skirt. Press under another ⁵/₈". Topstitch close to both folded edges, leaving one ¹/₂" opening in the bottom row of stitching for elastic insertion.

5. Cut a piece of ¹/₄" elastic 12" long. Attach a safety pin to each end of the elastic. Insert the safety pin into the casing through the gap in the stitching. Push the pin through the casing, emerging from the other end. Overlap the ends of the elastic ¹/₂". Stitch to secure. Topstitch over the gap in the stitching.

Overskirt

1. Press under ¹/₄" on both short edges of underskirt and one long edge. Press under another ¹/₄". Topstitch.

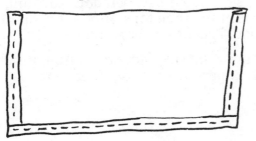

2. Press under ¹/₄" on remaining long raw edge. Press under another ⁵/₈". Topstitch close to both folded edges. Cut a piece of elastic 12" long. Insert into casing. Overlap ends ¹/₄" and stitch.

3. Put overskirt on doll over underskirt. Take bottom front corners of overskirt under itself and to the back. Tuck the corners into the waist of the skirt.

Apron

1. Press waist tie in half lengthwise. Fold long raw edges in to meet at center. Press.

2. Press one long edge of apron under ¹/₄" and 1¹/₄" again. Topstitch a scant ¹/₄" from folded edge. Press under ¹/₄" twice on short sides. Topstitch.

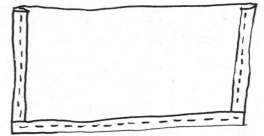

3. Using a long machine stitch, gather the long, unstitched (top) edge of the apron. Unfold the waist tie. To find center of tie fold the waist tie in half. Mark the center with a pin. Unfold. Measure 2" on either side of the center pin, and place a pin in both places. Match and pin the center and the side edges of the gathered top edge of the apron to the

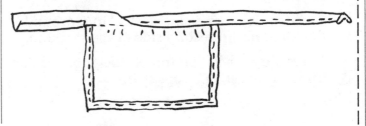

pins on the tie, right sides facing. Pull up on and adjust the gathering stitches on the apron between the pins. Pin and stitch.

4. Fold tie along pressed lines. Pin folded edge to apron. Pin fold evenly along remaining lengths of tie, matching top and bottom folds, turning ends to inside. Topstitch close to double-folded edge.

Cap

1. Stitch darts in two bonnet sides and two bonnet side linings.

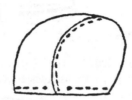

2. Stitch rounded bonnet top/back seams, right sides facing.

3. Pin bonnets to bonnet linings at lower, straight edge, right sides facing. Stitch, leaving a 1"-wide opening at the back for turning.

4. Apply interfacing to one side of bonnet flap. Fold bonnet flap in half along foldline, right sides facing. Stitch along both short edges. Trim corners. Turn. Press.

5. Sandwich bonnet flap inside two bonnet front edges, having raw edges even. Pin. Stitch. Turn right side out. Handstitch opening at bottom back closed. Press.

6. Cut two pieces of the white ¼"-wide ribbon, each 7" long. Turn under ¼" at one end of each and handstitch in place as shown.

Both Dolls

Stockings

1. Stitch down one side of stocking, around the toe, and up second side of the stocking.

2. Press under ¼" on top of stocking. Turn under another ¼". Topstitch.

Shoes

1. Stitch front seams in shoe sides, right sides facing.

2. Pin one shoe side to one sole, right sides together, matching the large dots at the back of the shoe side to those on the shoe sole and the small dot on the shoe sole to the seam on the shoe side. Stitch. Repeat for second side and sole.

3. Turn one set right side out. Put inside-out set inside this one. Match top back edges. Pin. Topstitch between dots as shown, ⅛" from edge.

4. Match two shoe tops, wrong sides facing. Topstitch ⅛" from edge between dots as shown. Repeat for second shoe.

5. Cut a piece of 1"-wide ribbon 2¼" long. Put a buckle on it. Pin edges of ribbon to right side of shoe top, having top of ribbon ¾" from the top (topstitched) edge of the shoe top. Baste in place. Repeat for second shoe.

6. Pin shoe top to shoe side, right sides facing, between dots as illustrated, matching dot at front of shoe top to seam at front of shoe side. Stitch between dots, catching both layers of the shoe tops, shoe sides, and the ribbon. Repeat for second shoe.

7. Turn right side out. Shape from inside with fingers. Repeat for other shoe.

VICTORIAN DOLL

Step back in time with this elegant little lady. She is dressed in a shiny moire dress, silky French drawers, fancy (store-bought) tights, and a frilly bonnet. Her high-top, buttoned shoes are made of sumptuous imitation leather. This is your chance to buy just a bit of that exquisite lace and dazzling dress-up fabric you've been admiring. Since so little is required for the doll, your pocketbook will not balk.

MATERIALS

One skein yarn
Matching thread
$3/4$ yard of $2^{1}/2$"-wide (or so) lace for collar and cuffs
1 yard moire
Matching thread
$3/8$ yard satin-like polyester fabric for drawers and bonnet brim ruffle
Matching thread
Two squares felt for underlining bonnet
$1/4$ yard Stitch Witchery™
$2^{2}/3$ yards of $1^{1}/2$"- or 2"-wide ribbon
$2/3$ yard matching $5/8$"-wide ribbon for drawers trim
Four snaps
$1/4$"-wide elastic
Doll tights (see Sources)
$1/8$ yard Ultraleather® double-sided suede, or vinyl (see Sources)
Matching thread
One 1" buckle
Three snaps
Three $1/4$" round black buttons or beads for shoes

INSTRUCTIONS

Note: All seam allowances are ¼" unless instructed otherwise.

Make the patterns and cut out the clothing pieces according to the instructions in chapter 1. For the dress skirt, cut a piece of fabric 4¾" x 30". For the middle underskirt, cut a piece 6¼" x 30". For the bottom underskirt, cut a piece 7" x 30". Cut bonnet bottom ruffle 2½" x 25".

HAIR

1. To form yarn into banana curls: Wind four lengths of the yarn as one around long (about 16") knitting needles, shish kebab skewers, or similar metal objects. Run under water until soaked. Put in preheated 275 degree F oven for 20 minutes or until completely dry. Remove from oven. Allow to cool. Remove from skewers. Repeat until you have about 30 lengths of curls.

2. To form bangs and hair at back of head, fold 10 lengths of curled yarn in half. Thread a needle, knot the thread, and take a stitch in the head, lodging the knot 1" in front of the junction of the four seams at the center top of the head. Take another stitch to one side. Pull up on the thread until there is a loop of several inches of thread. Insert the fold of the curled yarn into the loop from the back, so that the yarn loop is about ¾" long. Tighten the thread around the yarn. Add yarn in a row to one side until you reach the other seam. Repeat for the other side.

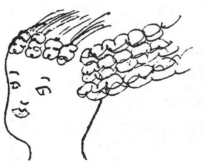

3. Fold another ten lengths of yarn in half. Starting just below the last stitched length of yarn on one side of the head stitch the fold of the yarn to the head. Add yarn as shown until you have used the ten pieces. Repeat for the other side.

4. Open the folded yarn on one side of the head so that the lengths are in continuous pieces. Pull the free end of the piece which lies to the back to where the middle of that piece of yarn is stitched. Stitch it to the first stitching, leaving a ½" or so piece at the end extending to the front. Repeat for all the back facing ringlets on that side of the head. Repeat for the other side of the head.

5. Pull other half of the ringlets which are now laying to the front of the doll to the top back of the doll's head and tie with a short piece of string. Clip the string close to the knot.

6. Cut a piece of the wide ribbon 24" long. Form it into a bow. Tack over string.

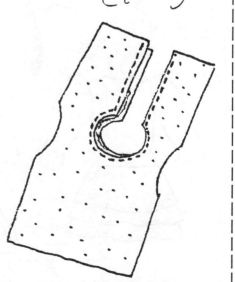

Dress

1. Stitch front to back bodices at shoulders and side seams. Repeat for second set: one will be the bodice, one the lining.

2. Pin lace to right side of one neck edge. Baste in place.

Match second bodice to first bodice's neck and back edges, right sides facing, matching shoulder seams. Pin. Stitch, catching lace in neck seam and in straight back seam as far as it goes.

Trim corners. Turn. Press.

3. Pin lace to bottom edges of two sleeves. Baste lace to sleeves. Stitch underarm seams of all four sleeves (the two without the lace are the sleeve linings), catching lace edges in the stitching of the two that have it. Match bottom edges of sleeves to sleeve linings, right sides facing. Pin. Stitch. Turn so sleeves with lace are on the outside. Press.

4. Gather top edges of sleeves between dots, treating the two layers of the sleeves as one. Pin to dress armhole, matching dots. Adjust gathers. Stitch.

5. Stitch short ends of one of the three skirt tiers together, right sides facing. Repeat for remaining tiers. Press seams open. To form hems, press under $1/4"$ and then another $1/4"$ on the bottom edge of each of the skirts. Topstitch.

6. Put the middle skirt tier inside the outer, shortest skirt and then the longest skirt inside both. Match the top edges. Baste the three layers together. Treat them as one to attach them to the dress.

Using two rows of gathering stitches, gather the top edge of the skirt from the back seam all the way around the skirt top and to the other side of the back seam. Pin the skirt to the bottom edge of the bodice, right sides facing, overlapping the backs of the dress $1/2"$ at center back. Adjust gathers. Pin. Stitch.

7. Sew snaps to dress back as marked.

8. Cut the wide ribbon in half. Tie one half around lower waist and make a bow in back. Reserve second half of ribbon for bonnet.

Drawers

1. Press under $1/4"$ at bottom legs. Turn under an additional $1^3/4"$.

2. Cut two pieces of elastic, each 6" long. Zigzag stitch the elastic to the inside of the legs, over the $1/4"$ you turned under, stretching the elastic as you sew.

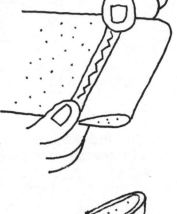

3. Stitch the inside leg seams.

4. Turn one leg right side out. Put it inside the other leg. Match the crotch seams. Pin and stitch. Turn right side out.

5. To form a casing, press under $1/4"$ along the top edge of the drawers. Press under an additional $5/8"$. Topstitch close to both folded edges, leaving a $1/2"$-wide opening in the bottom stitching. Cut a piece of elastic 11" long. Insert into the casing with a safety pin attached to the leading end. Overlap the ends of the elastic $1/2"$. Stitch them together securely. Push elastic back into casing. Stitch gap in topstitching closed.

6. Make two bows from the $5/8"$-wide ribbon. Tack to the outside of the legs over the elastic.

Bonnet

1. Pin and stitch the bonnet brim to the convex curve of the bonnet body and the concave curve of the bonnet body to the long curve of the bonnet back, matching large and small dots.

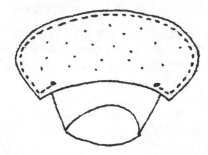

2. Using the Stitch Witchery™, apply the felt underlining to one bonnet brim, one body and one back. These will form the lining of the bonnet.

3. Pin and stitch the bonnet brim lining to the bonnet brim between the small dots.

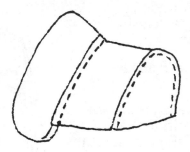

4. Right sides facing, pin and stitch the long outside curves of the two bonnet brim ruffle pieces together. Turn. Press. Gather the raw edges. Pin to the raw edge of the bonnet brim lining. Adjust gathers. Stitch.

5. Pin and stitch the concave curve of the bonnet lining body to the bonnet lining back.

6. Fold the bonnet bottom ruffle in half lengthwise. Stitch the short ends together, right sides facing. Turn. Press. Gather the long raw edges of the ruffle as one. Pin to bottom edges of right side of bonnet back and body lining. Adjust gathers. Baste. Lay this over the bonnet back and body, right sides together. Pin, matching seams and raw edges. Stitch. Turn right side out. Press.

7. Turn 1/4" on raw edge of bonnet body lining to inside. Pin over seam allowances of brim ruffle. Pin. Handstitch in place.

8. Put hat on doll. Cut a piece of ribbon 36" long. Put over hat. Tie a bow in the ribbon at one side of the hat.

Shoes

1. Stitch front seams in shoe sides from bottom to dot, right sides facing. Clip seam allowances to dot, as shown.

2. Pin one shoe side to one sole, right sides together, matching dots to front seam and center back of shoe side. Stitch. Repeat for second side and sole. Trim seam allowances to 1/8".

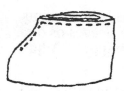

3. Turn one set right side out. Put the other, inside-out set, inside. Match top back edges. Pin. Topstitch 1/8" from edge between dots as shown. Repeat for second shoe.

4. Match two shoe extensions, wrong sides facing. Topstitch between dots as shown, 1/8" from edge. Repeat for second extension, reversing the direction of the extension as shown, to make a left and right extension.

5. Pin extension to untopstitched side of front as shown, right sides facing. Stitch. Repeat for second shoe, pinning and stitching to the other side of the front.

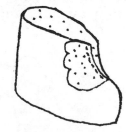

6. Shape shoe from inside with fingers. Repeat for other shoe.

7. Stitch buttonholes. Sew buttons in places.

NATIVE AMERICAN INDIAN BRAVE & SQUAW

These true native Americans are dressed in modern re-creations of authentic clothing made from animal skins. Looking at the patterns, you can see how the shirts made use of the natural shape of animal skins. The garments are held together by strips of hide. All are heavily fringed, thereby diverting rain and breaking the runoff into droplets.

Choose a warm brown cotton fabric for the doll and a tan imitation suede, leather, or felt for the clothing.

Both Dolls

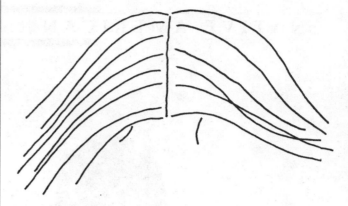

Hair

1. Cut 150 pieces of yarn, each 28" long.

2. Draw a straight 4" line on a piece of paper. Find the centers of the yarn and lay them over the line, distributing the yarn to fill the 4" evenly. Machine stitch through the yarn and paper.

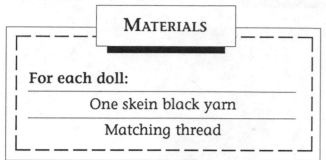

Carefully tear the paper away.

3. Place the stitched "part" of the hair piece on the center top of the doll's head, starting at the forehead about 1¼" to the front of the union of the four seams at the top of the head with the bottom of the part at the nape of the neck. In the process of tearing the paper from the yarn the stitching will have stretched, so ease the fullness between these two points. Handstitch along the machine stitching.

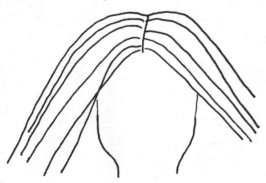

4. Cut folds in ends of hair. Braid the hair. Tie the ends with a piece of yarn. Tie ¼" wide-strips of suede from outfit below over ends of braids.

Native Indian Brave

INSTRUCTIONS

Note: All seam allowances are ¼" unless instructed otherwise.

Make patterns and cut and mark the fabric as instructed in chapter 1. Cut one strip of the fabric ½" x 18". This will be the belt. Cut the breechcloth 3" x 16". Cut two strips of the fabric, both the full width of the fabric and about 3/16" wide. These will be cut into thongs which will be laced through the garment to hold it together. Cut a piece of fabric 2" x 10" for war bonnet. For the decorative bands on shoulders and war bonnet, cut two pieces 1" x 6" and one piece 1" x 10" from white Ultrasuede™ or felt. Cut the decorations as indicated on pattern.

Breechcloth and Leggings

1. Glue the colored cut outs to the breechcloth. Let dry. Tie the belt on the doll, inserting the breechcloth as illustrated. The breechcloth should be longer in the front than the back.

2. Cut fringe on leggings as marked on pattern. Cut slits. Run a thong through the series of holes at the outside of the legs as shown. Knot ends close to fabric.

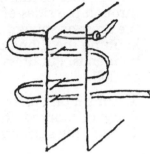

3. Run a shorter piece of thong through the top set of holes and tie the leggings on the belt as shown.

Shirt

1. Cut fringe all around shirt as indicated on pattern.

2. Glue cut out decorations to 1" x 6" decorative backings. Allow to dry. Glue to shirt as indicated on pattern.

3. Cut slits in shirt sides as marked. Run thong through the slits as shown. At the last hole at each end, tie a knot on the fabric.

4. Cut slits at shoulder of shirt, and shoulder and underarm of sleeves as marked. Run thong through the underarm slits as above, knotting the thong at both ends. Attach sleeve to shirt with a piece of thong, tying the thong in a knot at the shoulder as shown.

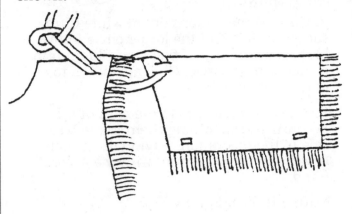

War Bonnet

1. Cut brim from sailor hat at bottom fold.

2. Dip top inch of feathers in black dye. Lay on waxed paper. Allow to dry.

3. Glue undyed short, soft feathers all around hat to cover.

4. Glue dyed feathers over fluffy feathers. Starting at the center top, glue one feather. Add one feather at one side and then the other, keeping the tips of the feathers even. The feathers at the center top of the hat will point straight back. Those toward the sides will point down farther. Stop adding feathers when you have about 2" left at the back.

5. Glue 2" x 10" piece of fabric to hat over feather tips, encasing the hat edges.

6. Glue decorations to decorative strip. Glue over Ultrasuede™ or felt as shown.

7. Cut two medallions out of white Ultrasuede™ or felt. Cut the larger circle from blue. Glue to back of first two. Glue star to center of front circle. Glue medallion to ends of decorative strip.

8. Add a few feathers to the ends of the decorative strip, gluing them to the back side of the medallion, having them point down, almost horizontal with the decorative band.

Native Indian Squaw

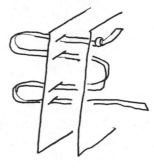

2. Cut slits on dress and on medallions as marked. Run thong through the dress and medallions as shown. Add three beads, one of each color. Knot ends of beads.

3. Cut slits along sides of dress as marked. Run a piece of thong through the sides of the dress as shown, knotting the thong at both ends. Put dress on doll.

4. Cut slit on either side of top back of shawl as marked. Run a piece of thong through the slits, put on the doll, and knot.

MATERIALS

One skein black yarn
Matching thread
3/8 yard double-sided suede, Ultrasuede™, or felt (see Sources)
Matching thread
6- x 9-mm pony beads: red, yellow, and turquoise
One feather

Headband

1. Cut headband into three strips, leaving 1/2" uncut at one end as shown. Braid. Tie a knot a few inches from the ends. Tack to doll's head as shown.

INSTRUCTIONS

Note: All seam allowances are 1/4" unless instructed otherwise.

As instructed in chapter 1 make patterns, cut and mark fabric. Cut two 3/8"-wide strips of fabric the width of the material. These will be used as thongs to hold the dress together. Cut headband 3/4" x 20".

Dress

1. Cut fringe all around dress and shawl as indicated on pattern.

2. Put feather into back of headband.

ALL OTHER DOLLS
Face diagram/stencils

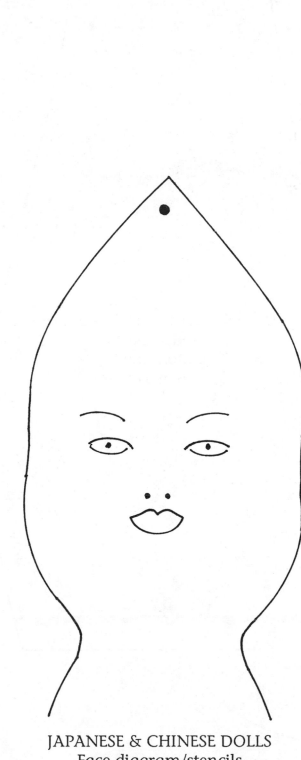

JAPANESE & CHINESE DOLLS
Face diagram/stencils

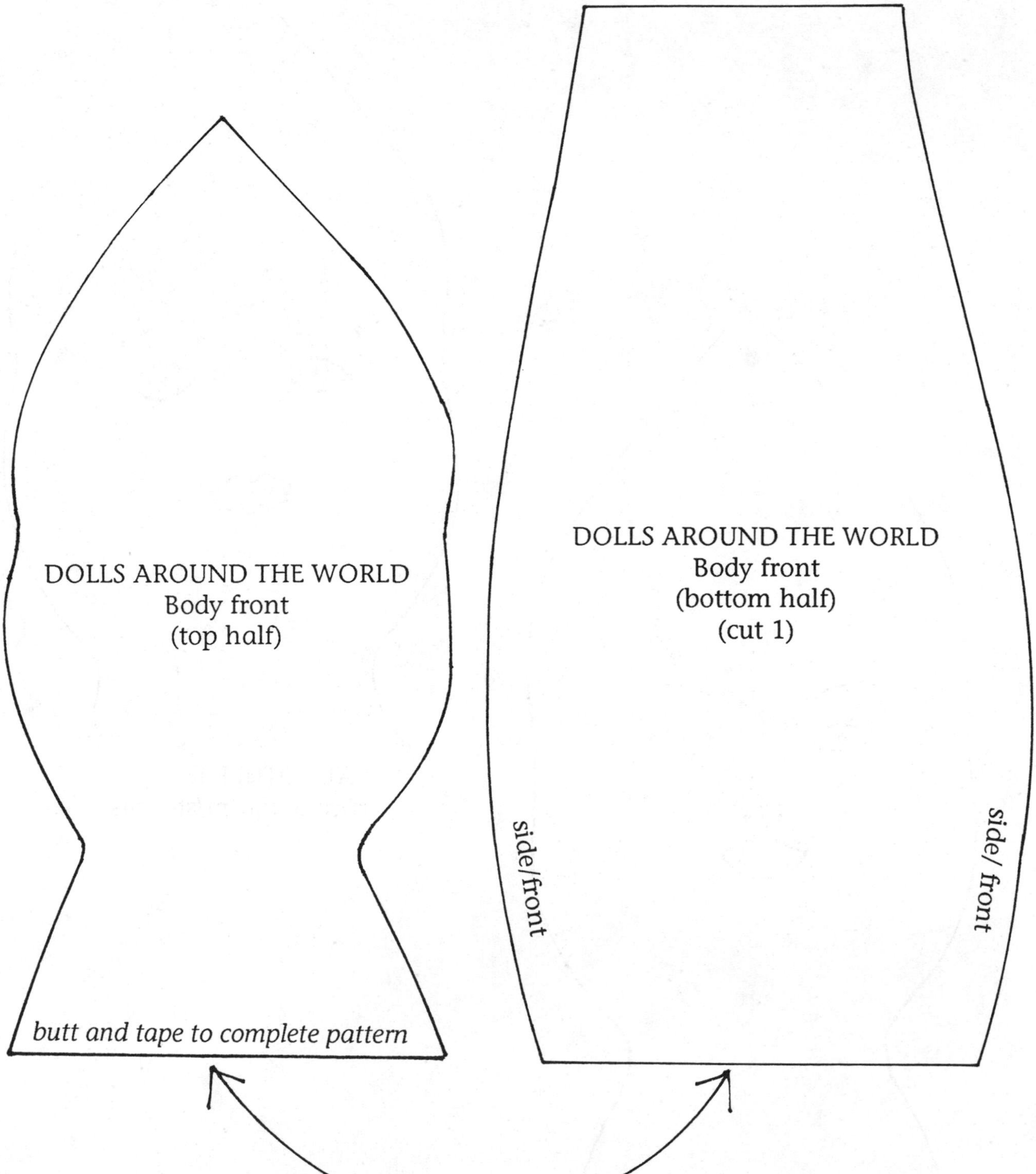

DOLLS AROUND THE WORLD
Body front
(top half)

DOLLS AROUND THE WORLD
Body front
(bottom half)
(cut 1)

side/front

side/front

butt and tape to complete pattern

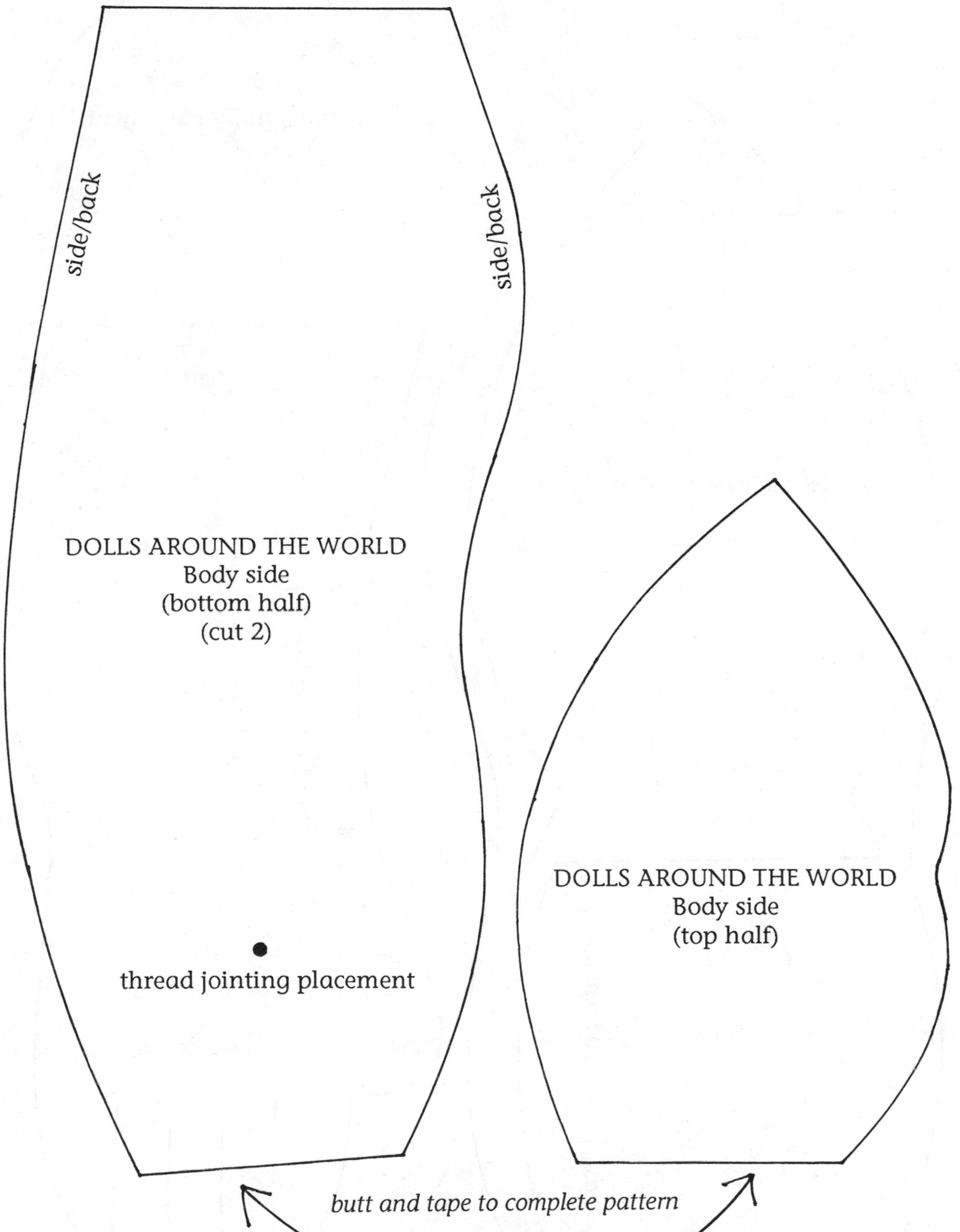

side/back

side/back

DOLLS AROUND THE WORLD
Body side
(bottom half)
(cut 2)

DOLLS AROUND THE WORLD
Body side
(top half)

thread jointing placement

butt and tape to complete pattern

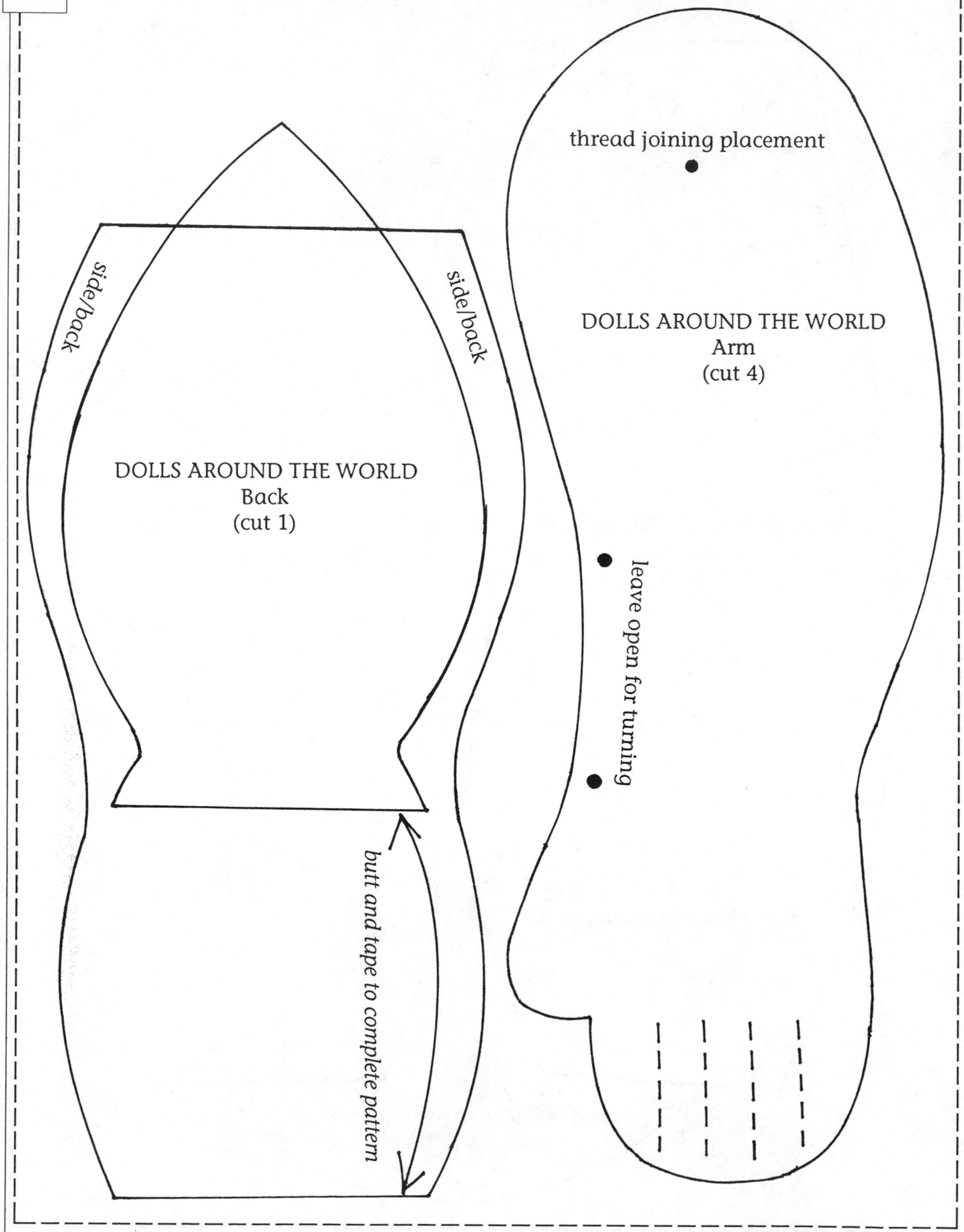

thread joining placement

DOLLS AROUND THE WORLD
Arm
(cut 4)

leave open for turning

side/back

side/back

DOLLS AROUND THE WORLD
Back
(cut 1)

butt and tape to complete pattern

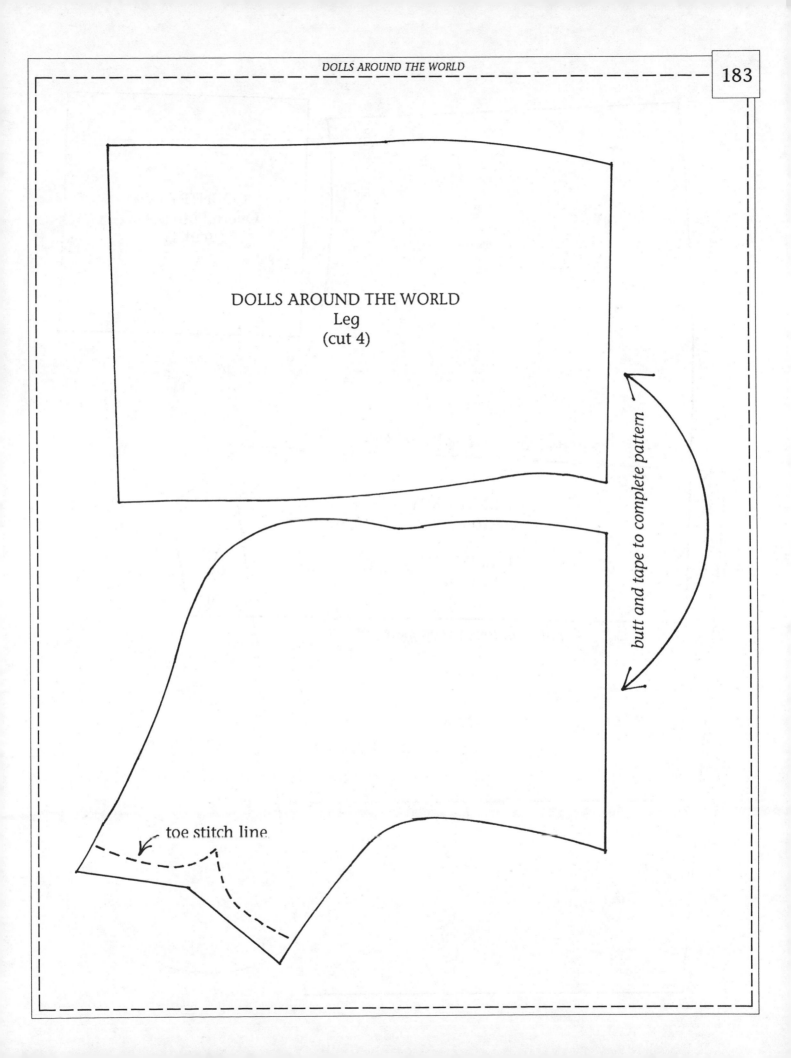

DOLLS AROUND THE WORLD
Leg
(cut 4)

butt and tape to complete pattern

toe stitch line

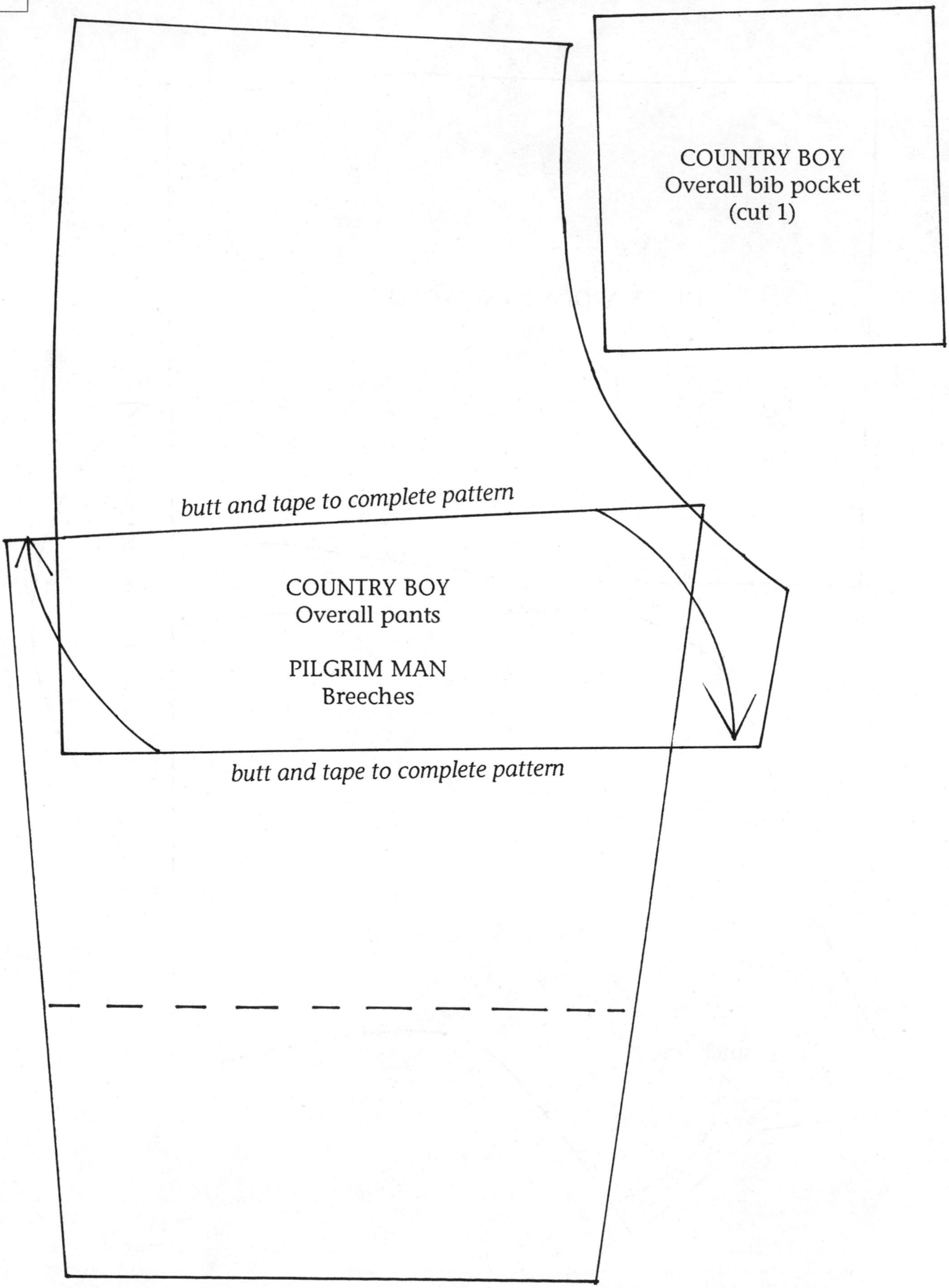

COUNTRY BOY
Overall bib pocket
(cut 1)

butt and tape to complete pattern

COUNTRY BOY
Overall pants

PILGRIM MAN
Breeches

butt and tape to complete pattern

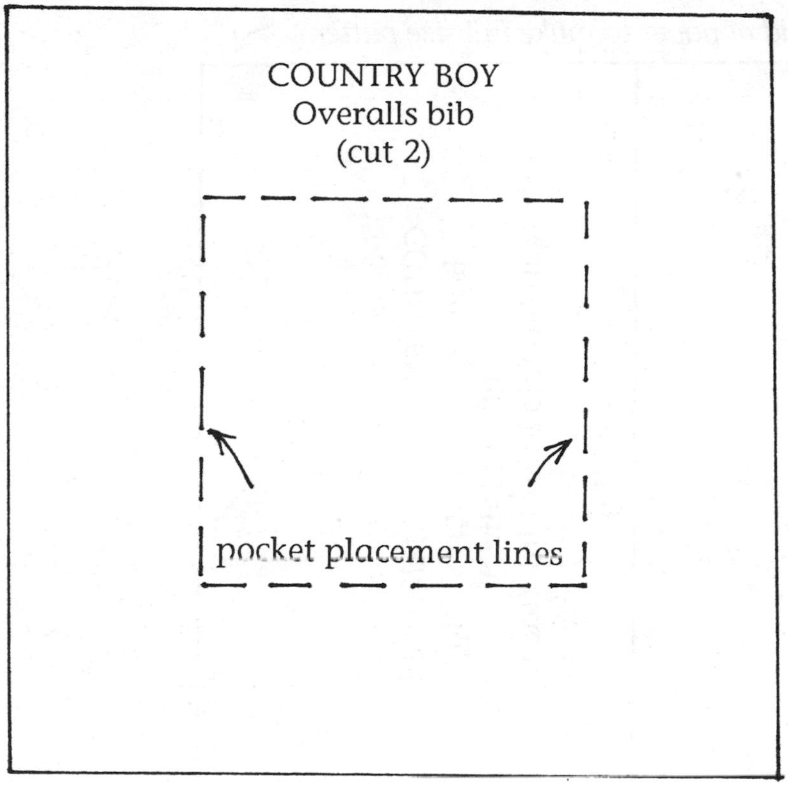

COUNTRY BOY
Overalls bib
(cut 2)

pocket placement lines

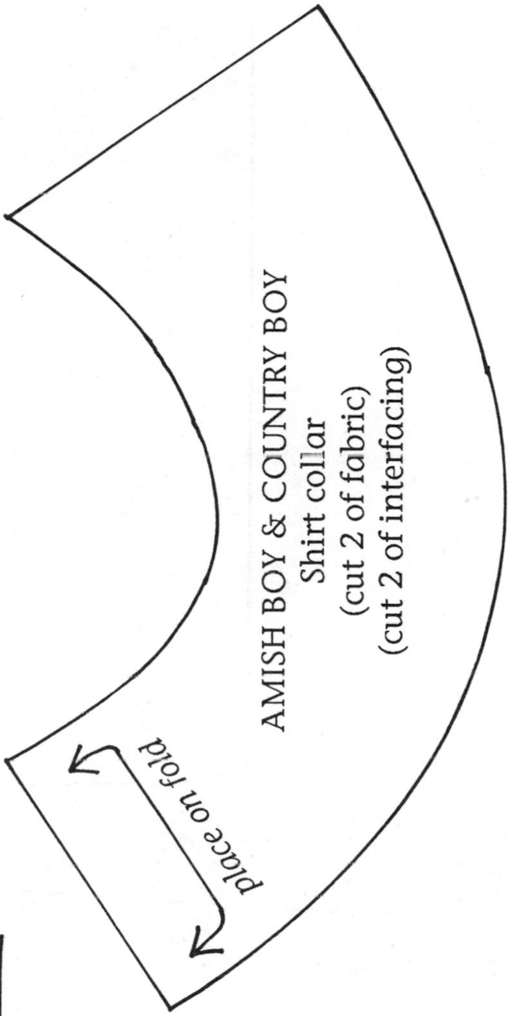

AMISH BOY & COUNTRY BOY
Shirt collar
(cut 2 of fabric)
(cut 2 of interfacing)

place on fold

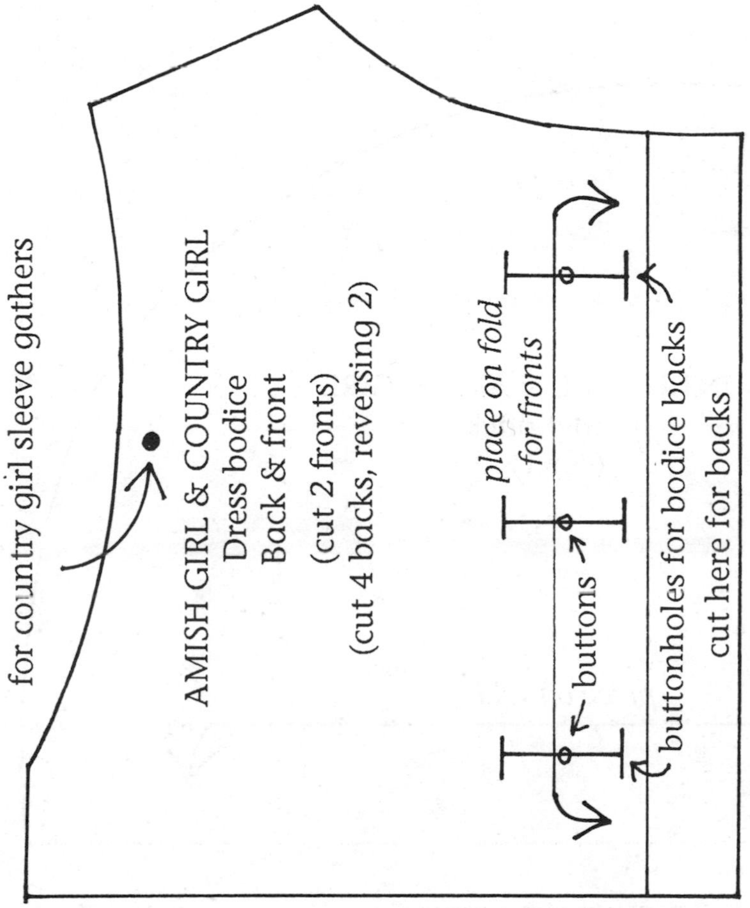

for country girl sleeve gathers

AMISH GIRL & COUNTRY GIRL
Dress bodice
Back & front
(cut 2 fronts)
(cut 4 backs, reversing 2)

place on fold
for fronts

buttons

buttonholes for bodice backs
cut here for backs

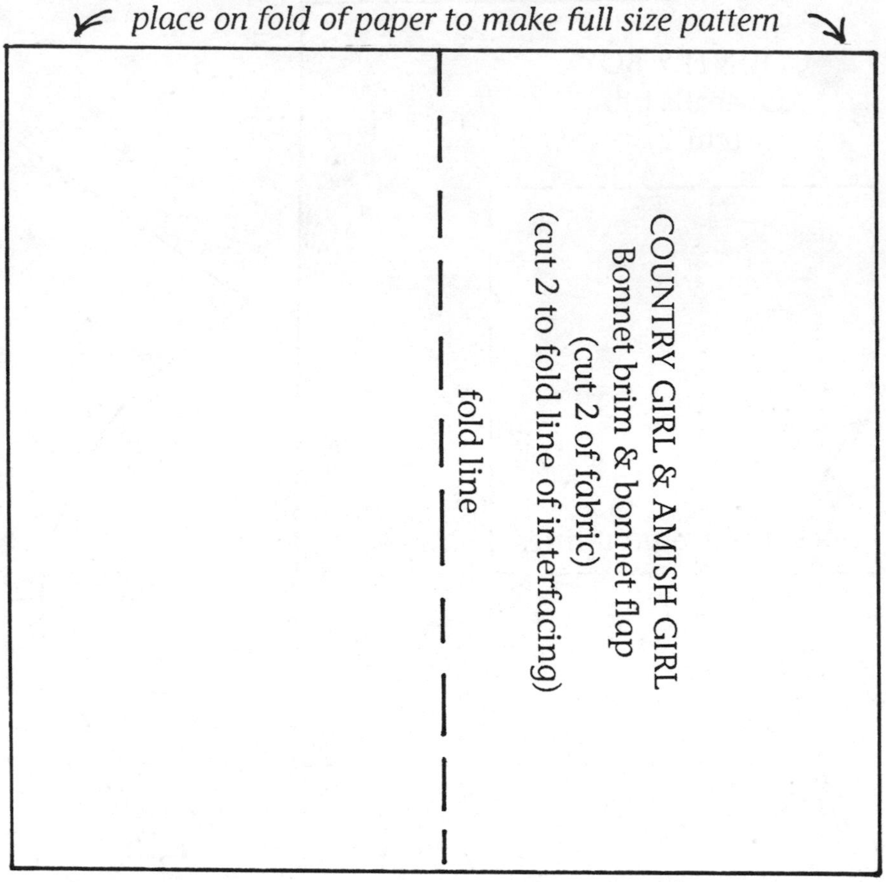

place on fold of paper to make full size pattern

COUNTRY GIRL & AMISH GIRL
Bonnet brim & bonnet flap
(cut 2 of fabric)
(cut 2 to fold line of interfacing)

fold line

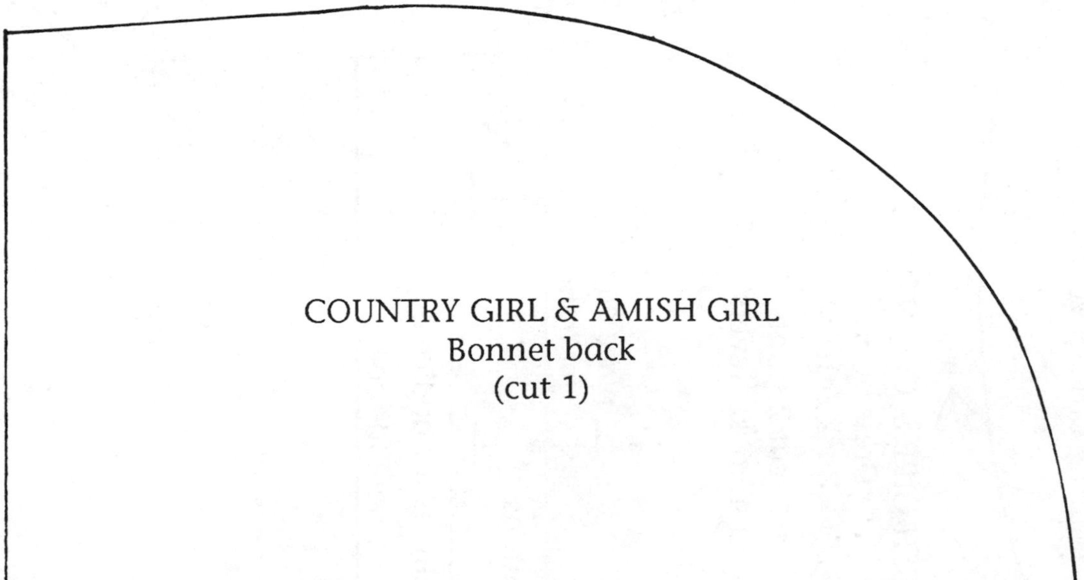

COUNTRY GIRL & AMISH GIRL
Bonnet back
(cut 1)

place on fold

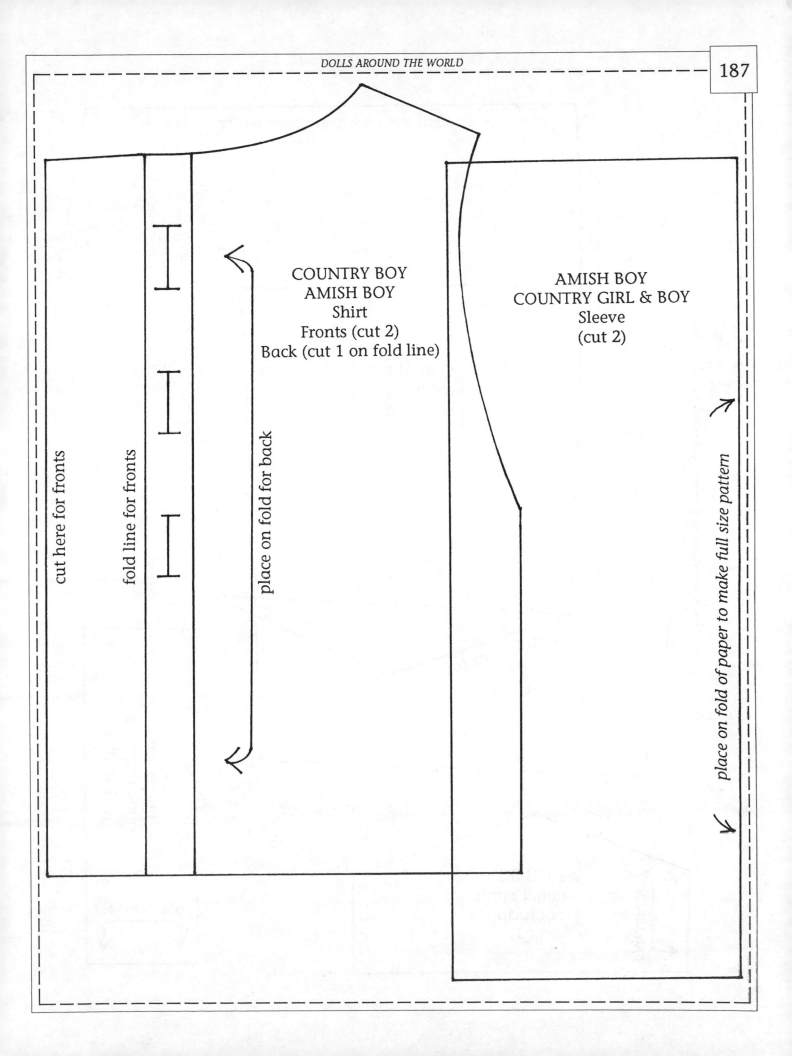

cut here for fronts

fold line for fronts

place on fold for back

COUNTRY BOY
AMISH BOY
Shirt
Fronts (cut 2)
Back (cut 1 on fold line)

AMISH BOY
COUNTRY GIRL & BOY
Sleeve
(cut 2)

place on fold of paper to make full size pattern

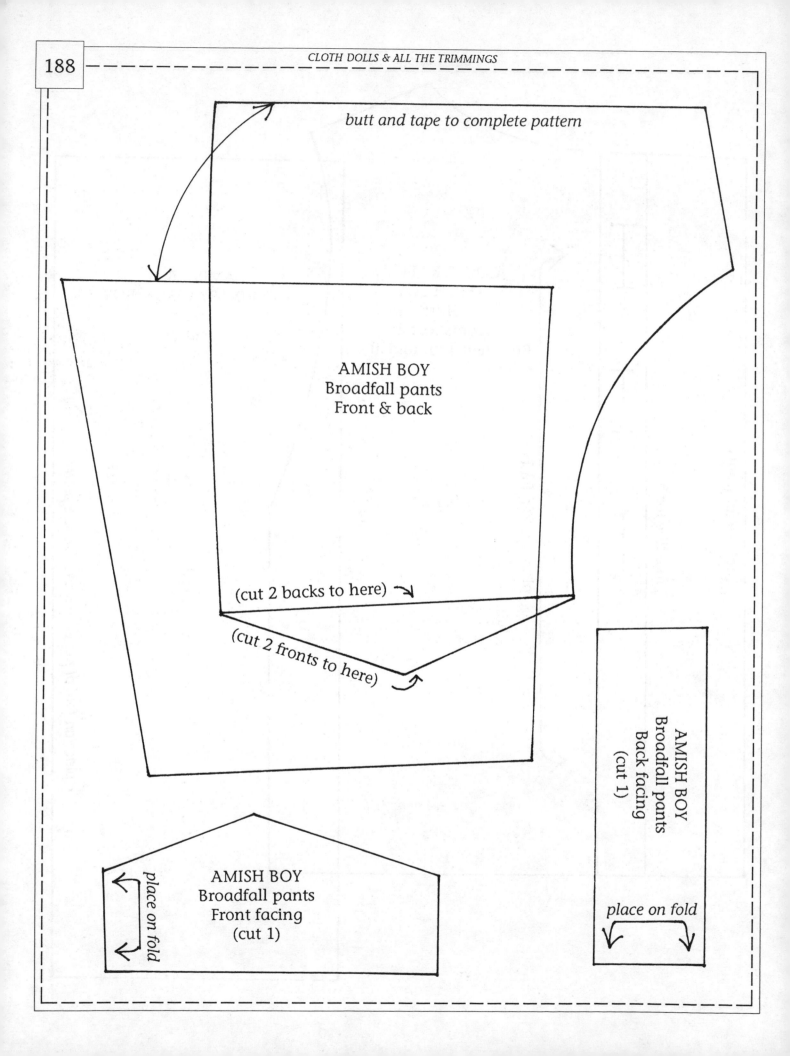

butt and tape to complete pattern

AMISH BOY
Broadfall pants
Front & back

(cut 2 backs to here)

(cut 2 fronts to here)

AMISH BOY
Broadfall pants
Back facing
(cut 1)

place on fold

AMISH BOY
Broadfall pants
Front facing
(cut 1)

place on fold

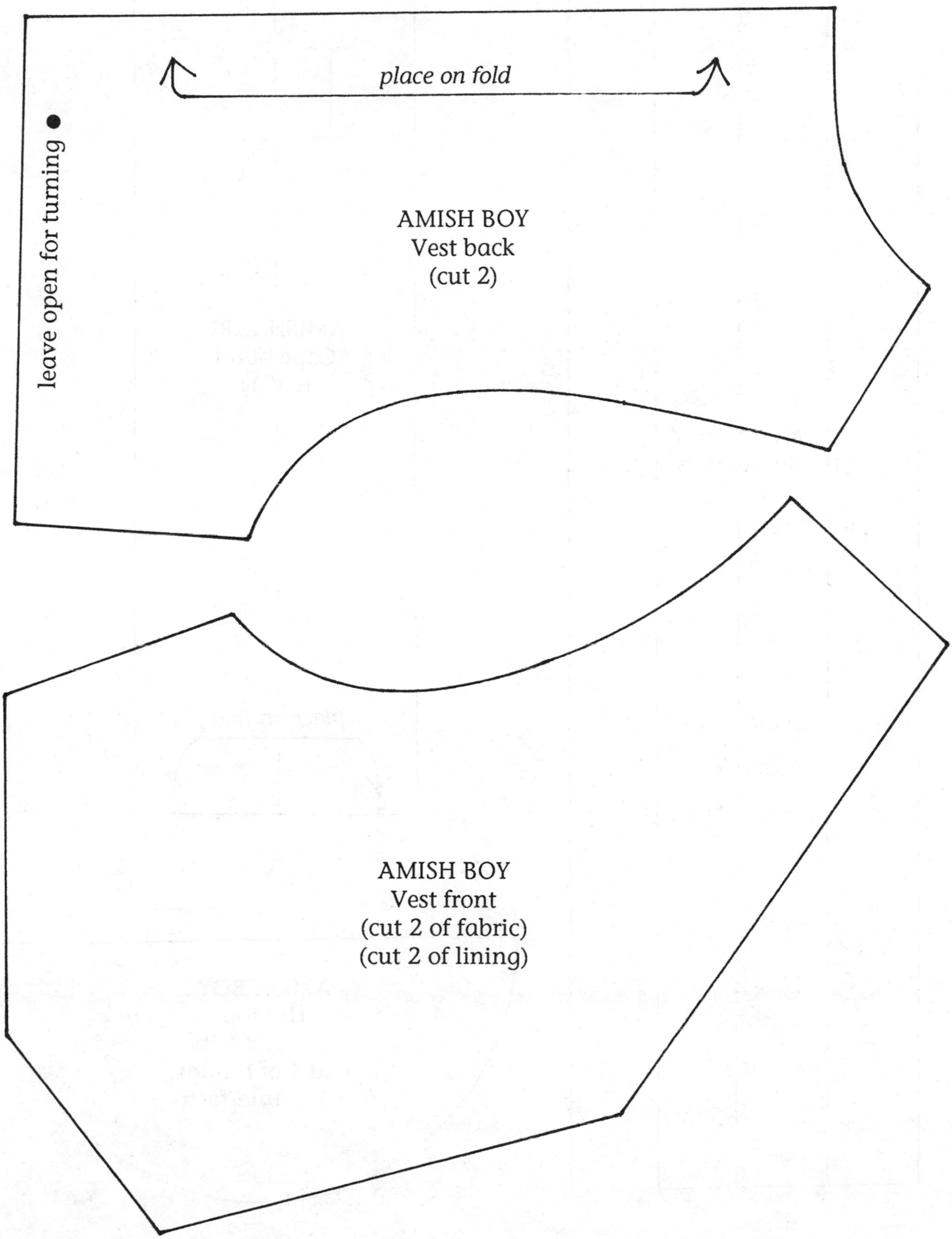

place on fold

leave open for turning

AMISH BOY
Vest back
(cut 2)

AMISH BOY
Vest front
(cut 2 of fabric)
(cut 2 of lining)

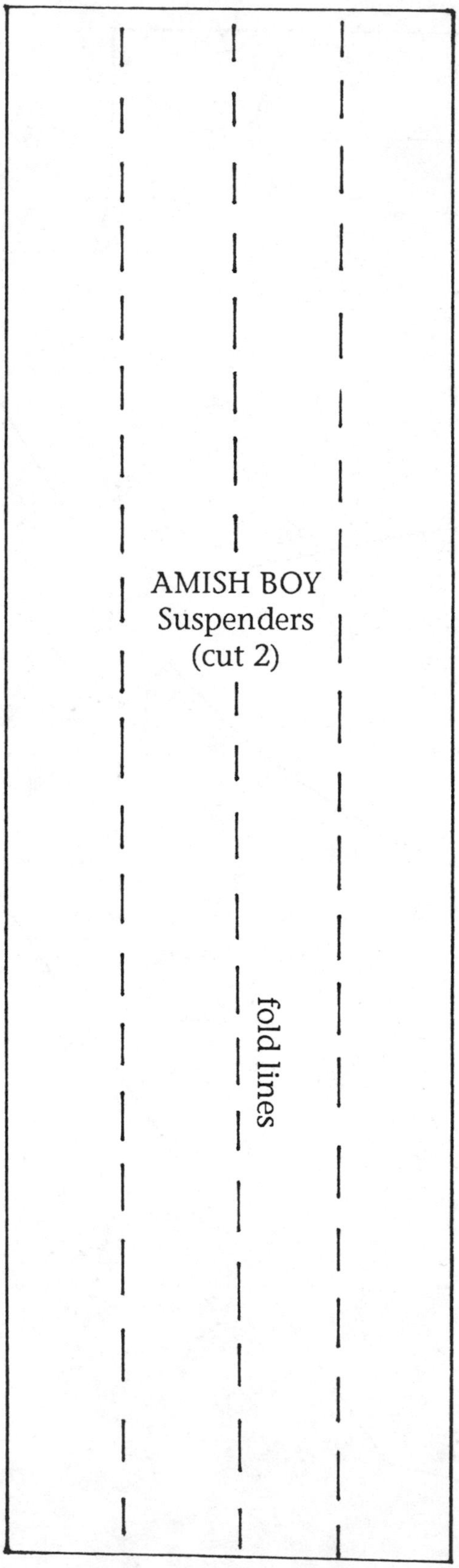

AMISH BOY
Suspenders
(cut 2)

fold lines

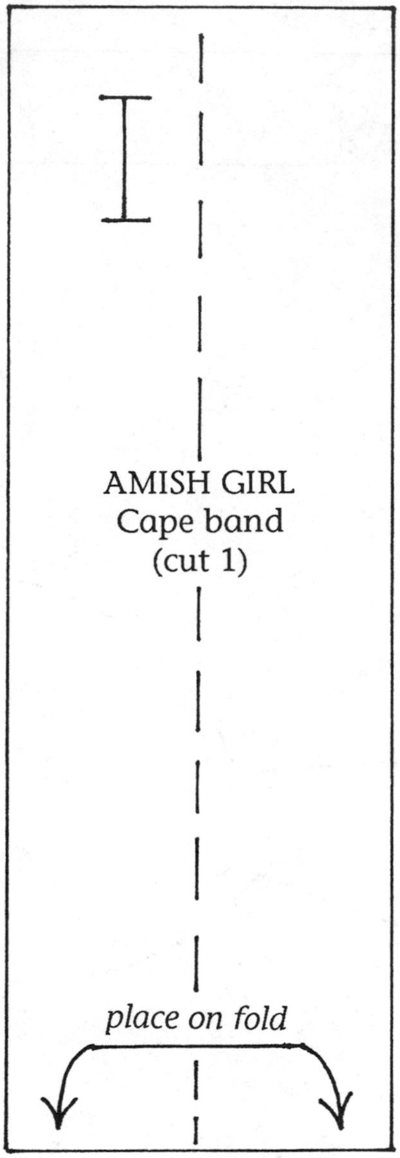

AMISH GIRL
Cape band
(cut 1)

place on fold

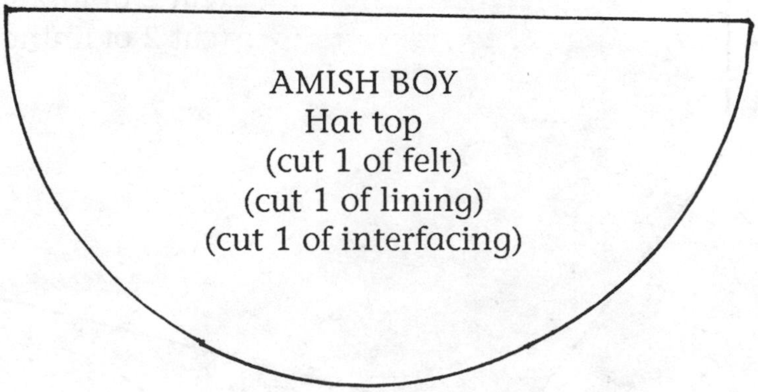

AMISH BOY
Hat top
(cut 1 of felt)
(cut 1 of lining)
(cut 1 of interfacing)

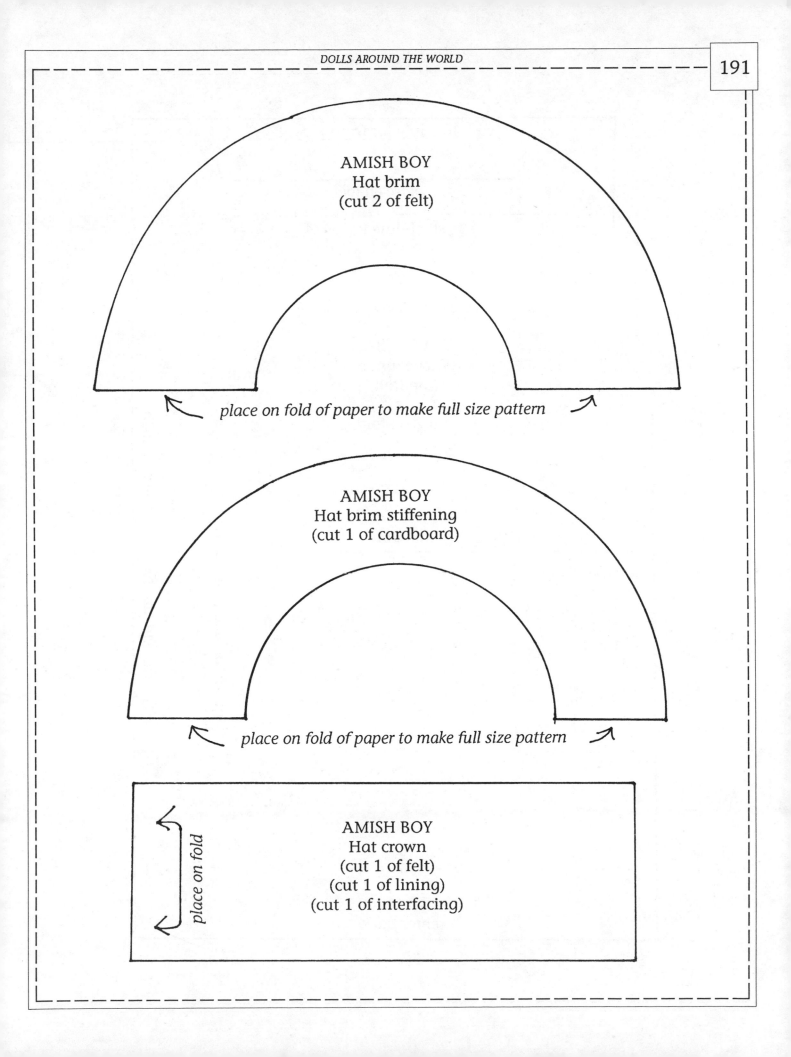

AMISH BOY
Hat brim
(cut 2 of felt)

place on fold of paper to make full size pattern

AMISH BOY
Hat brim stiffening
(cut 1 of cardboard)

place on fold of paper to make full size pattern

AMISH BOY
Hat crown
(cut 1 of felt)
(cut 1 of lining)
(cut 1 of interfacing)

place on fold

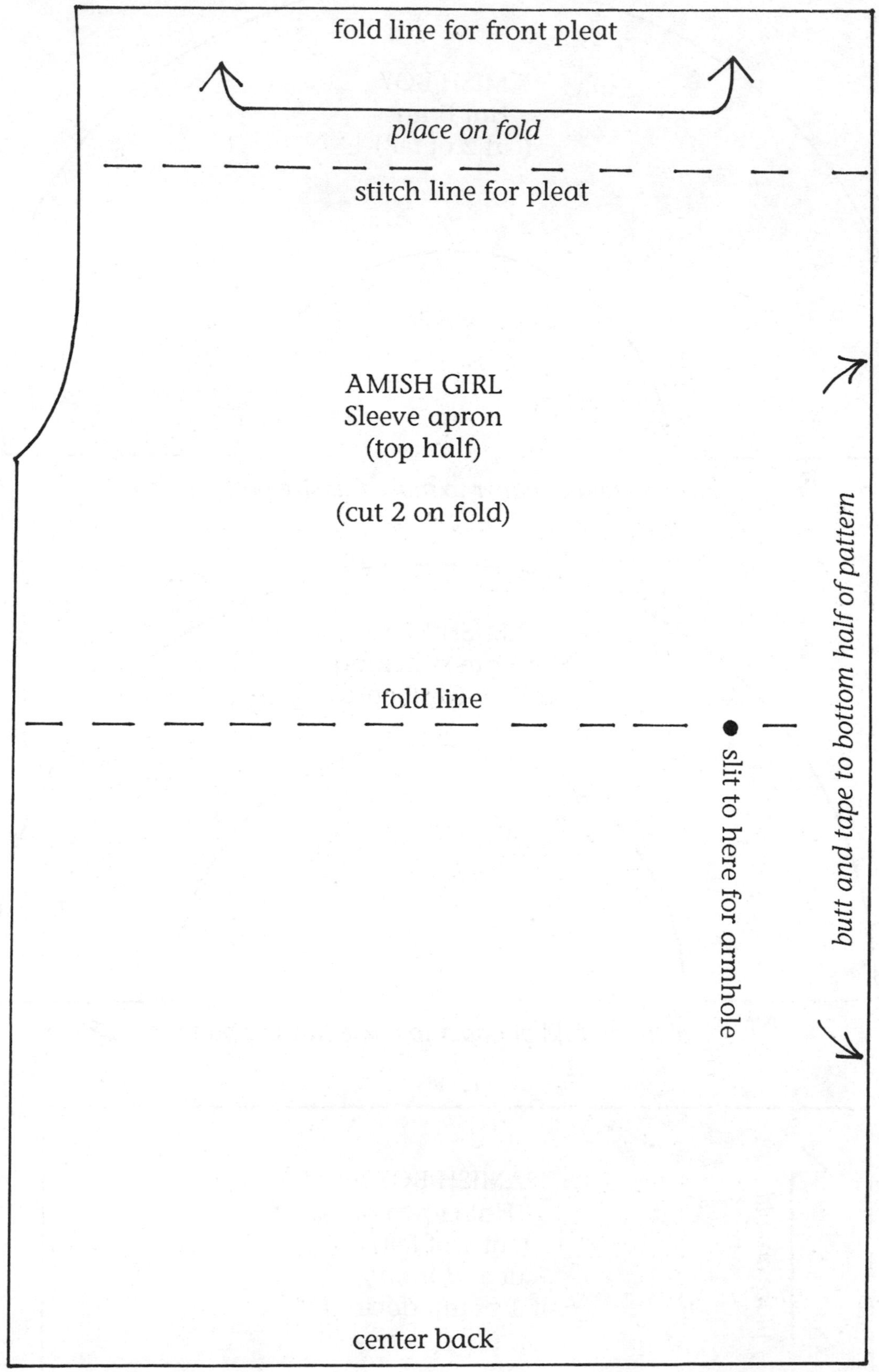

fold line for front pleat

place on fold

stitch line for pleat

AMISH GIRL
Sleeve apron
(top half)

(cut 2 on fold)

fold line

● slit to here for armhole

butt and tape to bottom half of pattern

center back

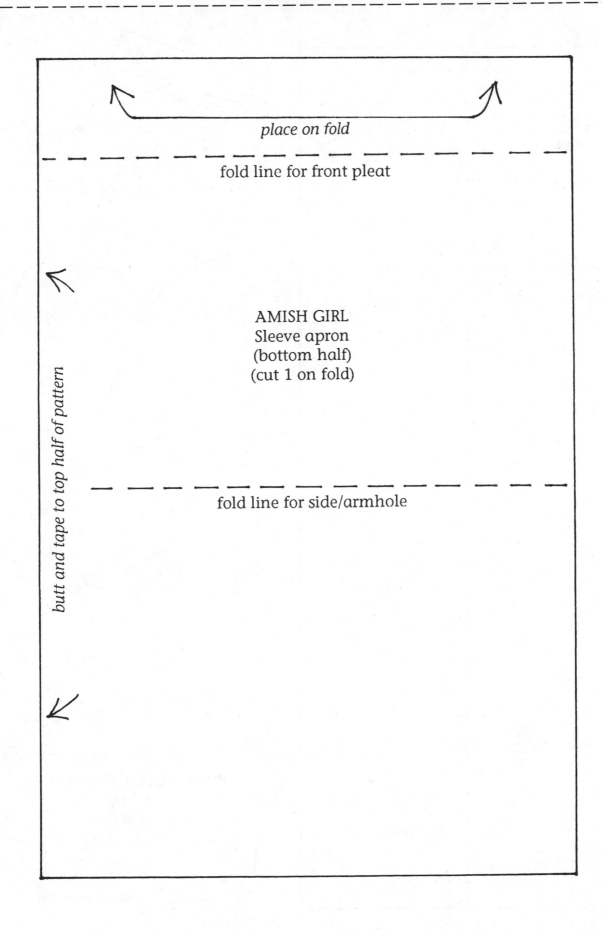

place on fold

fold line for front pleat

butt and tape to top half of pattern

AMISH GIRL
Sleeve apron
(bottom half)
(cut 1 on fold)

fold line for side/armhole

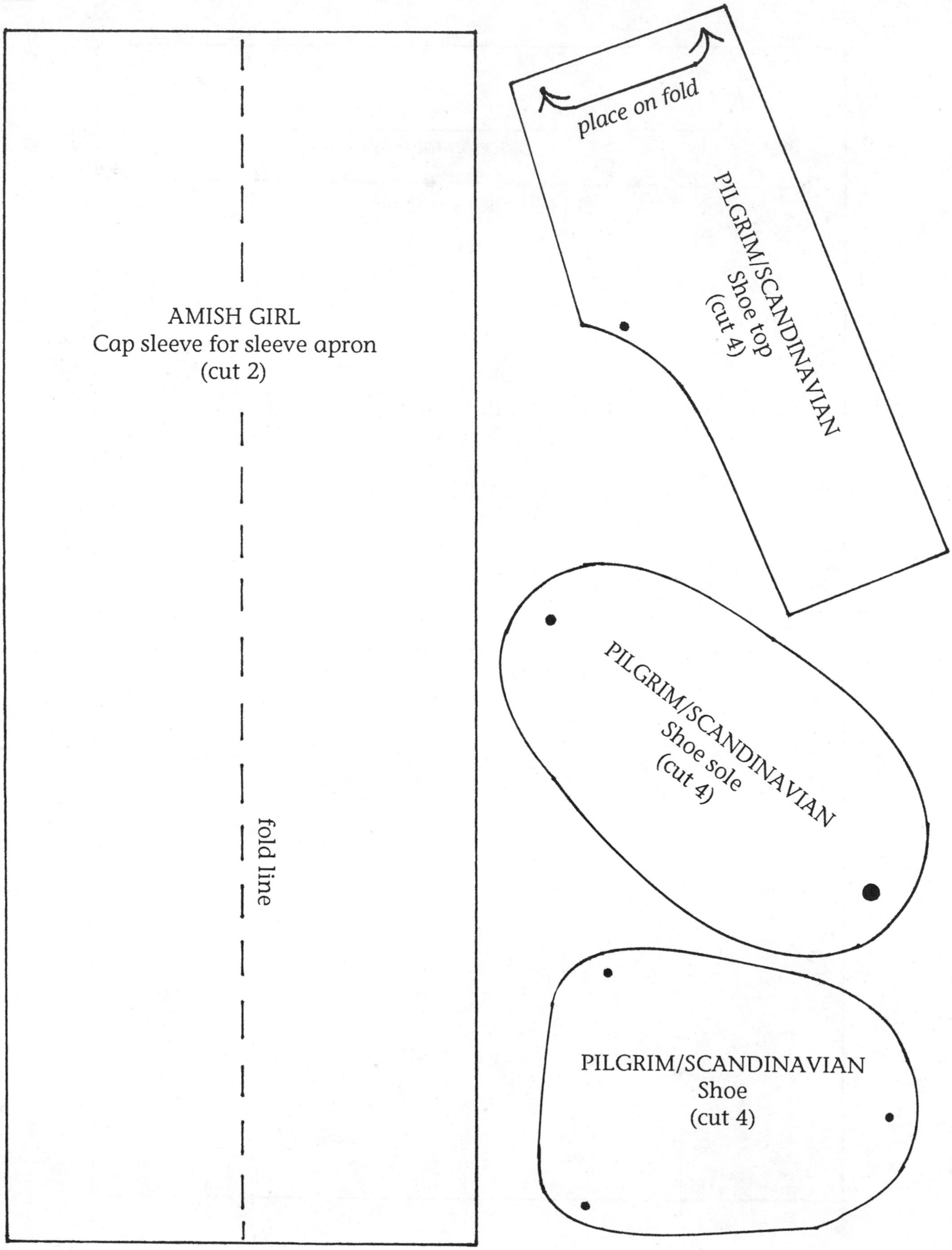

AMISH GIRL
Cap sleeve for sleeve apron
(cut 2)

fold line

place on fold

PILGRIM/SCANDINAVIAN
Shoe top
(cut 4)

PILGRIM/SCANDINAVIAN
Shoe sole
(cut 4)

PILGRIM/SCANDINAVIAN
Shoe
(cut 4)

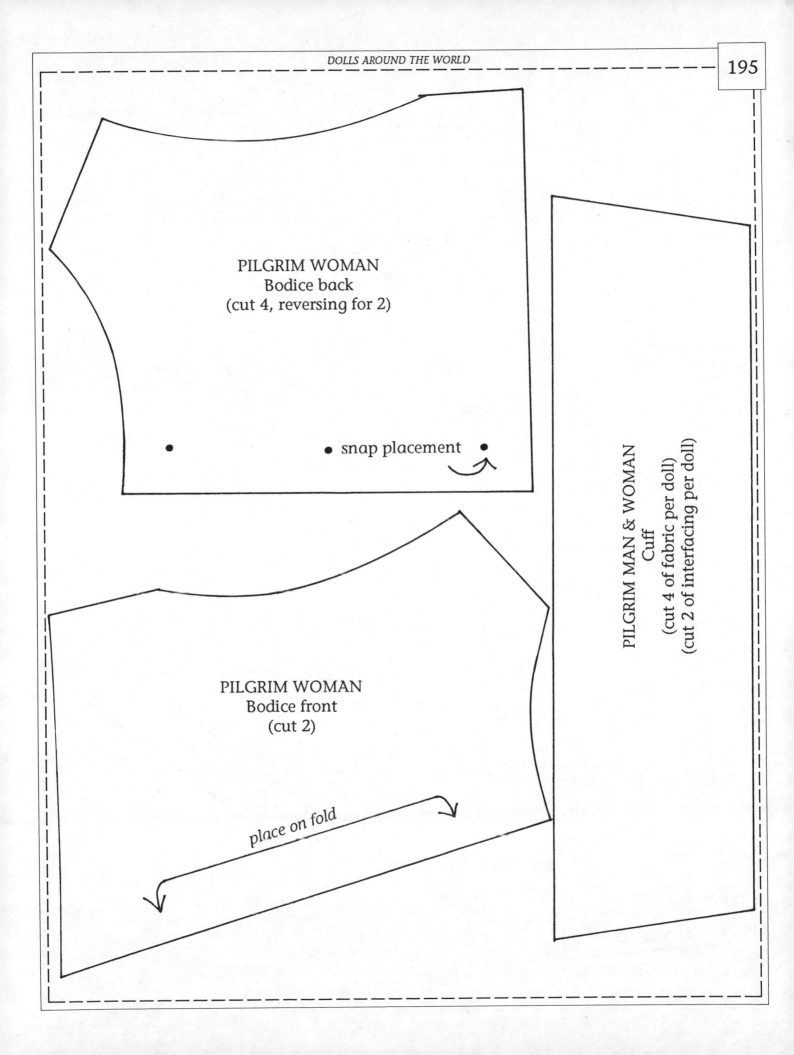

PILGRIM WOMAN
Bodice back
(cut 4, reversing for 2)

● snap placement

PILGRIM WOMAN
Bodice front
(cut 2)

place on fold

PILGRIM MAN & WOMAN
Cuff
(cut 4 of fabric per doll)
(cut 2 of interfacing per doll)

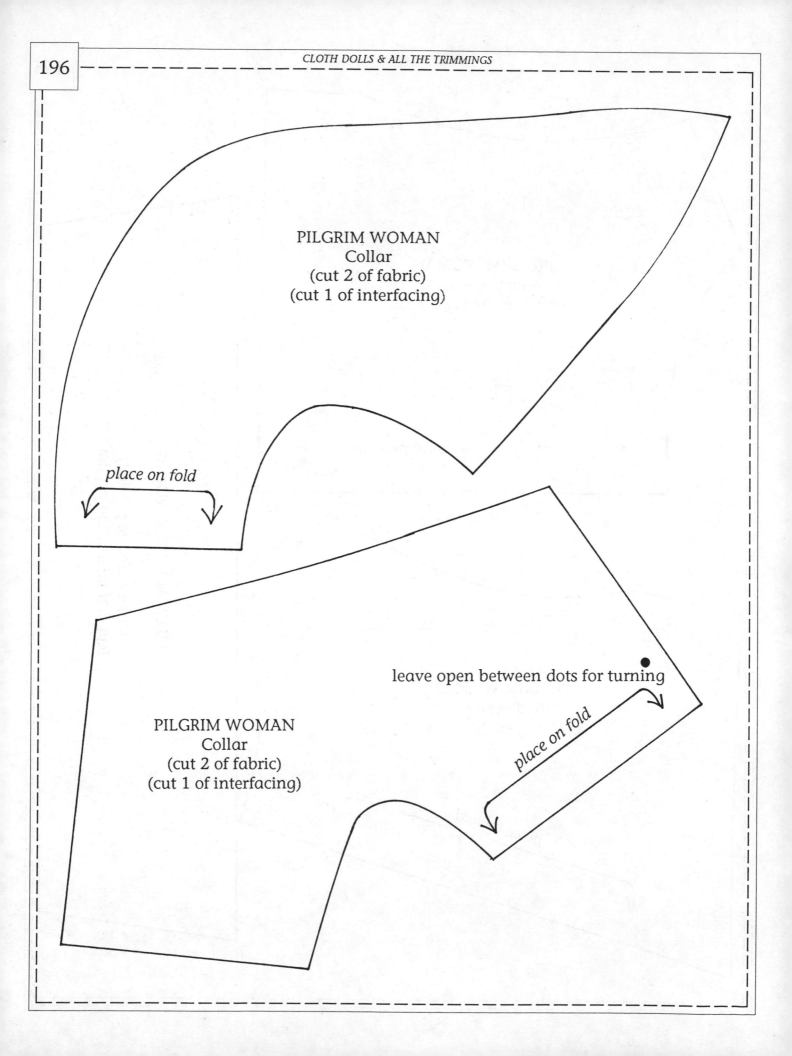

PILGRIM WOMAN
Collar
(cut 2 of fabric)
(cut 1 of interfacing)

place on fold

PILGRIM WOMAN
Collar
(cut 2 of fabric)
(cut 1 of interfacing)

leave open between dots for turning

place on fold

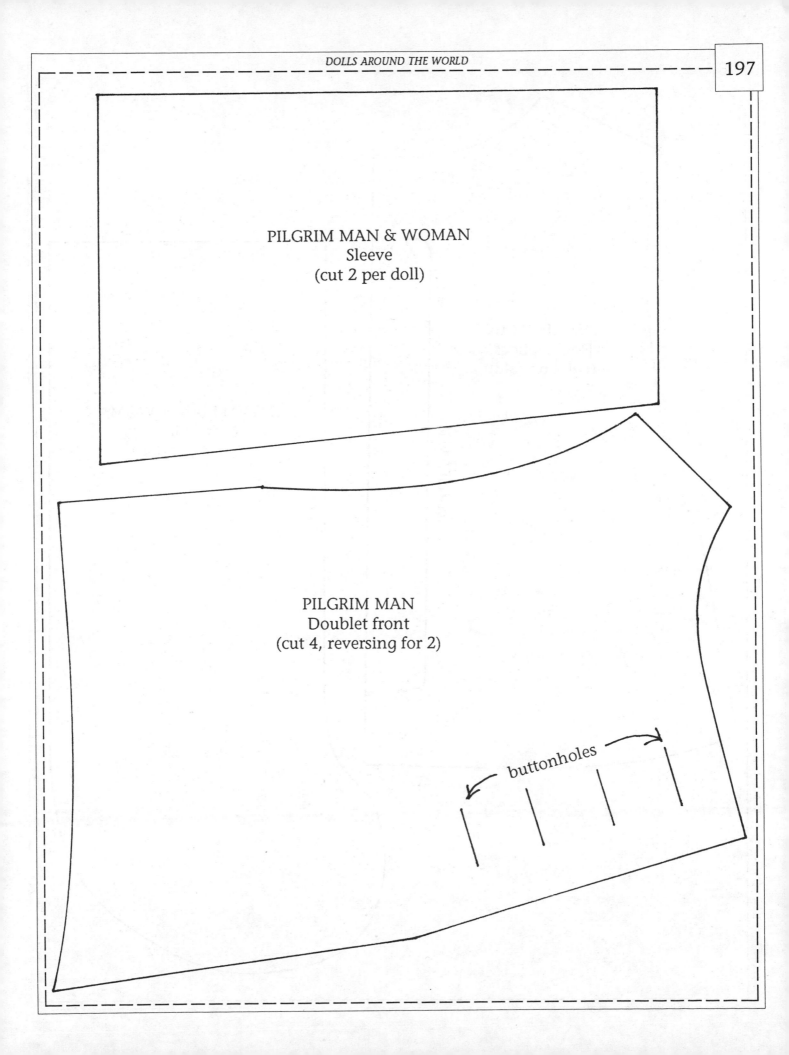

PILGRIM MAN & WOMAN
Sleeve
(cut 2 per doll)

PILGRIM MAN
Doublet front
(cut 4, reversing for 2)

buttonholes

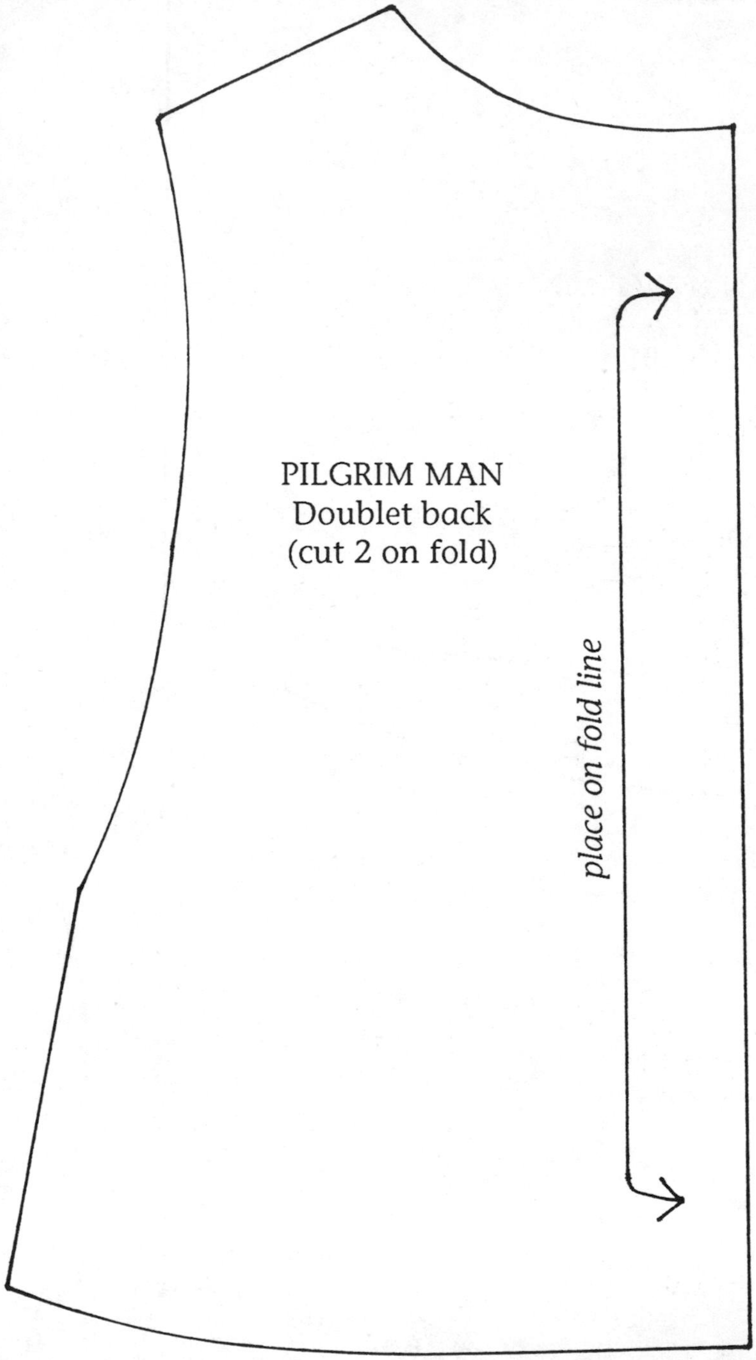

PILGRIM MAN
Doublet back
(cut 2 on fold)

place on fold line

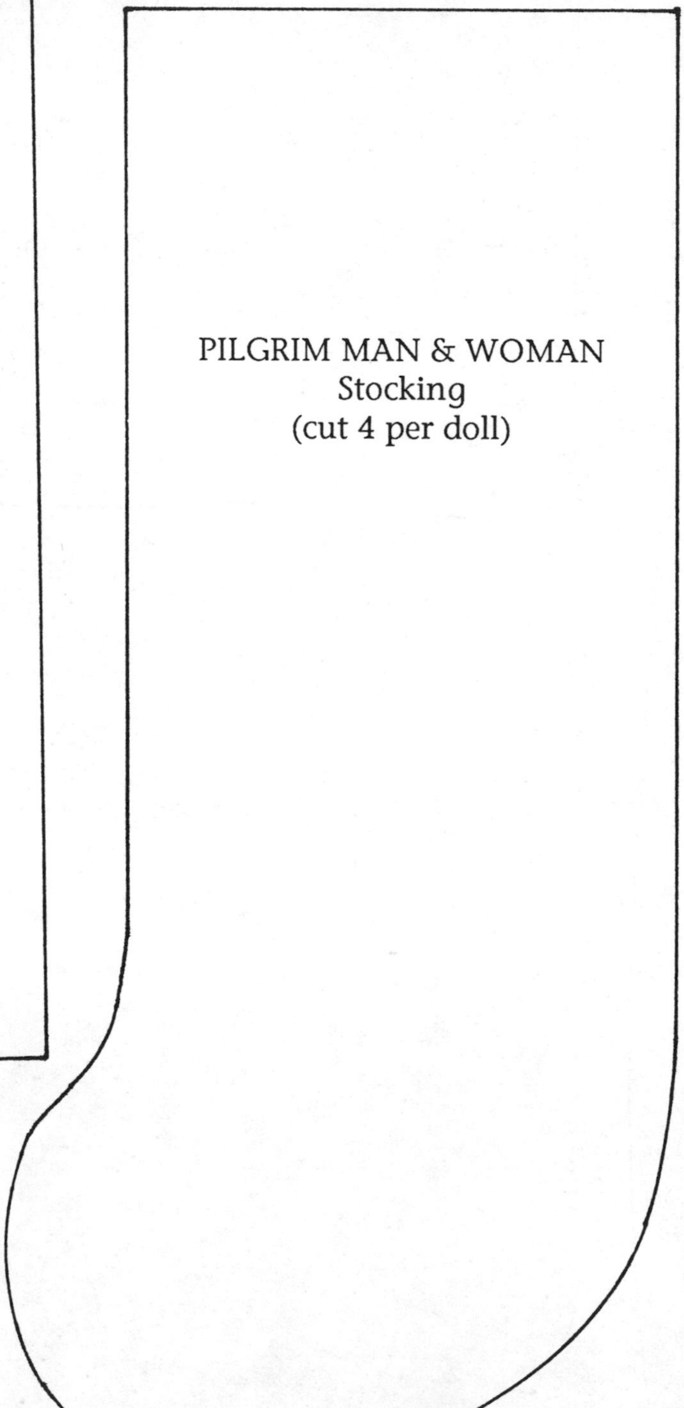

PILGRIM MAN & WOMAN
Stocking
(cut 4 per doll)

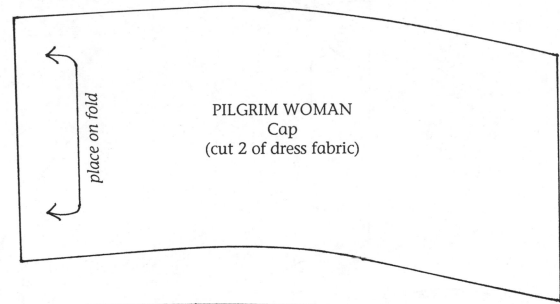

place on fold

PILGRIM WOMAN
Cap
(cut 2 of dress fabric)

stitch line

fold line

dart

front edge

bottom edge

PILGRIM WOMAN
Cap contrast
(cut 2 of white fabric)
(cut 1 of interfacing)

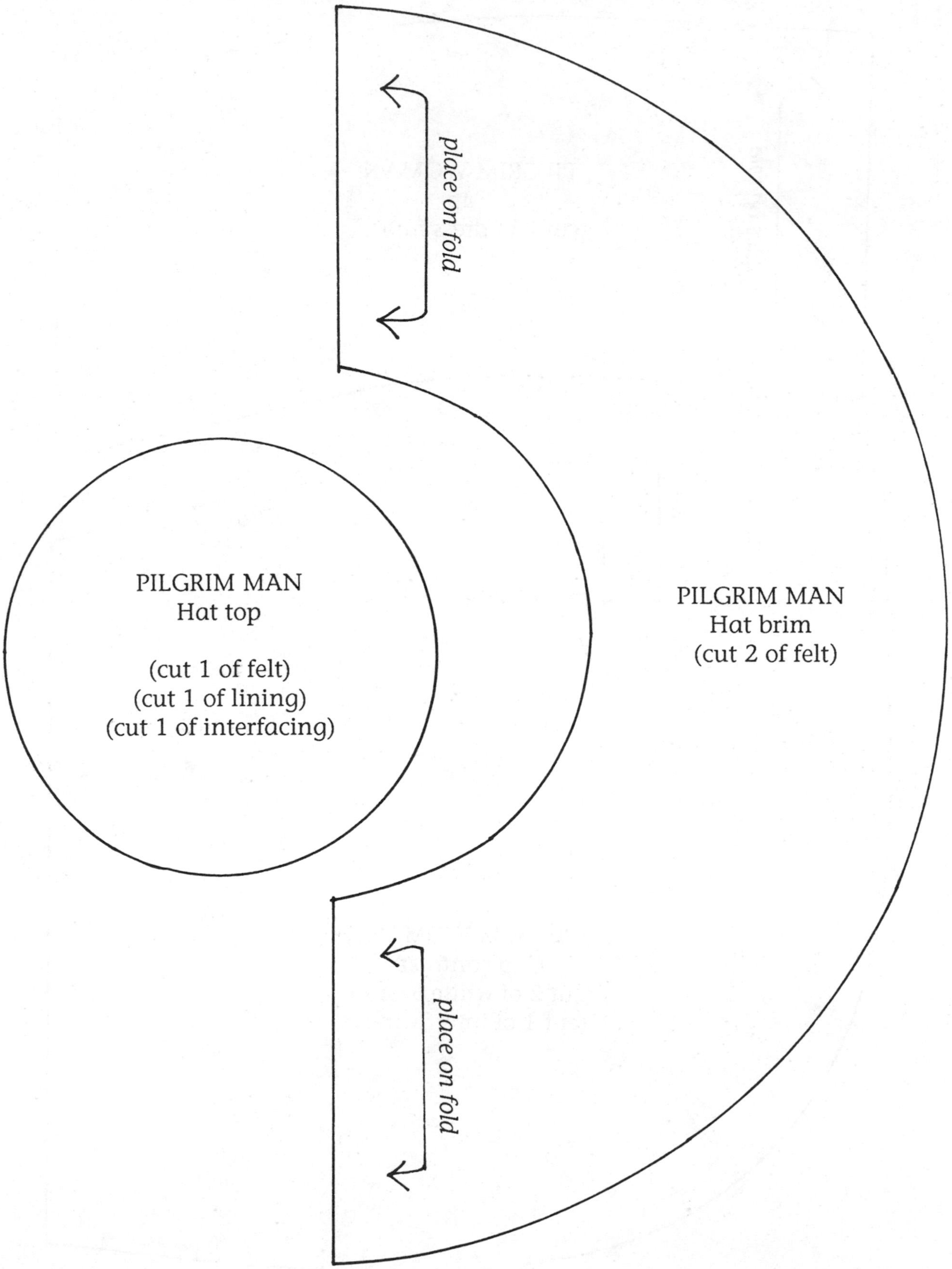

place on fold

PILGRIM MAN
Hat top

(cut 1 of felt)
(cut 1 of lining)
(cut 1 of interfacing)

PILGRIM MAN
Hat brim
(cut 2 of felt)

place on fold

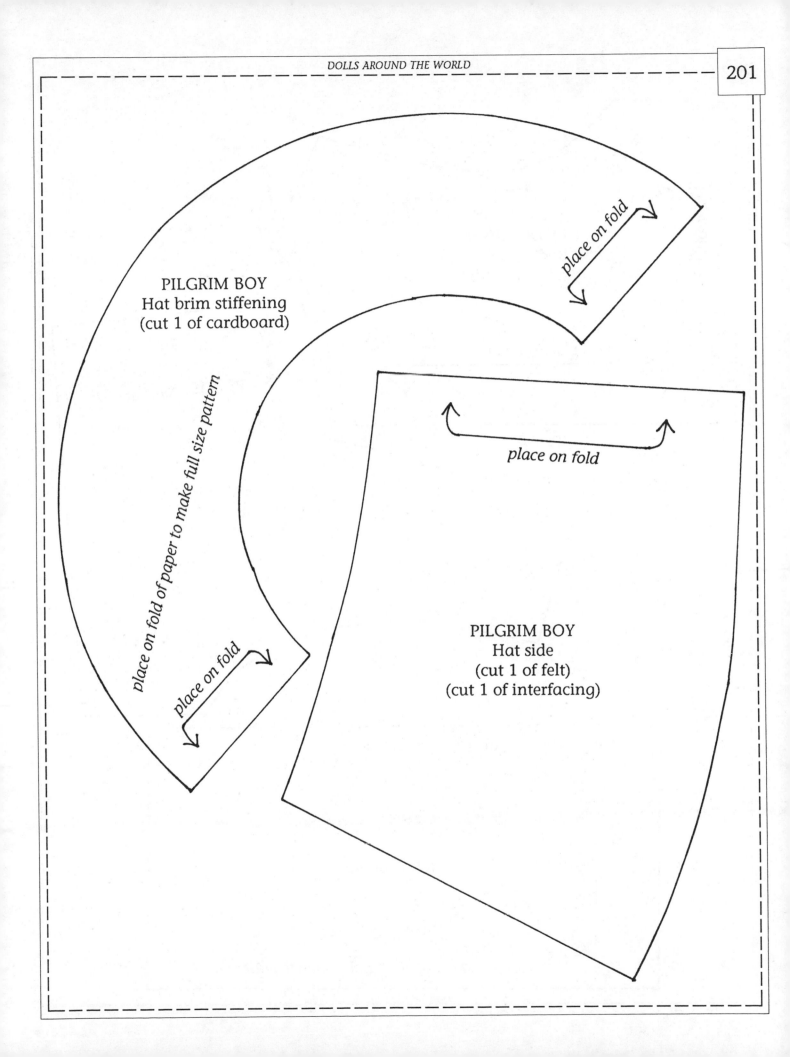

PILGRIM BOY
Hat brim stiffening
(cut 1 of cardboard)

place on fold of paper to make full size pattern

place on fold

place on fold

place on fold

PILGRIM BOY
Hat side
(cut 1 of felt)
(cut 1 of interfacing)

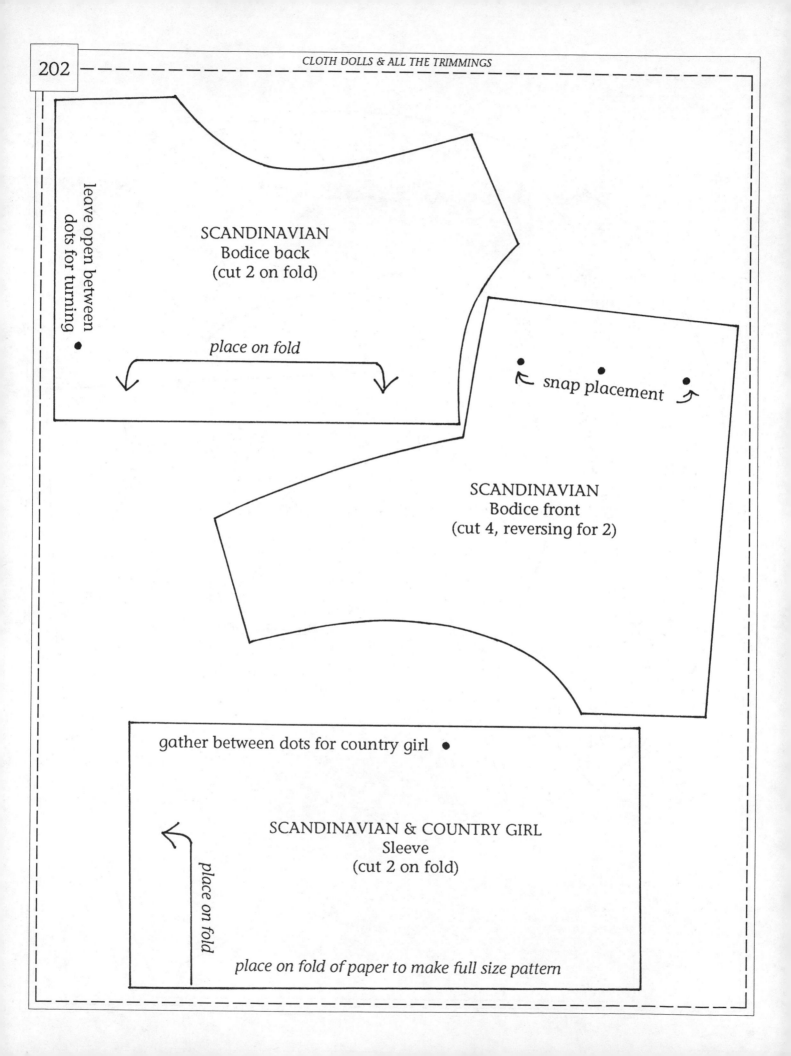

leave open between
dots for turning

SCANDINAVIAN
Bodice back
(cut 2 on fold)

place on fold

snap placement

SCANDINAVIAN
Bodice front
(cut 4, reversing for 2)

gather between dots for country girl ●

SCANDINAVIAN & COUNTRY GIRL
Sleeve
(cut 2 on fold)

place on fold

place on fold of paper to make full size pattern

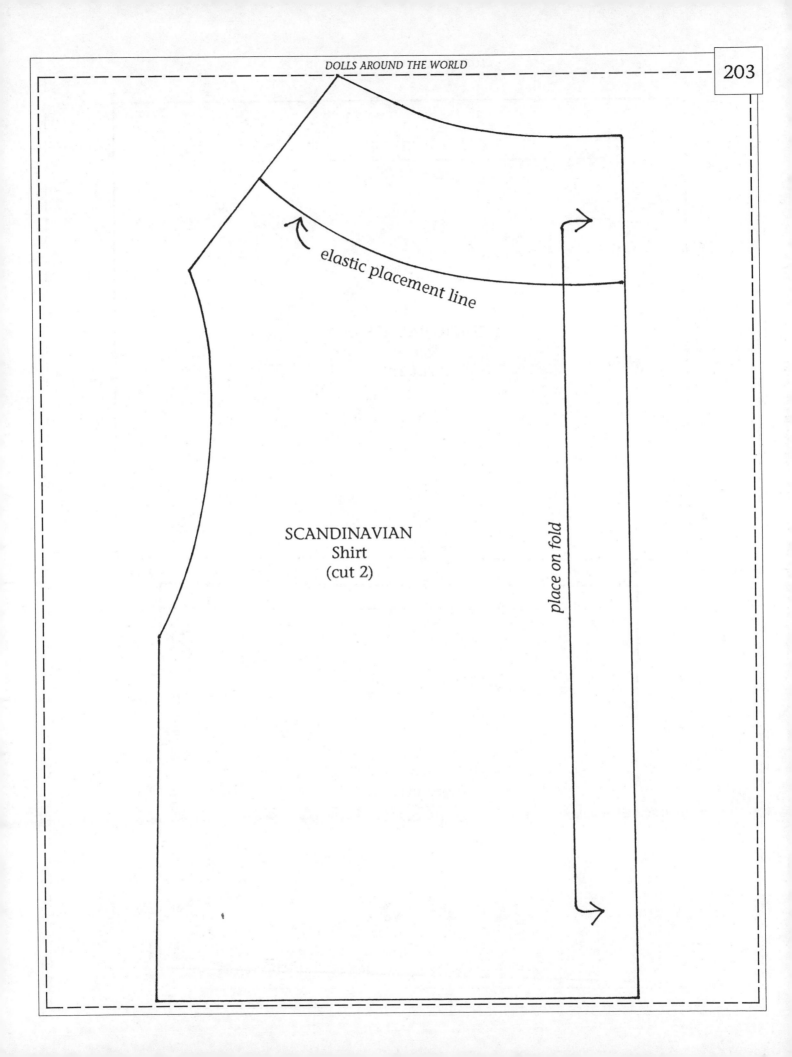

elastic placement line

SCANDINAVIAN
Shirt
(cut 2)

place on fold

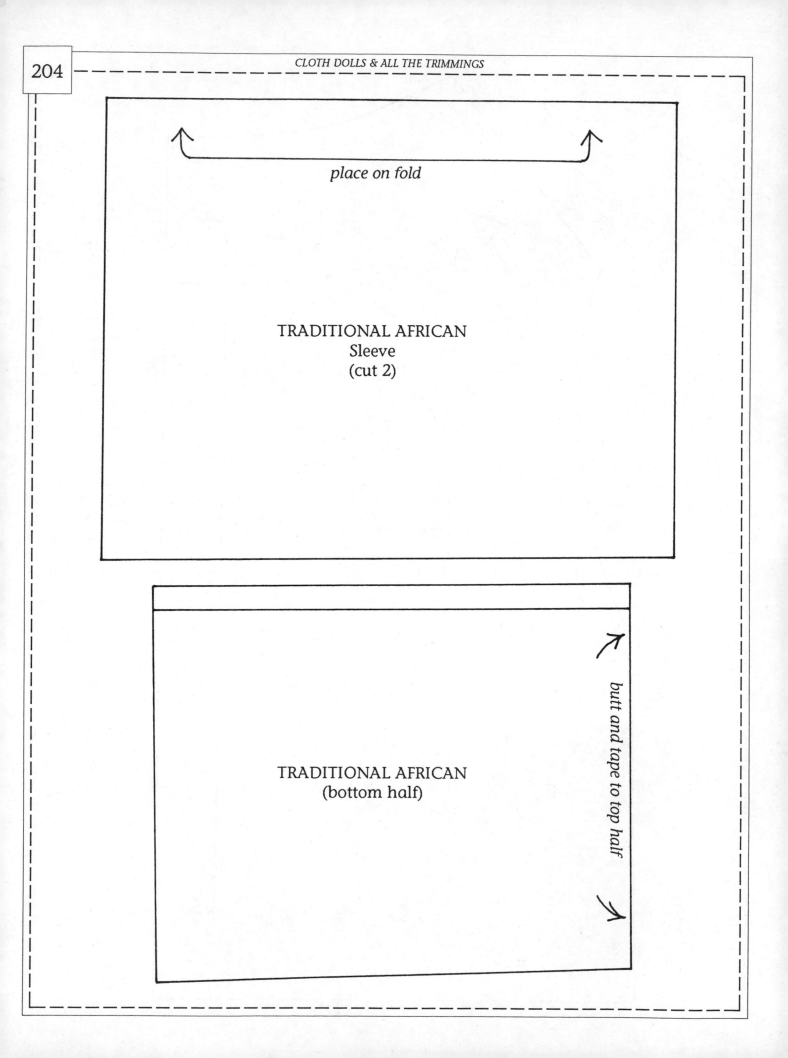

place on fold

TRADITIONAL AFRICAN
Sleeve
(cut 2)

TRADITIONAL AFRICAN
(bottom half)

butt and tape to top half

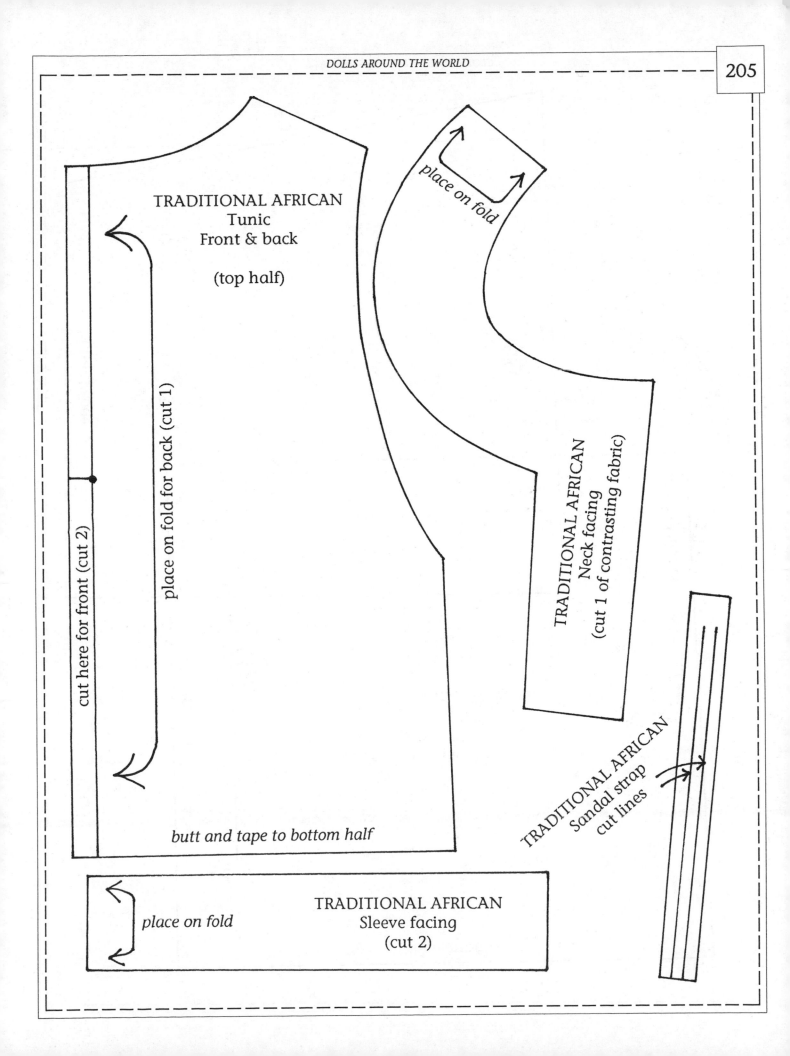

TRADITIONAL AFRICAN
Tunic
Front & back

(top half)

place on fold for back (cut 1)

cut here for front (cut 2)

butt and tape to bottom half

place on fold

TRADITIONAL AFRICAN
Neck facing
(cut 1 of contrasting fabric)

place on fold

TRADITIONAL AFRICAN
Sleeve facing
(cut 2)

TRADITIONAL AFRICAN
Sandal strap
cut lines

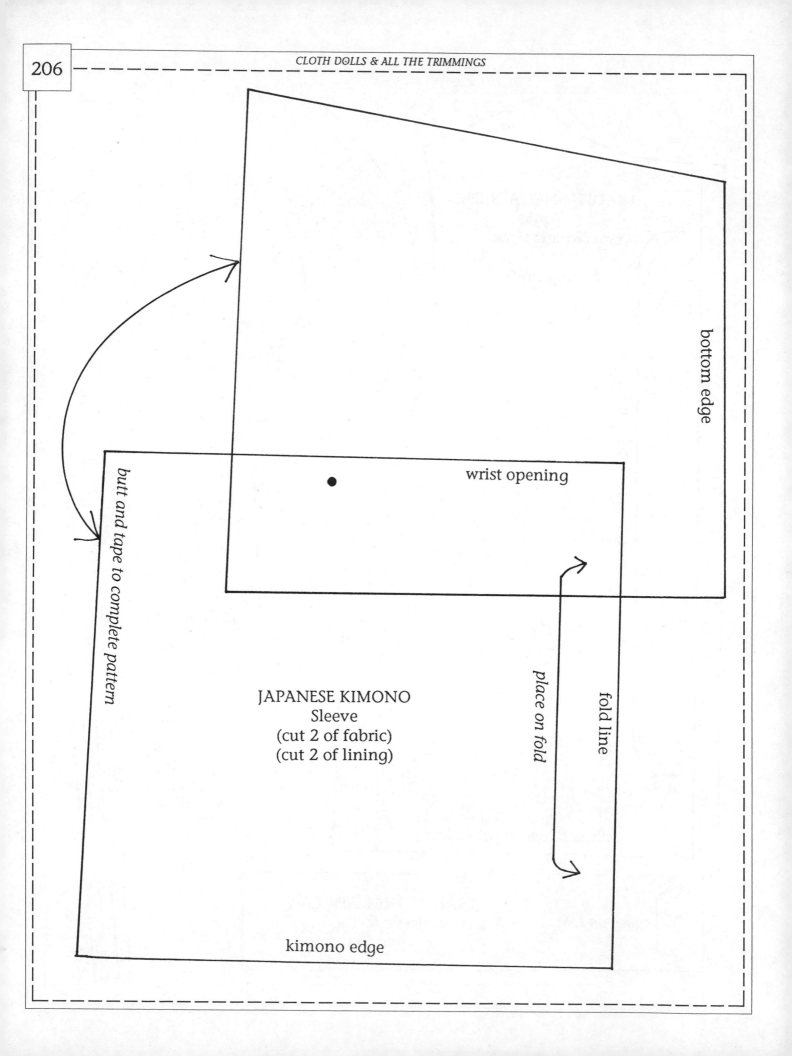

bottom edge

wrist opening

butt and tape to complete pattern

JAPANESE KIMONO
Sleeve
(cut 2 of fabric)
(cut 2 of lining)

place on fold

fold line

kimono edge

JAPANESE KIMONO
Front
Top
(cut 1 of fabric)
(cut 1 of lining)

butt and tape to top half

butt and tape to bottom half of pattern

JAPANESE KIMONO
Front
(bottom half)

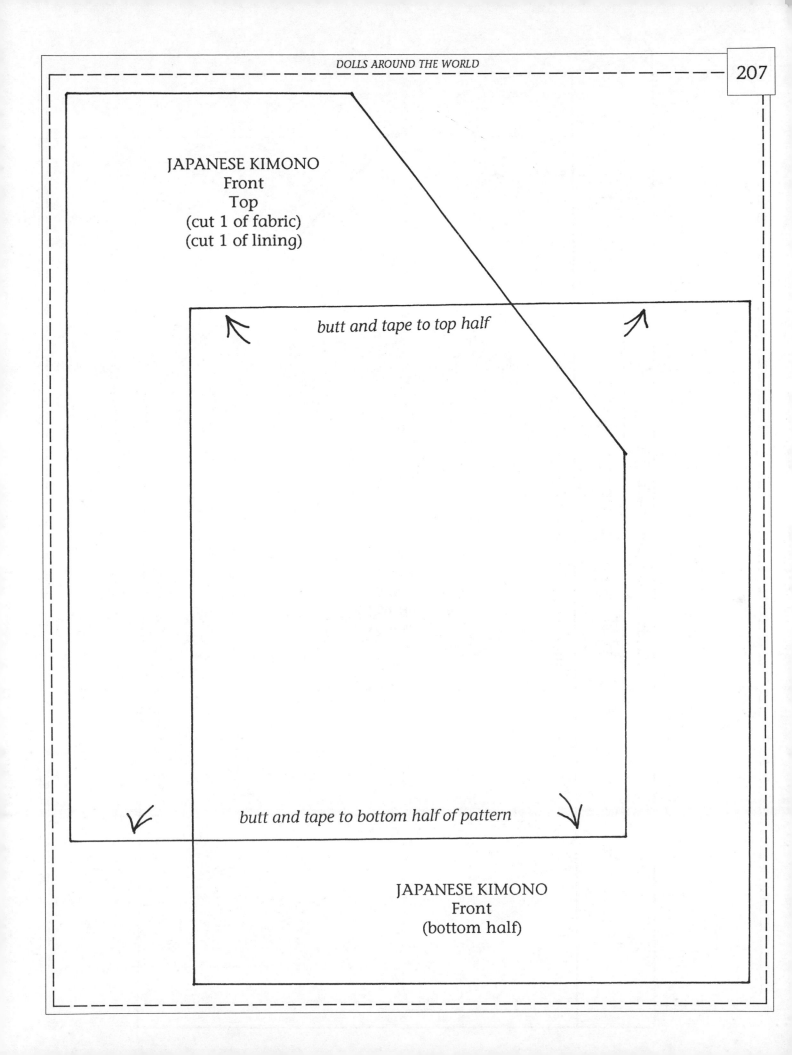

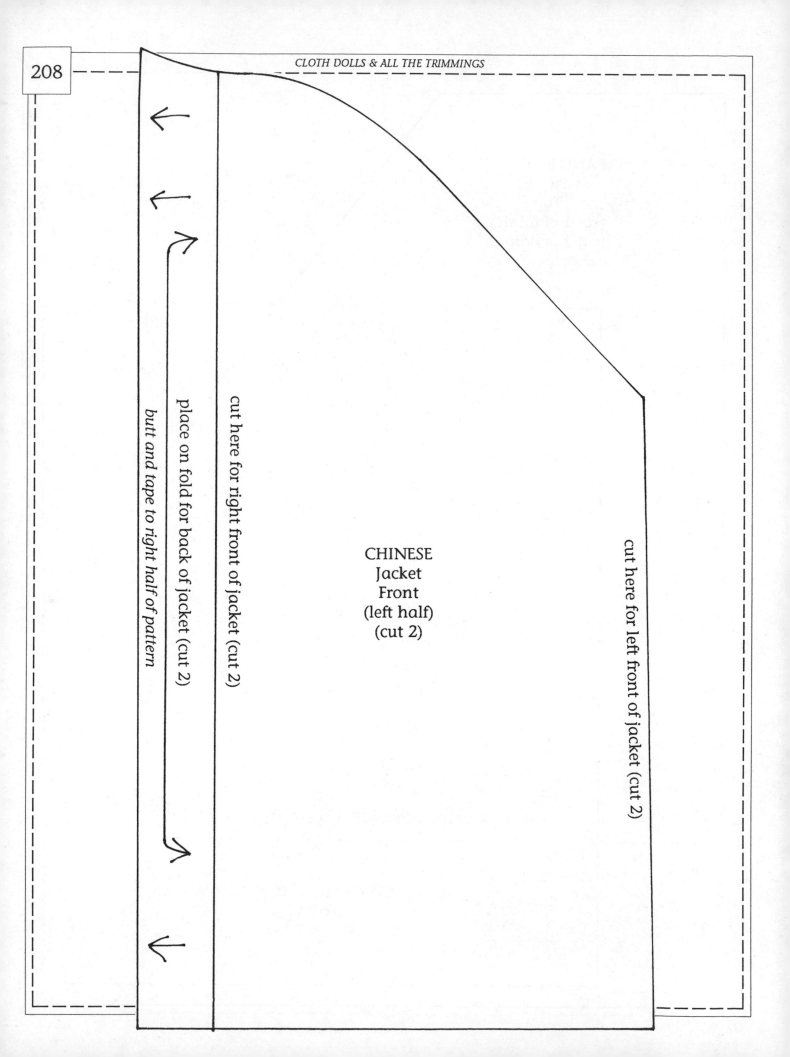

butt and tape to right half of pattern

place on fold for back of jacket (cut 2)

cut here for right front of jacket (cut 2)

CHINESE
Jacket
Front
(left half)
(cut 2)

cut here for left front of jacket (cut 2)

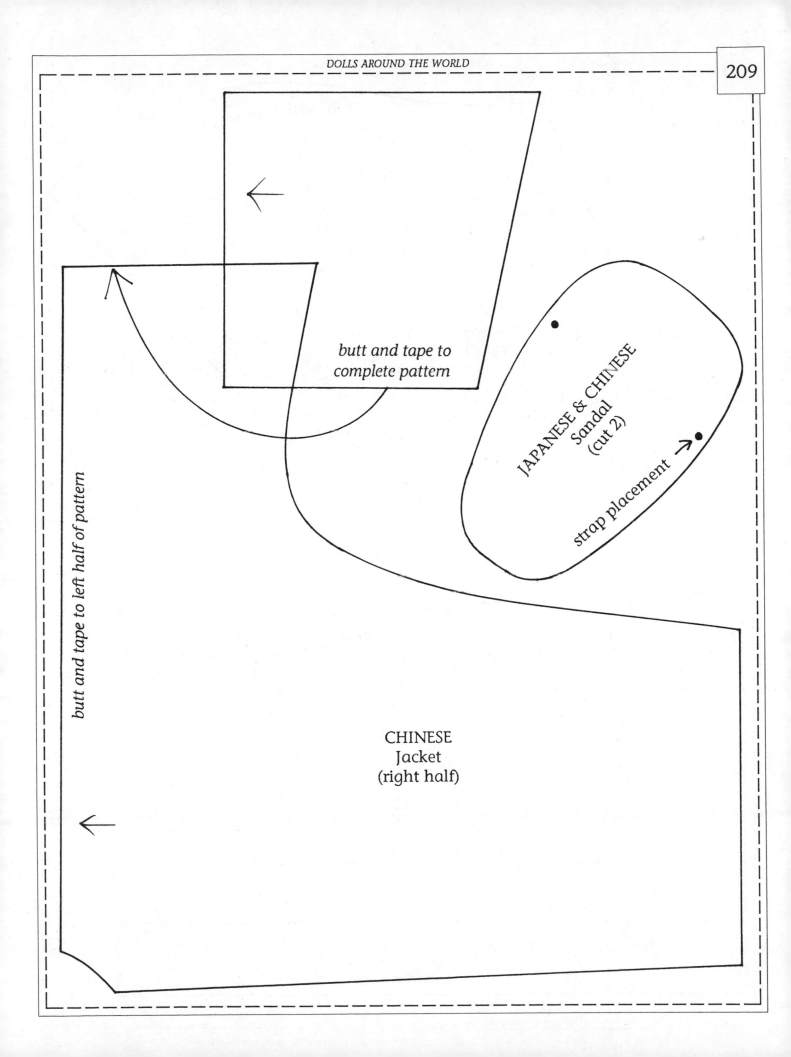

butt and tape to complete pattern

JAPANESE & CHINESE
Sandal
(cut 2)

strap placement

butt and tape to left half of pattern

CHINESE
Jacket
(right half)

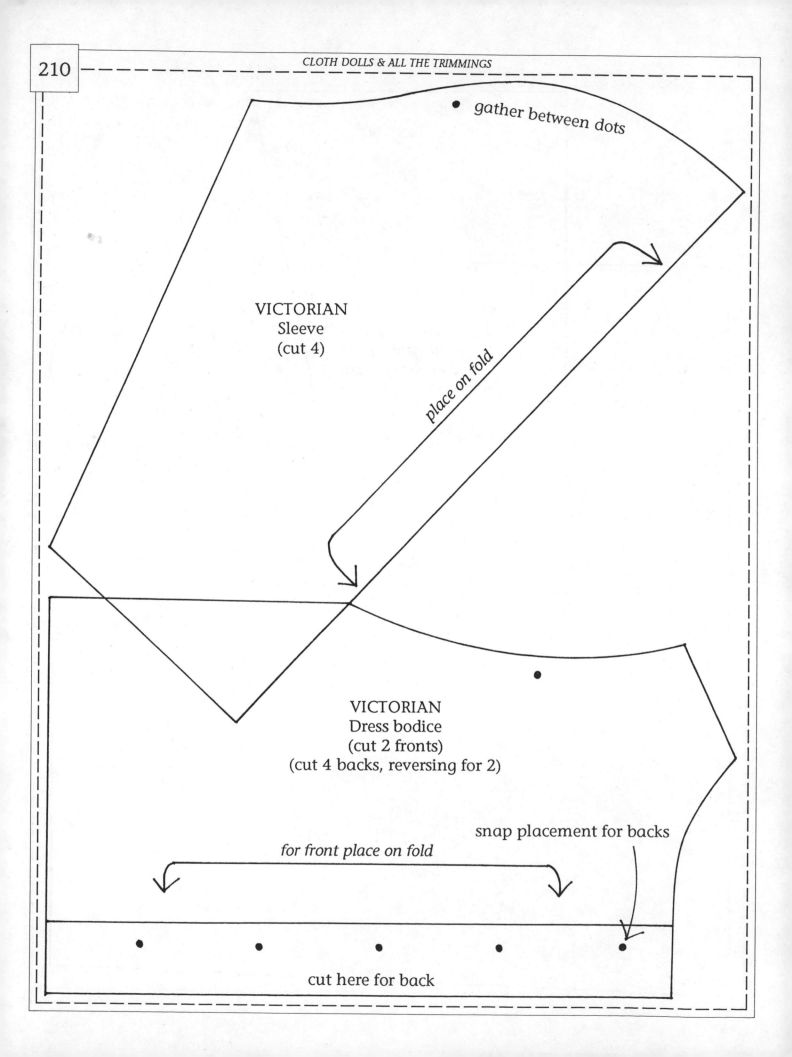

● gather between dots

VICTORIAN
Sleeve
(cut 4)

place on fold

VICTORIAN
Dress bodice
(cut 2 fronts)
(cut 4 backs, reversing for 2)

snap placement for backs

for front place on fold

cut here for back

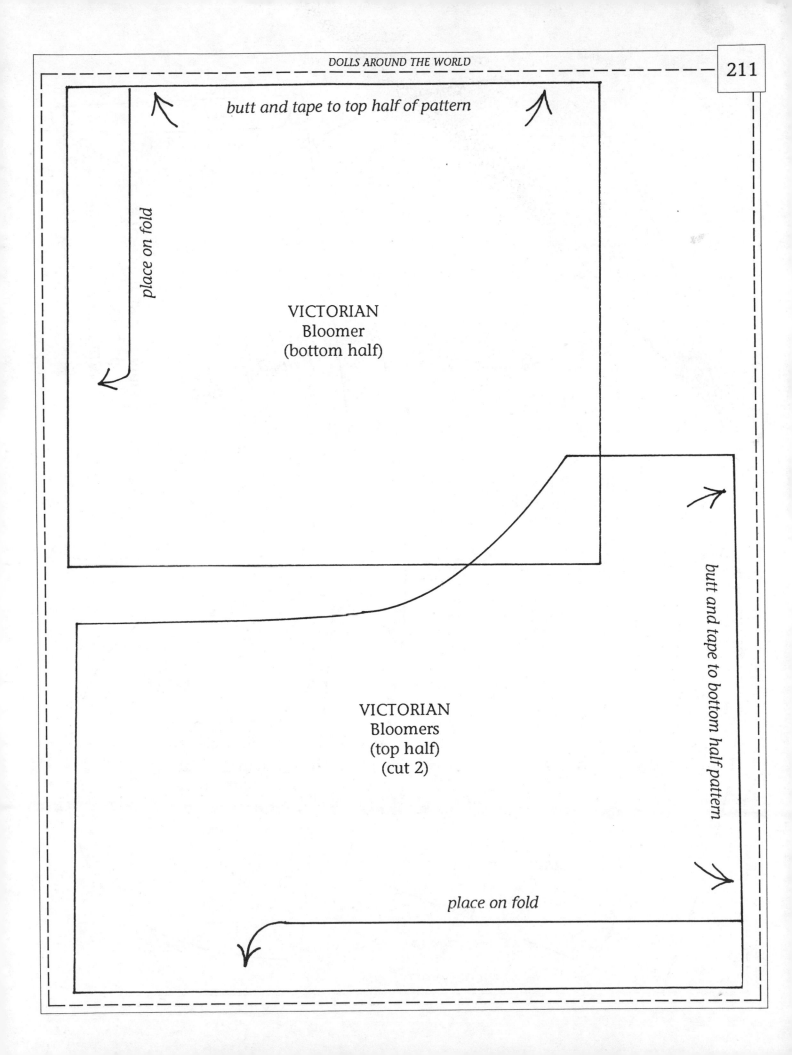

butt and tape to top half of pattern

place on fold

VICTORIAN
Bloomer
(bottom half)

butt and tape to bottom half pattern

VICTORIAN
Bloomers
(top half)
(cut 2)

place on fold

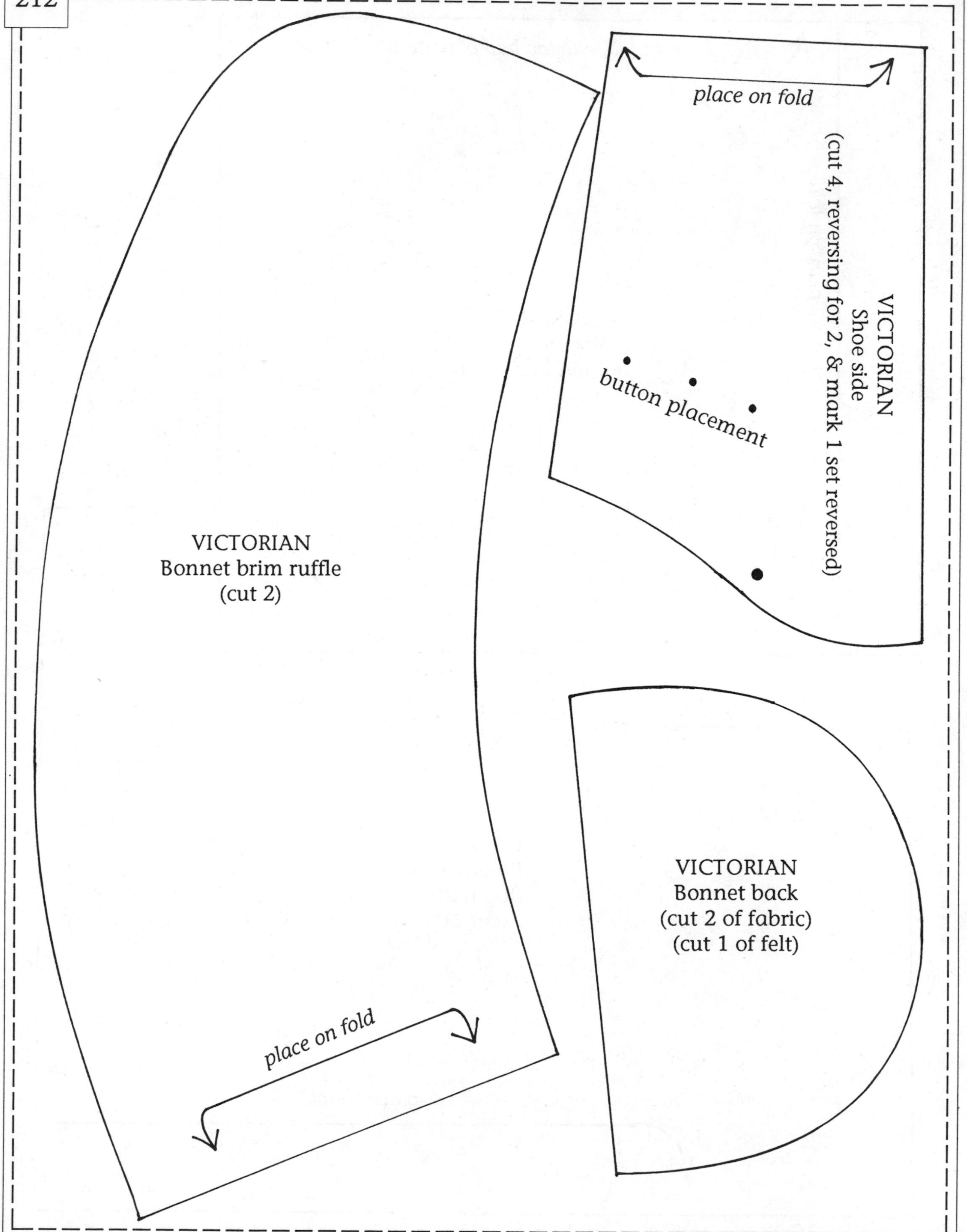

VICTORIAN
Bonnet brim ruffle
(cut 2)

place on fold

VICTORIAN
Shoe side
(cut 4, reversing for 2, & mark 1 set reversed)

place on fold

button placement

VICTORIAN
Bonnet back
(cut 2 of fabric)
(cut 1 of felt)

VICTORIAN
Shoe extension
(cut 4, reversing for 2
& mark 1 set,
reversed)

VICTORIAN
Hat brim
(cut 2 of fabric)
(cut 1 of felt)

place on fold of paper for full size pattern

VICTORIAN
Bonnet side
(cut 2 of fabric)
(cut 1 of felt)

VICTORIAN
Shoe sole
(cut 4)

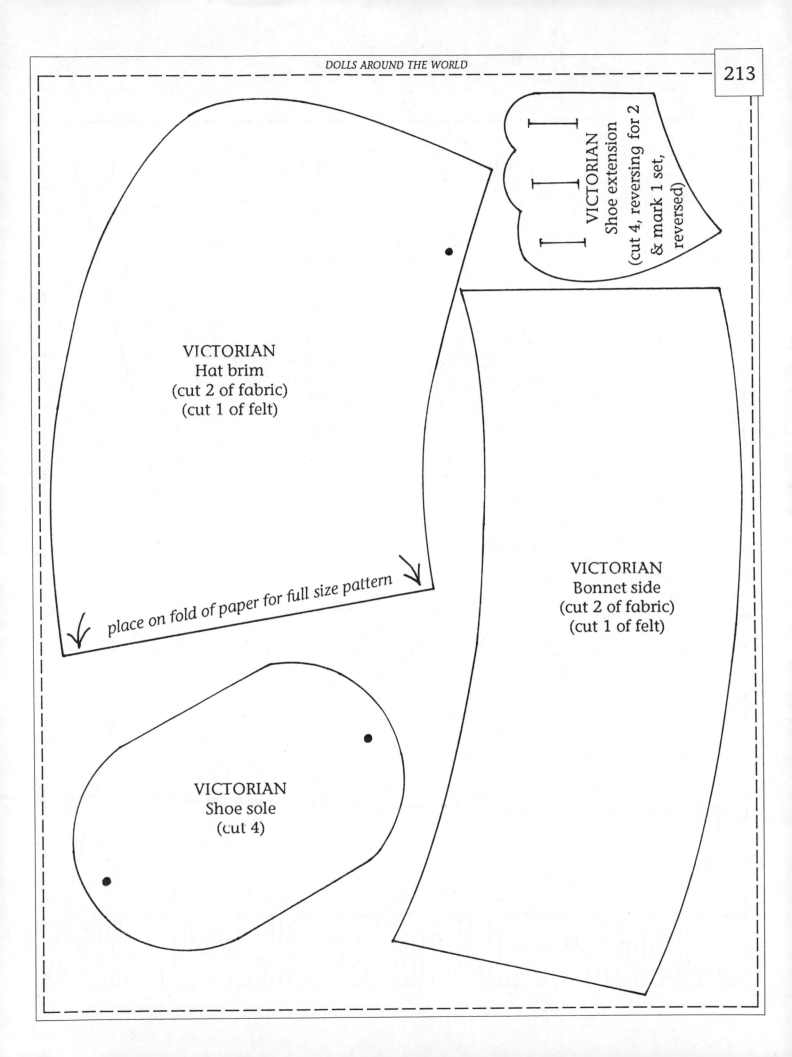

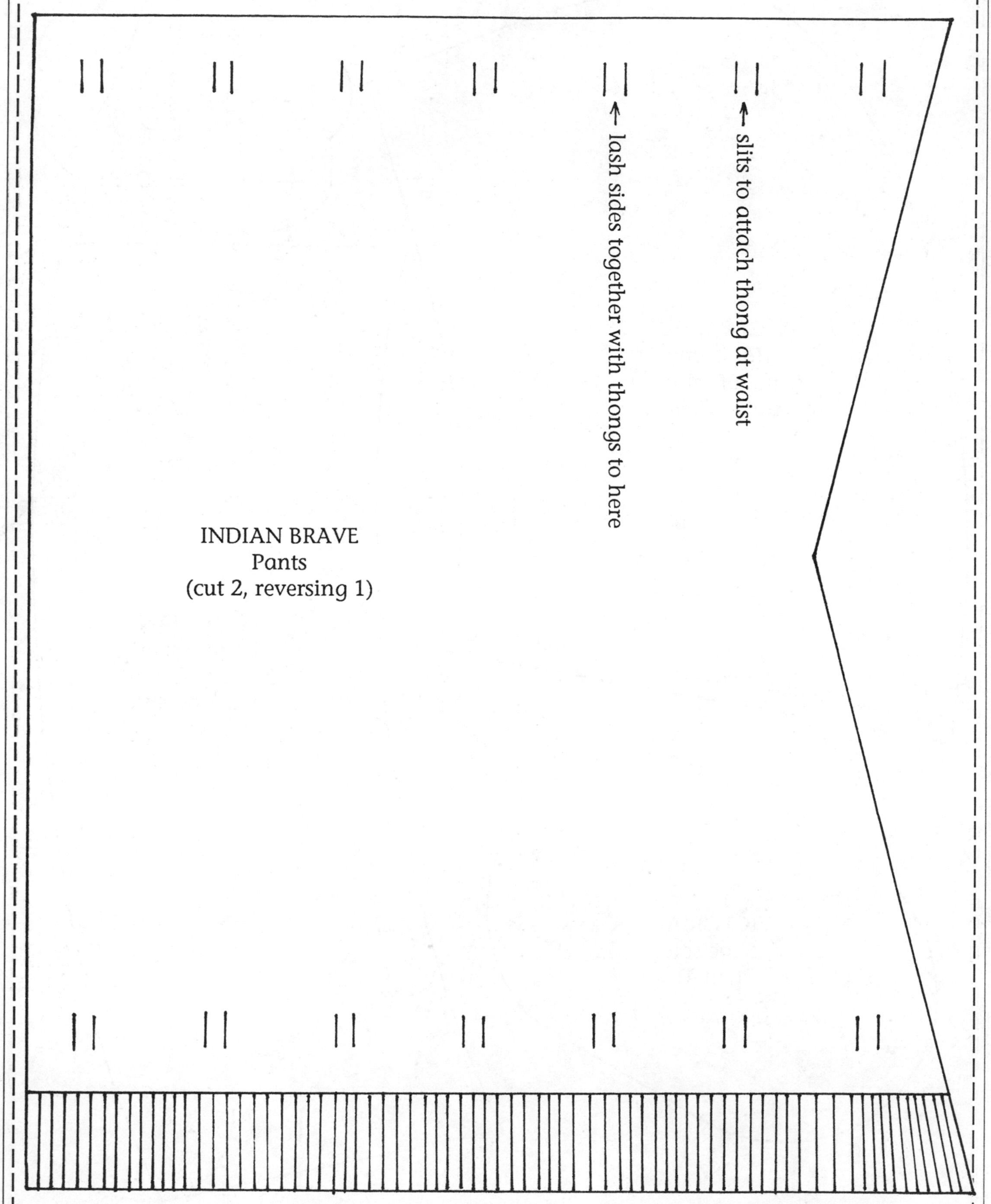

→ slits to attach thong at waist

→ lash sides together with thongs to here

INDIAN BRAVE
Pants
(cut 2, reversing 1)

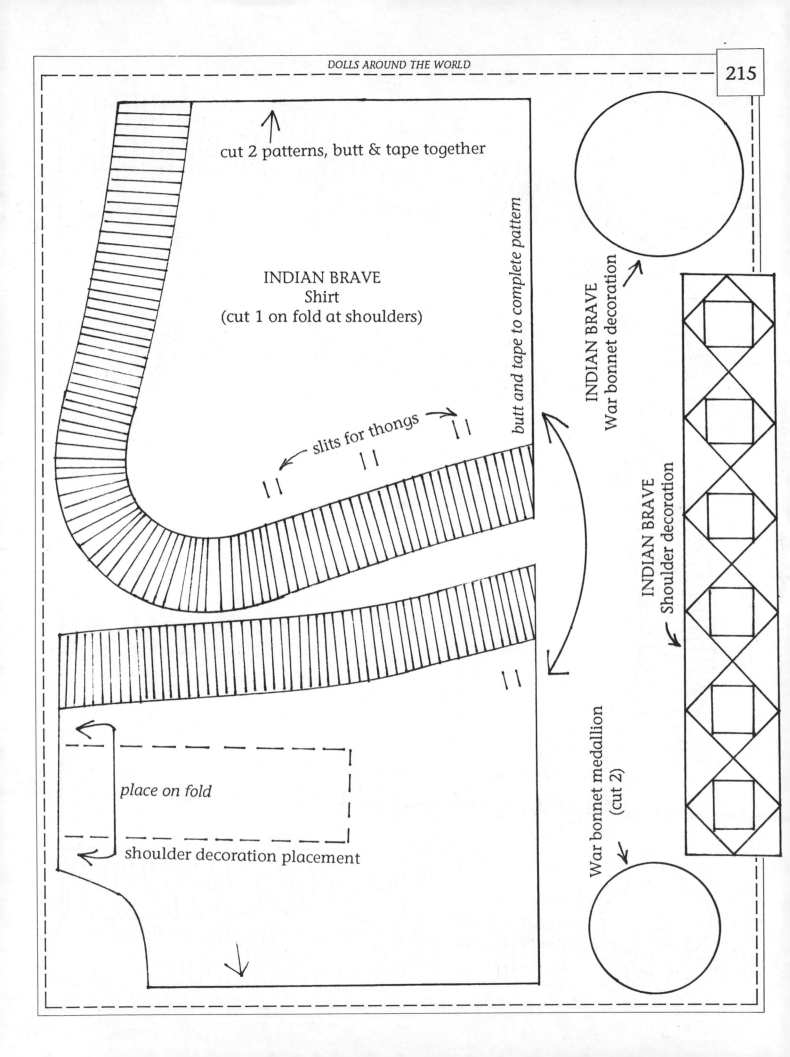

cut 2 patterns, butt & tape together

INDIAN BRAVE
Shirt
(cut 1 on fold at shoulders)

slits for thongs

butt and tape to complete pattern

INDIAN BRAVE
War bonnet decoration

INDIAN BRAVE
Shoulder decoration

War bonnet medallion
(cut 2)

place on fold

shoulder decoration placement

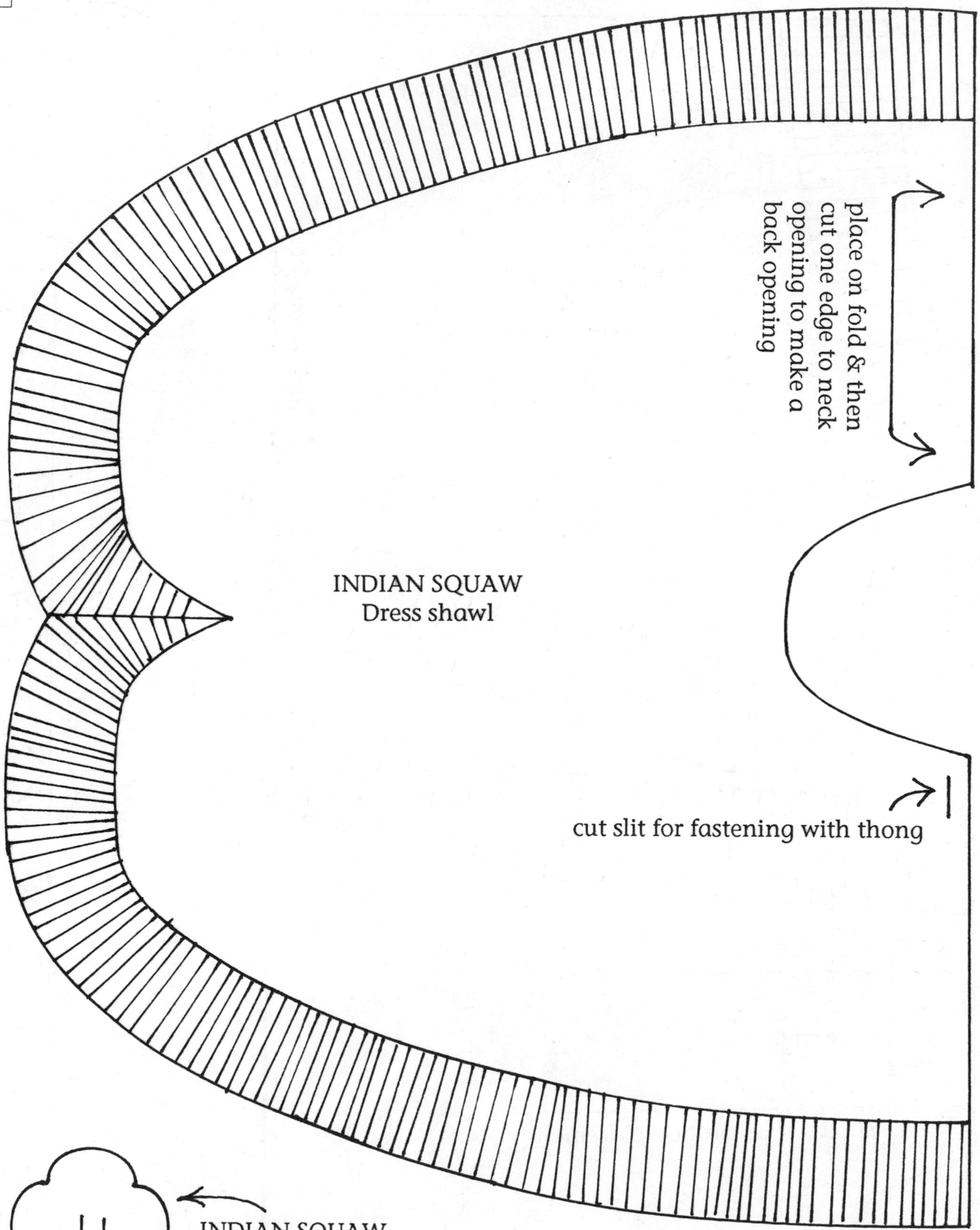

INDIAN SQUAW
Dress shawl

place on fold & then
cut one edge to neck
opening to make a
back opening

cut slit for fastening with thong

INDIAN SQUAW
Dress decoration
(cut 2)

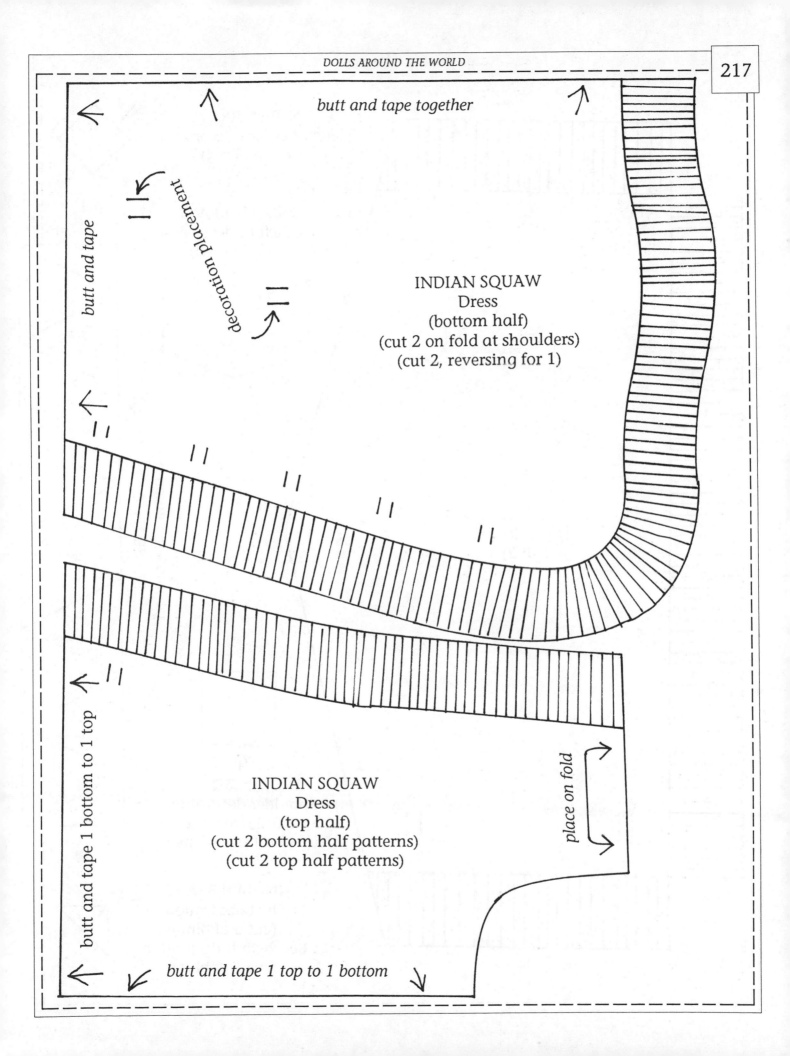

butt and tape together

butt and tape

decoration placement

INDIAN SQUAW
Dress
(bottom half)
(cut 2 on fold at shoulders)
(cut 2, reversing for 1)

butt and tape 1 bottom to 1 top

INDIAN SQUAW
Dress
(top half)
(cut 2 bottom half patterns)
(cut 2 top half patterns)

place on fold

butt and tape 1 top to 1 bottom

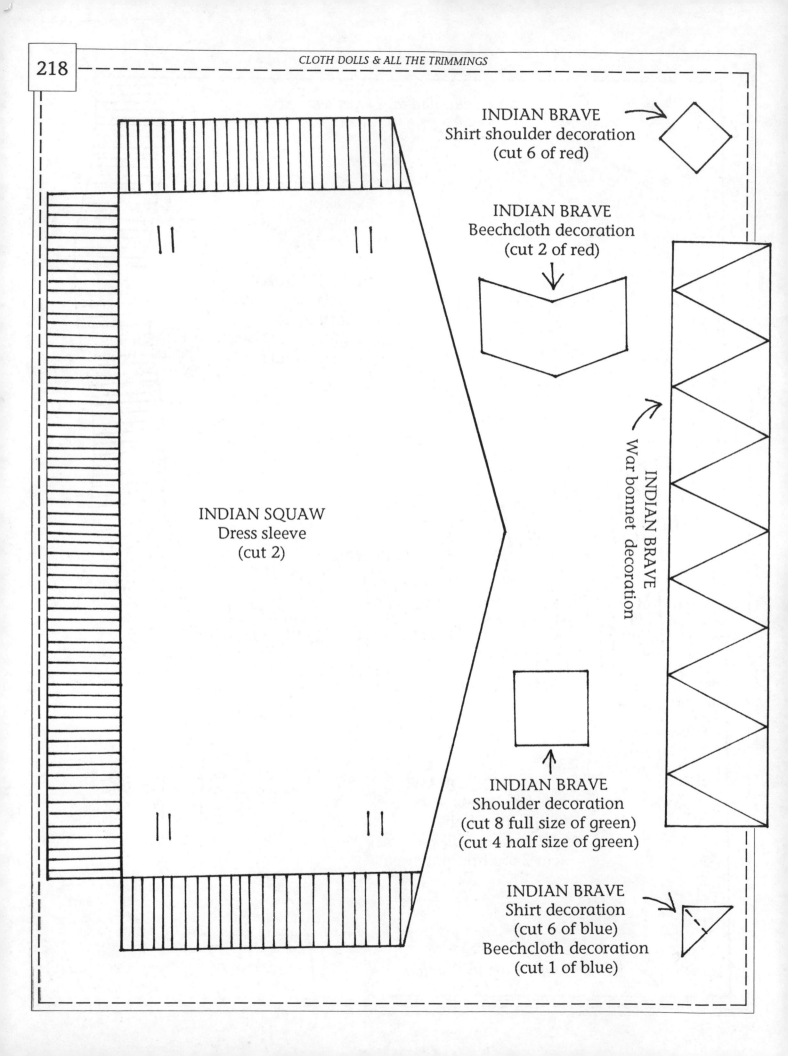

INDIAN BRAVE
Shirt shoulder decoration
(cut 6 of red)

INDIAN BRAVE
Beechcloth decoration
(cut 2 of red)

INDIAN BRAVE
War bonnet decoration

INDIAN SQUAW
Dress sleeve
(cut 2)

INDIAN BRAVE
Shoulder decoration
(cut 8 full size of green)
(cut 4 half size of green)

INDIAN BRAVE
Shirt decoration
(cut 6 of blue)
Beechcloth decoration
(cut 1 of blue)

SOURCES

By Diane
1126 Ivon Ave.
Endicott, NY 13760
Catalog: $1.50

Diane's double-sided suede was used for the Indians' clothing. It is less expensive than Ultrasuede®, is easy to sew, and works up beautifully.

Carolee Creations
787 Industrial Drive
Elmhurst, IL 60126
Catalog: ($1.00)

If these patterns have whet your appetite for yet more dollmaking, call (708) 530-7175 to request a catalog or to ask any questions.

CR'S Crafts
Box 8
Leland, IA 50453
Catalog: $2.00

This catalog is full of a large selection of goodies for dollmaking and general crafts. Patterns for dolls, porcelain dolls, and stuffed animals are pictured in the color sections at the beginning and end of the catalog. Order the Pretty Hair™ and plastic beads for the baby doll, sailor hat (5") for the Native Indian brave, the Victorian and Scandinavian dolls' tights, and the Dress-up doll's feather boa from this source.

Clotilde, Inc.
P.O. Box 22312
Ft. Lauderdale, FL 33332
Catalog: $1.00

Here you will find every sewing notion imaginable — all discounted at least 20 percent.

G Street Fabrics
Mail Order Service
11854 Rockville Pike
Rockville, MD 20852
No catalog.

Send $10 for a fabric sample chart of Ultrasuede® or Ultraleather®. The latter was used to make the Victorian, Pilgrim, and Scandinavian doll shoes. Or call their 800 number to order: 1-800-333-9191.

Home Sew
Dept. JD
Bethlehem, PA 18018
Catalog: Free

Great source for elastic, lace, trims, and other goodies at fantastic prices. Prudence's cluny lace came from this source.

National Artcraft Co.
23456 Mercantile Rd.
Beachwood, OH 44122
Catalog: $3.00

Your dolls will appreciate a little help standing up from this company's doll stands.

Patterncrafts
Box 25370
Colorado Springs, CO 80936-5370
Catalog: $2.00

More than 700 patterns, many of them dolls and all pictured in color, are featured in this inspiring catalog.

Mimi's Books & Suppplies For the Serious Dollmaker
P.O. Box 662
Point Pleasant, NJ 08742
Catalog: $2.00

This catalog is a handbook full of useful tips and instructions for the dollmaker, as well as the best selection of supplies available. From hair to body fabric to patterns and books, Mimi's catalog is a must. This is the source for the 55 mm joints for the baby doll (chapter 5) and the 30 mm joints for the dolls around the world (chapter 6). Mimi also publishes a wonderful quarterly magazine. Full of artist profiles and all the latest tips, tools and techniques, *Let's Talk About Dollmaking* offers you an inside look at all the current happenings in the cloth doll world.

Platypus
Box 396, Planetarium Station
New York, NY 10024
Catalog: $1.50

Open this catalog and you'll fall in love with these gorgeous dolls. They are all beautifully constructed and detailed.

Ragpats
P.O. Box 175
Caroga Lake, NY 12032
Catalog: $3.00

Over 200 patterns from the 1930s to 1970s are included in this catalog. All are reprinted directly from the original.

REFERENCES

Cherished Dolls You Can Make For Fun by Better Homes and Gardens Editors, Better Homes and Gardens Books.

Cloth Doll Magazine
P.O. Box 1089
Mount Shasta, CA 96067
Subscription: $13.95

This is the periodical for the cloth dollmaker.

The Cloth Dollmaker's Sourcebook by Diane Patterson Dee,
Betterway Publications, Inc., White Hall, VA 22987

In this book you'll find sources for a variety of cloth doll, stuffed animal, and toy patterns. Contemporary designers are featured as well as suppliers of materials and accessories.

Reader's Digest Complete Guide To Sewing, Reader's Digest Books.

An excellent general guide to sewing.

More good books from WILLIAMSON PUBLISHING

To order additional copies of Easy-to-Make **CLOTH DOLLS & All THE TRIMMINGS**, please enclose $13.95 per copy plus $2.00 shipping and handling. Follow "To Order" instructions on the last page. Thank you.

Easy-to-Make
TEDDY BEARS AND ALL THE TRIMMINGS
by Jodie Davis

Here's Jodie Davis' first fabulous book! Now you can make the most lovable, huggable, plain or fancy teddy bears imaginable, for a fraction of store-bought costs. Step-by-step instructions and easy patterns drawn to actual size for large, soft-bodied bears, quilted bears, and even jointed bears. Plus patterns for clothes, accessories—even teddy bear furniture!

192 pages, 8 1/2 x 11, illustrations and patterns,
Quality paperback, $12.95

GOLDE'S HOMEMADE COOKIES
by Golde Soloway

Over 50,000 copies of this marvelous cookbook have been sold. Now its in its second edition with 135 of the most delicious cookie recipes imaginable. Publishers Weekly says, "Cookies are her chosen realm and how sweet a world it is to visit." You're sure to agree!

162 pages, 8 1/4 x 7 1/4 , illustrations,
Quality paperback, $8.95

THE BROWN BAG COOKBOOK:
Nutritious Portable Lunches for Kids and Grown-Ups
by Sara Sloan

Bette Midler says she couldn't live without this book in her kitchen, now that she is raising a healthy child, and thousands of others agree. Here are more than 1,000 brown bag lunch ideas with 150 recipes for simple, quick, nutritious lunches that kids will love. Breakfast ideas, too! This popular book is now in its seventh printing!
192 pages, 8 1/4 x 7 1/4, illustrations,
Quality paperback, $8.95

CARING FOR OLDER CATS & DOGS:
Extending Your Pet's Healthy Life
by Robert Anderson, DVM and Barbara J. Wrede

Here's the only book that will help you distinguish the signs of natural aging from pain and suffering, that will help you care for your pet with compassion and knowledge. How to help your older pet, how to nourish, nurture, and nurse your cat or dog, and finally when and how to let go. Medially sound with reasonable homeopathic remedies too, mixed with practical advice and compassion.
Every older pet deserves an owner who has read this!

192 pages, 6 x 9, illustrations
Quality paperback, $10.95

THE COMPLETE AND EASY GUIDE TO SOCIAL SECURITY & MEDICARE
by Faustin F. Jehle

A lifesaver of a book for every senior citizen— in fact every citizen— you know. Do someone a special favor, and give this book as a gift. Written in "plain English," here's all that red tape unravelled. Over 300,000 copies sold!

175 pages, 8 1/2 x 11, charts and tables,
Quality paperback, $10.95

KID'S CREATE!
Art & Craft Experiences for 3- to 9-year-olds
by Laurie Carlson

What's the most important experience for children ages 3 to 9? Why to create something by themselves. Carlson provides over 150 creative experiences ranging from making dinosaur sculptures to clay cactus gardens, from butterfly puppets to windsocks. Plenty of help for the parents working with the kids, too! A delightfully innovative book. A choice of Scholastic and Better Homes & Gardens Book Clubs.

160 pages, 11 x 8 1/2, over 400 illustrations,
Quality paperback, $12.95

ADVENTURES IN ART
Art & Craft Experiences for 7- to 14-year-olds
by Susan Milord

Imagine an art book that encourages children to explore, to experience, to touch and to see, to learn and to create...imagine a true adventure in art. Here's a book that teaches artisan's skills without stifling creativity. Covers making handmade papers, puppets, masks, paper seascapes, seed art, tin can lantern, berry ink, still life, silk screen, batiking, carving and so much more. Perfect for the older child. Let the adventure begin!

160 pages, 11 x 8 1/2, 500 illustrations
Quality paperback, $12.95

THE KIDS' NATURE BOOK:
365 Indoor/Outdoor Activities and Experiences
by Susan Milord

Winner of the Parents' Choice Gold Award for learning and doing books, The Kids' Nature Book is loved by children, grandparents. and friends alike. Simple projects and activities emphasize fun while quietly reinforcing the wonder of the world we all share.
Packed with facts and fun!

160 pages, 11 x 8 1/2, 425 illustrations
Quality paperback, $12.95

DOING CHILDREN'S MUSEUMS:
A Guide to 225 Hands-On Museums
by Joanne Cleaver

Turn an ordinary day into a spontaneous "vacation" by taking a child to some of the 225 participatory children's museums, discovery rooms, and nature centers covered in this highly acclaimed, one-of-a-kind book. Filled with museum specifics to help you pick and plan the perfect place for the perfect day, Cleaver has created a most valuable resource for anyone who loves kids!

224 pages, 6 x 9,
Quality paperback, $12.95

PARENTS ARE TEACHERS, TOO:
Enriching Your Child's First Six Years
by Claudia Jones

Be the best teacher your child ever has. Jones shares hundreds of ways to help any child learn in playful home situations. Lots on developing reading, writing, math skills. Plenty on creative and critical thinking, too. A book you'll love using!

192 pages, 6 x 9, illustrations,
Quality paperback, $9.95

MORE PARENTS ARE TEACHERS, TOO:
Encouraging Your 6- to 12-Year-Old
by Claudia Jones

Help your children be the best they can be! When parents are involved, kids do better. When kids do better, they feel better, too. Here's a wonderfully creative book of ideas, activities, teaching methods and more to help you help your children over the rough spots and share in their growing joy in achieving. Plenty on reading, writing, math, problem-solving, creative thinking. Everything for parents who wants to help but not push their children.

226 pages, 6 x 9, illustrations,
Quality paperback, $10.95

THE HOMEWORK SOLUTION
by Linda Agler Sonna

Put homework responsibilities where they belong - in the student's lap! Here it is! The simple remedy for the millions of parents who are tired of waging the never-ending nightly battle over kids' homework. Dr. Sonna's "One Step Solution" will relieve parents, kids and their siblings of the ongoing problem within a single month.

192 pages, 6 x 9,
Quality paperback, $10.95

To Order:

At your bookstore or order directly from Williamson Publishing. We accept Visa and MasterCard (please include number and expiration date), or send check to:

Williamson Publishing Company
Church Hill Road, P.O. Box 185
Charlotte, Vermont 05445
Toll-free phone orders with credit cards:
1-800-234-8791

Please add $2.00 for postage and handling. Satisfaction is guaranteed or full refund without questions or quibbles.